DISCOVER QGIS 3.X

A WORKBOOK FOR THE CLASSROOM OR INDEPENDENT STUDY

KURT MENKE

loca e
PRESS

Credits & Copyright

Discover QGIS 3.x

by Kurt Menke

Published by Locate Press LLC

Direct permission requests to info@locatepress.com or mail:
Locate Press LLC, PO Box 671897, Chugiak, AK, USA, 99567-1897

Editor   Gary Sherman
Interior Design   Based on Memoir-LaTeXdocument class
Publisher Website   http://locatepress.com
Book Website   http://locatepress.com/dq3

Contents

CONTENTS

Foreword

It is a great honor to present Discover QGIS 3.x. This is a GIS workbook, which takes novices and experts alike through an entire GIS universe, using QGIS 3.x—the latest version of the leading open source GIS. As an educator I can use Discover QGIS 3.X as a curriculum and textbook for several courses. It covers the entire spectrum of GIS tasks and it works well for every level of education, from high school to university. New and experienced GIS users will find this workbook useful.

The entire workbook is written in a consistent manner. For each chapter there is an introduction, objectives, several tasks, questions, conclusions, and discussion questions. New terms are explained before starting—easy to read and follow along. As reader I feel confident that I can accomplish each task with the help from the author.

It´s easy to see that Kurt Menke has great experience in both a pedagogical teaching approach and in combining real life work and solving problems using GIS as a toolbox.

I highly recommend this book as a guided tour through the GIS jungle. I can also recommend Kurt Menke as lecturer in GIS. I have participated in several of his well-organized workshops at international QGIS meetings, and always gained new knowledge.

Lene Fischer
Associate Professor
University of Copenhagen
Department of Geoscience and Natural Resource Management
Forest and Landscape College

About this Book

It is with great pleasure that I welcome you to Discover QGIS 3.x, an update to the orginal Discover QGIS title published in 2016. QGIS has evolved substantially, as has this workbook. Since 2016, there have been six new QGIS releases, two of which were long-term releases. The move from the 2.x line to 3.x included significant changes *under the hood*. QGIS migrated from Python 2 to 3, and to the latest version of the Qt library(v5). With these changes many aspects of the interface improved. The upgrade most obvious to the everyday user is the updated Browser Panel which replaces the out moded stand-alone QGIS Browser application. In addition, the new unified Data Source Manager simplifies the basic task of adding data. With improved processing, streamlined workflows, and a multitude of search options, it is an exciting time to be learning QGIS. The improvements in QGIS 3.x allow this second edition of Discover QGIS to be 70 pages shorter than its predeccesor and cover many more features.

Of the 32 exercises in this workbook, 15 are brand new and 2 have seen considerable changes. Part 4 - Cartographic Design focuses on the substantial cartographic features found natively in QGIS 3.x., eliminating the reliance on Inkscape. In accordance with user feedback, Part 5 - Advanced Data Visualization replaces the seldom used section on Remote Sensing. There was a time when cartography was a weakness of QGIS. Today it is one of it's greatest strengths. These final two parts teach you many modern cartogaphic and data visualization features unique to QGIS. All of the exercises are up to date with QGIS 3.6 - Noosa, yet will still work with the long-term release version 3.4 Madeira. The one exception to this is Part 4 - Exercise 4 - Task 3, which can only be accomplished with version 3.6. Another new feature is a series of Appendices which cover keyboard shortcuts, useful plugins and contributing to the QGIS project. This workbook will serve you for a long time.

As with the first edition, Discover QGIS 3.x is largely based on The GeoAcademy. The first three parts are updates to the original GeoAcademy material. In addition, I augment that material with features I find invaluable in my day-to-day work as a GIS consultant. This workbook represents the best parts of the GeoAcademy combined with my diverse experience teaching QGIS, and using it in an applied work setting. The notes included throughout introduce features not explicitly addressed by the exercise, but of which you should be aware. I hope you enjoy the book!

The GeoAcademy

The GeoAcademy was founded in 2013, when Dr. Phil Davis brought together subject matter experts to author the first ever GIS curriculum based on a national standard—the U.S. Department of Labor's Geospatial Competency Model (GTCM). The GTCM is a hierarchical model of the knowledge, skills, and abilities (KSA's) needed to be a working GIS professional in today's marketplace. Forty U.S. college GIS educators vetted these KSA's. Since 95% of U.S based colleges and universities use a single vendor's GIS software, the GeoAcademy decided to offer an alternative free and open source GIS curriculum. A cost effective and accessible alternative. Over the summer of 2014 the exercises were beta tested on Canvas by over 3,000 students. The first edition of the GeoAcademy was released in September 2014. The GeoAcademy's mission was an attempt to teach GIS using QGIS, versus the creation of a QGIS manual.

Since its development, the GeoAcademy curriculum has been presented at several FOSS4G conferences and is relied on by many professors in their GIS programs. Over 5,000 people enrolled in the online GeoAcademy MOOC. In 2015 the GeoAcademy team won the Global Educator of the Year Team Award by GeoForAll (http://www.geoforall.org/).

Who This Book is For

The orginal motivation behind the GeoAcademy was to produce material that could be easily used, in whole or in part, by instructors wanting to incorporate QGIS into their curricula. This motivation holds true for Discover QGIS 3.x. It is designed for the classroom. It introduces the QGIS interface and covers: basic GIS concepts, spatial analysis, modeling, data creation and editing, cartographic design and data visualization. The material is modular. Instructors can opt to use the book in its entirety or select specific exercises to augment their courses. There are solution files for each exercise and many exercises include a challenge exercise. Each exercise also features discussion questions.

Discover QGIS 3.x also serves as an independent study resource for beginners and experts alike. New to GIS? This workbook guides you on an introductory path. Wishing to learn the new workflows and features in QGIS 3.x.? It's in here too.

The Data

The data for this book are available for download at `http://locatepress.com/workbook_qgis3`. They are organized by part and exercise. Each exercise includes solution files and answers to exercise questions. The package for the entire workbook is 1.18 Gb in size. The size of the data package is in part due to the fact that this workbook deals with many different types of data such as imagery and mesh data. It is also due to the author's belief that it is beneficial to learn using data from numerous sources covering different topic areas. All the data are in the public domain.

About the Author

A former archaeologist, Kurt Menke is a geospatial generalist based out of Albuquerque, New Mexico, USA. He received a Master's degree in Geography from the University of New Mexico in 2000. That same year he founded Bird's Eye View (`https://www.birdseyeviewgis.com/`) to apply his expertise with GIS technology towards solving the world's mounting ecological, economic and social issues. His areas of focus are public health, conservation and education. Kurt Menke has a broad skillset. He is a spatial analyst, cartographer, web map developer, trainer/teacher and author. He has a long history using QGIS. He first downloaded it in 2005 when it was at version 0.7 Seamus. He is an open source GIS authority, having co-authored Mastering QGIS for Packt Publishing and authoring Discover QGIS through Locate Press. He can frequently be found speaking at FOSS4G and QGIS conferences. In 2015 he became an OsGeo Charter Member. He is an experienced FOSS4G educator and is a co-author of the GeoAcademy. He is now a QGIS Certified Instructor. His offerings range from a semester long Intro to FOSS4G course he originally developed in 2009, to short courses and professional workshops. In 2015 he was awarded the Global Educator of the Year Team Award by GeoForAll as part of the GeoAcademy team.

Acknowledgments

I would like to thank Tom Armitage for doing a thorough technical review of this workbook. His feedback was invaluable. Saber Razmjooei and Peter Petrik with Lutra Consulting were intrumental in helping me understand the new QGIS support for mesh data, and where to find interesting datasets. Martin Dobias, also with Lutra Consulting, helped answer my questions about extruding vector features into 3D space. Nyall Dawson was the inspiration for creating the random dot boundary for the Colorful U.S. State map and for creating wedge buffers via geometry generators. Mathieu Pellerin inspired the use of raster imager markers. Klas Karlsson was the inspiration for the live layer effects applied to bathymetry data and created the Made with QGIS logo used in the blending modes exercise. The geometry generator task for creating label callouts was influenced by Keith Jenkins' excellent write up on GitHub.

I would also like thank each of my original GeoAcademy co-authors: Dr. Richard (Rick) Smith (British Petroleum), Nate Jennings (City of Sacramento), and Dr. John van Hoesen (Green Mountain College). The GeoAcademy, and by extension this workbook, would not have been developed if it had not been for the leadership of Dr. Phil Davis (Del Mar College), the principal investigator for the GeoAcademy.

Finally, I would like to thank editor and publisher Gary Sherman, the founder of QGIS and owner of Locate Press for his immediate and kind answers to my Latex and RST questions. He also helped edit this workbook.

Part I

Introduction to Geospatial Technology

Exercise 1

Spatial Data Models

Objective – Explore and Understand Spatial Data Models

1.1   Introduction

In this exercise, you'll explore and manage geospatial data using both the Browser panel and the Data Source Manager of the FOSS4G software QGIS. Both the Browser panel and the Data Source Manager allow you to locate data in your local file system, get some information about the data and and add it to QGIS. As you will see, the Data Source Manager also has a version of the Browser panel available. Therefore, there is a lot of duplicate functionality between the two. Overall the Data Source Manager has more functionality. However, the Browser panel can also be a handy way to add data. It is analogous to Windows Explorer, but works specifically with geospatial datasets.

This exercise will also introduce you to the QGIS interface, which is used throughout the workbook. It is important to learn the concepts in this exercise as future exercises will require the skills covered here.

This exercise includes the following tasks:

- Task 1 – Working with the Browser panel.

- Task 2 – Become familiar with geospatial data models.

- Task 3 – Working with the Data Source Manager.

1.2   Objective: Explore and Understand Geospatial Data Models

Geographic Information Systems model the real world with representations of objects such as lakes, roads and towns. Geospatial data models are the means used to represent these features. They are composed of two parts: spatial features and attributes. When these two components are combined they create a model of reality (Figure 1.1, on the following page).

There are two main geospatial data models: vector and raster. Geospatial features can be represented in either data model.

Vector Data Model – This model is best for representing discrete objects. It comes in three forms: point, line, and polygon. Vector representations have more precision than rasters. This is because points, lines and polygons are defined by X/Y coordinates. Vector is best when precise distances, lengths and areas are needed. It is also ideal for network analyses, for example the shortest distance between two points across a linear network. It is also well suited to cartography since you can use different icons for points, patterns for lines and different outlines and fills for polygons.

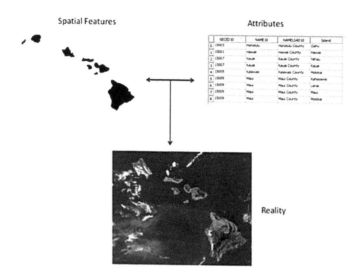

Figure 1.1: Two parts of the geospatial data model

Raster Data Model – This model is ideal for representing continuous phenomena such as elevation or precipitation. A raster is composed of a matrix of contiguous cells, with each cell (pixel) holding a single numeric value. Cells are typically square and have a characteristic known as resolution. This is the dimension of a cell. Typically resolution is expressed in coordinate units such as meters or feet. Rasters are also used for aerial photography and satellite imagery. Furthermore, they are a great choice for site suitability modeling. For example, rasters can be combined via mathematical operations (raster algebra) to compute potential locations for things like species habitat, disease vectors or store locations.

1.3   Task 1 - Working with the Browser panel

In this task, you will become familiar with the Browser panel. The first step in working on a project with geospatial datasets is to organize your workspace. It is important that we organize datasets logically on the computer and make them easy to find. In this task, you will obtain a copy of the exercise data and explore how the data is organized using the Browser panel.

Open QGIS. The way you open QGIS will vary depending on your operating system. For this series of exercises, we will explain how to open and use QGIS using the Microsoft Windows 10 operating system.

1. Click `Start | All Programs | QGIS | QGIS Desktop 3.x.`

> NOTE: You may see more than one version of QGIS. One with GRASS 7 support and one without. GRASS is another open source GIS software package. It has its own data structure named a GRASS database. QGIS with GRASS 7 is configured with support for GRASS databases. Since you are not working with a GRASS database, either version will work.

The interface to QGIS is straightforward. Both the Browser and Layers panels are docked to the left side of QGIS (Figure 1.2, on the next page). Most of the remaining space is taken up by the Map canvas. Above are toolbars and menus.

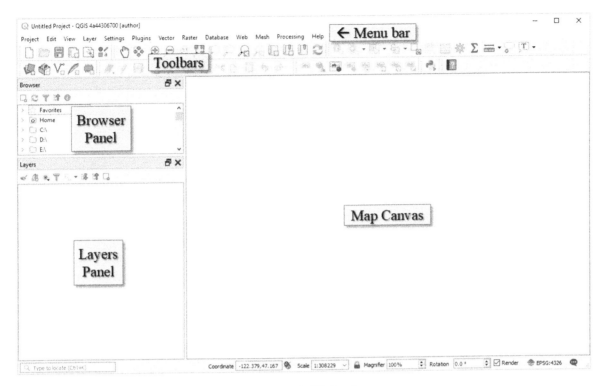

Figure 1.2: QGIS Desktop

Your QGIS window may look slightly different than the one pictured above. To reset your display back to the default settings, click the Settings | Options | System tab | Settings section | Reset button, then click OK and restart QGIS. Also note that many of the QGIS screenshots in this book contain the word [author] in the title bar. QGIS allows you to set up User Profiles. To do so go to the menu bar and choose Settings | User Profiles. Each profile has settings for the plugins installed, toolbars enabled, arrangement of toolbars etc. This book has been written using a Profile named author which has the default QGIS settings. You may also choose to set up profiles for specific analyses, particular projects or clients.

For this task you will focus on the Browser Panel which displays the file tree. It shows your computer's files and folders. Your machine may have a different set and number of drives listed here—this is fine. Below the drives are Database and Web Server connections. There are no connections of either type at this point.

2. Look at the file tree. Click the arrow to the left of the C: drive to expand it. You will now see all of the subfolders directly under the C:/ drive.

3. Expand the `Discover_QGIS_2ndEd\Part_1_Introduction_to_Geospatial_Technology\Exercise_1_Data` folder in the file tree by clicking the arrows to the left of each folder. You will now see the contents of the `Exercise_1_Data` folder for the exercise (Figure 1.3, on the following page).

4. Take a moment to read the names of the files. There are three folders and several files listed with different icons. The vector file icon ⌇ indicates that the dataset is a vector layer. This icon ▓ is used to represent raster data but is also used for other files such as the XML files you see here. The ⊟ icon indicates that the dataset is a database.

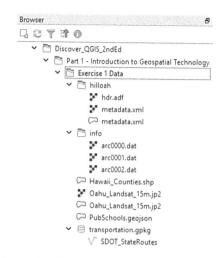

Figure 1.3: Exercise data in Browser panel

> Note that QGIS includes different User Interface (UI) Themes. To access these go to the menu bar and choose *Settings* / *Options* and select the *General* tab. In the *Application* section find *UI Theme*. There is a *Night Mapping* theme which has been greatly improved in recent releases. Using this while working in the evening can make your mapping exerience more pleasant. After switching to one of these you will need to close and relaunch QGIS for the change to take effect. In QGIS 3.6 Noosa there is another new UI them named *Blend of Gray*.

1.4 Task 2 - Become Familiar with Geospatial Data Models

Now that you are familiar with the basic layout of the Browser Panel, you will explore some geospatial data. You will learn how to access properties of a layer and begin adding data to QGIS.

1. Let's take a closer look at these data currently listed in the `Exercise_1_Data` folder.

2. Right-click on the `Hawaii_Counties.shp` layer in the file tree. From the context menu choose Layer Properties (Figure: 1.4). Also notice that there is an option to Export Layer. This allows you to export a layer to a new format without having to first load the layer into QGIS.

Figure 1.4: Browser Panel Context Menu

3. A Layer Properties window opens with some basic information about the dataset. You will notice that the Storage type is ESRI shapefile. You can also see that it has a Geometry type of Polygon(MultiPolygon) and it has 9 features (Figure 1.5, on the facing page).

> This Layer Properties window also has a Preview tab for seeing a preview of the spatial features and an Attributes tab for previewing the attribute table.

4. Close the Layer Properties window.

Figure 1.5: Layer Properties

In addition to data models (vector and raster) we have to understand file formats. Some file formats are designed to store vector, and others raster data. Shapefiles are vector file format. In fact, they are probably the most common vector file format. An individual shapefile can only contain one geometry type (polygon, line, or point). A shapefile is actually a collection of files on the computer with a common name, but different extensions. There are three files that are mandatory to have a functioning shapefile:

- .shp -- stores the feature geometry

- .shx -- an index linking the .shp to the .dbf

- .dbf -- a database file which stores the attributes

> The shapefile format is considered a mostly open specification. The specification is published but was not developed in an open forum. The format, while ubiquitous, has some significant limitations: A) Attribute column names are limited to 10 characters, B) lacks a time data type, C) only supports text fields of 255 characters in length, D) is limited to 2 GB in size and E) there is a maximum number of attribute columns of 255. The Esri whitepaper describing the format can be found here: `http://esri.com/library/whitepapers/pdfs/shapefile.pdf`

5. Now right-click on `PubSchools.geojson` and again choose Layer Properties. You will see that this is a GeoJSON dataset and that it has 287 point features. GeoJSON (`http://geojson.org/`) is an open standard format that stores spatial data as JavaScript. It is commonly used for displaying vector data in web maps.

6. Expand the `transportation.gpkg` database. Notice that is has a line geometry icon $\vee$.

7. Using what you know, open the Layers Properties for the SDOT_StateRoutes layer. The Storage reads GPKG. This is a fairly new file format known as a GeoPackage. It is a spatial database format based on the FOSS SQLite database. It can be used on any operating system. You can see this layer does indeed have line geometry with 122 features. Close the Layer Properties window.

> Paul Ramsey authored a very helpful blog entitled, *Beyond the Shapefile with File Geodatabase and GeoPackage*, comparing the limitations of the Shapefile with Esri File Geodatabases and GeoPackages. You can find the article here: `https://carto.com/blog/inside/fgdb-gpkg/`

8. Again right-click on `Hawaii_Counties.shp` but this time choose Add Layer to Project. The counties layer will be added to QGIS. It will appear on the map canvas and as a layer in the Layers Panel (Figure 1.6, on the next page).

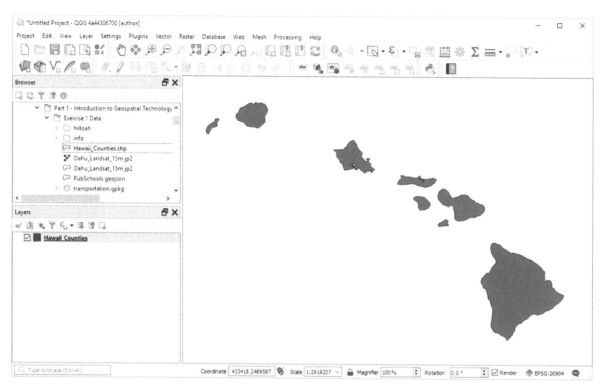

Figure 1.6: First Layer in QGIS

9. Now you will switch your attention to the Layers Panel. Right-click on the Hawaii_counties layer and choose Open Attribute Table from the context menu. The attribute table can also be opened by clicking the Open Attribute Table ⊞ button or by clicking F6. The table opens showing you the other component of the data model, the attributes (Figure 1.7). Each row corresponds to one polygon. If you recall from exploring this dataset with the Browser Panel, it has 9 features (9 polygons). The attribute table has 9 corresponding records. The columns are things we know about the polygons. There are columns with the County name (NAMELSAD10) and with the Island name Island). Close the table when done.

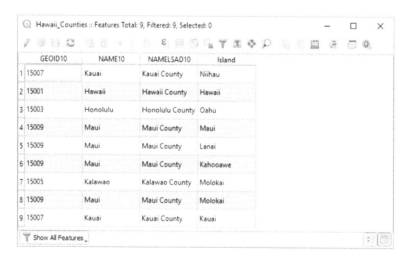

Figure 1.7: Attribute Table

10. Using what you know add the Oahu_Landsat_15m.jp2 dataset (with the raster icon) to the map canvas.

11. Right-click on the layer in the Layers Panel and choose Zoom to Layer from the context menu. This is an example of a raster dataset. Like a photograph, it is composed of cells or pixels. This raster is a satellite image of the island of Oahu, Hawaii (Figure 1.8). Close QGIS when done.

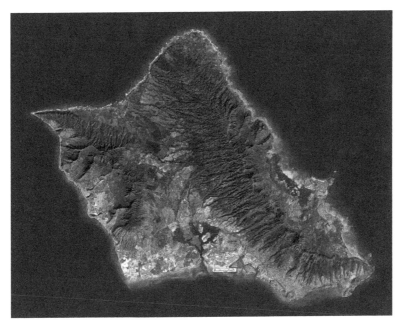

Figure 1.8: Oahu Satellite Image

1.5   Task 3 - Working with the Data Source Manager

Now that you know how geospatial datasets are stored on your computer, you will learn more about the data they contain. This next section will introduce you to working with the QGIS Data Source Manager.

1. Click Start | All Programs | QGIS | QGIS 3.x.

The QGIS interface is a little cluttered by default, so let's arrange the panels so the Layers panel and the Browser panel take up the same space.

Panels can be docked and undocked from the QGIS window. To undock a panel, click and drag the panel's top title bar (outlined in Figure 1.9) and drag it away from the sides. When you release your mouse button, the panel will be floating freely.

Figure 1.9: Area to drag when undocking a panel

To dock a floating panel, click and drag the title bar, and drag the panel to the left or right side of QGIS until a rectangle appears underneath the panel. To stack the Layers panel with the Browser panel drag the Layers Panel over the Browser Panel until it is highlighted and drop it. At the bottom of the panel you will now see a tab for each panel. Each are now available with a click of a button, and each panel has more space when you're working with it Docking action is shown in Figure 1.10, on the next page.

With the QGIS interface customized, let's add some data. In Task 2, you learned how to add data via the Browser panel. Here you will learn about the Data Source Manager.

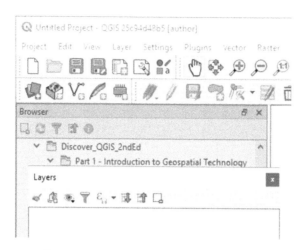

Figure 1.10: Docking the Layers Panel

On the Data Source Manager toolbar click the Open Data Source Manager button . The Data Source Manager window opens. Along the left side are tabs for the Vector and Raster data models along with database and web server connections. The top most tab is the Browser. With that selected the right side of the window shows a Browser window similar to the Browser Panel you have been working with so far (see Figure 1.11, on the facing page).

2. Click the Vector tab ⋁ Vector

3. The right portion of the window will switch to a dialog used for adding vector data to QGIS. Next you will add one of the ESRI shapefiles. Since this is a file based dataset you will keep the Source type File which is the default. Then click the Browse button. (Figure 1.12, on the next page).

4. The Open an OGR Supported Vector Layer window opens. The window defaults to all files. Click the All files dropdown box and change it to ESRI Shapefiles (shown in Figure 1.13, on page 28). Take a moment to peruse the other formats supported.

> NOTE: OGR is a FOSS4G project with the sole purpose of reading and writing geospatial vector data files. You can see which formats it supports here: https://www.gdal.org/ogr_formats.html

5. Once you are finished exploring, make sure it is still set to ESRI Shapefiles. This filters what you see in the exercise folder so that you only see the shapefile(s).

6. Select Hawaii_Counties.shp and click Open (see Figure 1.14, on page 28).

7. Now back at the Data Source Manager window, click Add to add the data to QGIS and Close to dismiss the Data Source Manager window.

8. You will now see Hawaii_Counties in the Layers Panel and the map features displayed in the map canvas. Vector GIS layers will come in with random colors. You will learn how to change layer styling in a future exercise.

9. In Task 1 you opened the attribute table. Another way to interact with both the spatial features and the attributes is the Identify Features button.

10. Click the Identify Features button

Figure 1.11: Data Source Manager

Figure 1.12: Add Vector Layer

11. Click on one of the features on the map. The Identify Results panel (Figure 1.15, on the following page) shows you the attributes for the feature you clicked on. *Note:* The Identify Results panel may initially be docked or floating. You can position it as needed.

Now you will learn how to add Raster data with the Data Source Manager .

12. Open the Data Source Manager .

13. Click the Raster tab ⬛ Raster .

14. Keep the source type as File and browse to your Exercise_1_Data folder.

```
All files (*)
GDAL/OGR VSIFileHandler (*.zip *.gz *.tar *.tar.gz *.tgz *.ZIP *.G.
Arc/Info ASCII Coverage (*.e00 *.E00)
Arc/Info Generate (*.gen *.GEN)
Atlas BNA (*.bna *.BNA)
AutoCAD DXF (*.dxf *.DXF)
AutoCAD Driver (*.dwg *.DWG)
Comma Separated Value (*.csv *.CSV)
Czech Cadastral Exchange Data Format (*.vfk *.VFK)
EDIGEO (*.thf *.THF)
EPIInfo .REC (*.rec *.REC)
ESRI Personal GeoDatabase (*.mdb *.MDB)
ESRI Shapefiles (*.shp *.SHP)
```

Figure 1.13: OGR Supported Vector Formats

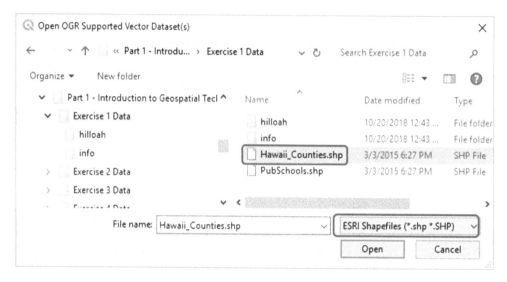

Figure 1.14: Open an OGR Supported Vector Layer

Figure 1.15: Identify Results

15. The Open a GDAL Supported Raster Data Source window opens. This is a very similar workflow to adding

vector data.

> Whereas QGIS uses OGR to open vector data files, here it uses another FOSS4G software library called GDAL. GDAL is used for reading and writing raster datasets. You can review the supported GDAL raster formats here: `https://www.gdal.org/formats_list.html`

16. The windows raster data filter is set to All Files by default, so you see the entire contents of the folder.

17. Set the filter to ERDAS JPEG2000. Also, note how many formats it will read! There are many more raster file types than vector. Once you have set the filter you'll see the one dataset: `Oahu_Landsat_15m.jp2` (Figure 1.16).

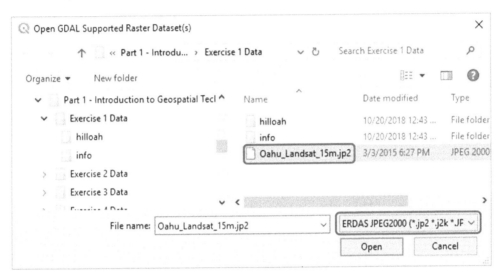

Figure 1.16: Open a GDAL Supported Raster Data Source

18. Select the `Oahu_Landsat_15m.jp2` raster dataset and click Open and then back at the Data Source Manager click Add and Close.

19. This dataset only covers a portion of Hawaii—just the island of Oahu. Right-click on the Oahu_Landsat_15m dataset in the Layers Panel and choose Zoom to Layer to zoom to the spatial extent of this raster (Figure 1.17, on the following page).

You may notice two folders in the exercise data folder that we have not discussed yet. One is named `hilloah` and the other `info`. Together, these combine to make another geospatial raster dataset format named a GRID. The info folder holds the attributes and always has the name "info". The other folder is the layer name and contains the spatial data. Let's add a GRID raster to our map.

20. Open the Data Source Manager and click the Raster tab again.

21. Set the filter to Arc/Info Binary Grid. Double click the `hilloah` folder to enter it. Select the `hdr.adf` file and click Open. Back at the Data Source Manager click Add and Close to add the raster to QGIS (Figure 1.18, on the next page).

22. This raster is a hillshade image of Oahu and it represents the terrain.

Data is often stored deep inside a series of folders. It is often tedious and time consuming to navigate deep inside the folders to gain access to the data. Favorites provide a way to create a shortcut directly to any folder so that you have one-click access. Let's create a favorite to our exercise folder for practice.

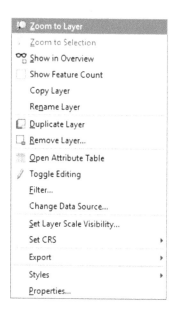

Figure 1.17: Zoom to Layer Extent

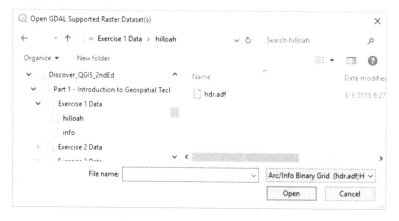

Figure 1.18: Adding a GRID

23. Look at the Browser Panel and scroll to the top. Note that there is a Favorites item. You can identify folders or locations as being favorites in order for them to appear here.

24. Navigate to the `Exercise_1_Data` folder in the Browser Panel. Right-click on it and choose Add as a Favorite (Figure 1.19, on the facing page).

25. Now expand Favorites and you will see your exercise folder listed there. You can remove a favorite anytime by right-clicking on it and choosing Remove favorite.

26. Expand the exercise folder under Favorites to expose the contents. Select `SDOT_StateRoutes.geojson` and drag it onto the map. This is a quick way to add data to your map.

1.6   Conclusion

In this exercise you explored datasets that use the two common geospatial data models: vector and raster. You have also used the Browser panel and the Data Source Manager to add data to QGIS. In future exercises, you will learn how to use QGIS to make maps and perform analyses.

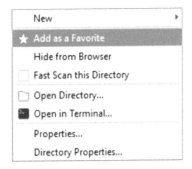

Figure 1.19: Add as a Favorite

1.7 Discussion Questions

1. How can Browser favorites make your workflow more efficient?

2. What are the two main parts of a GIS data model?

3. Name two ways of seeing feature attributes for a vector GIS layer.

Exercise 2

Displaying Geospatial Data

Objective – Explore and Understand How to Display Geospatial Data

2.1 Introduction

In this exercise, you'll learn how to complete a well-designed map showing the relationship between species habitat and federal land ownership, as well as how to symbolize GIS data layers in QGIS. In addition, you will learn how to use a QGIS Print Layout to design a well crafted map deliverable. The final map will include standard map elements such as the title and map legend.

This exercise will also continue to introduce you to the QGIS interface, as QGIS will be used throughout the book. It is important to learn the concepts in this exercise as future exercises will require the skills covered in this exercise.

This exercise includes the following tasks:

- Task 1 – Add data, organize map layers and set map projections.

- Task 2 – Style data layers.

- Task 3 – Compose map deliverable.

2.2 Objective: Create a Map that Meets the Customer's Requirements

Cartographers are frequently provided with a map requirements document from a coworker or customer. For this exercise, the you'll respond to a map requirements document from a customer who is writing a paper about the state of Greater sage-grouse habitat in the western United States. The map requirements from the customer are below.

Map Requirements from Customer:

Hi, my name is Steve Darwin. I am a wildlife biologist writing a paper on the state of Greater sage-grouse (see figure 2.1, on the next page) populations in the western United States. I need a letter sized, color, map figure that shows the relationship between current occupied Greater sage-grouse habitat and federal land ownership. I am interested in seeing how much habitat is under federal versus non-federal ownership.

I have been provided data from the US Fish and Wildlife Service depicting current occupied range for Greater sage-grouse. I also have federal land ownership, state boundaries and country boundaries from the US National Atlas. The land ownership data has an attribute column describing which federal agency manages the land (AGBUR).

I want to have the habitat data shown so that the federal land ownership data is visible beneath. I would like each different type of federal land styled with standard Bureau of Land Management colors. The map should also include a title ("Greater sage-grouse Current Distribution"), a legend, data sources and the date. The map should be a high-resolution (300 dpi) jpg image.

I trust that you will get the figure right the first time, so please just submit the completed figures to the managing editor directly.

Figure 2.1: Greater Sage-grouse

Image attribution: By Pacific Southwest Region from Sacramento, US (Greater Sage-Grouse) CC BY 2.0 (`http://creativecommons.org/licenses/by/2.0`), via Wikimedia Commons.

2.3   Task 1 - Add Data, Organize Map Layers and Set Coordinate Reference System

In this first task you will learn a new way to add data to QGIS Desktop. You will then set the projection for the map project, organize the data layers in the Table of Contents and change the layer names.

1. Open QGIS 3.x and make sure the Browser Panel is open.

2. Using the file tree in the Browser Panel navigate to the Exercise 2\Data folder.

3. Right click on the Exercise 2\Data folder and choose Add as a Favorite from the context menu.

4. Sometimes when recent changes have been made, such as setting a folder as a favorite, the Refresh button needs to be pressed in order to see the changes. Click the Refresh button (Figure: 2.2, on the facing page).

5. Now expand Favorites near the top of the file tree in the Browser Panel by clicking the plus sign to the left. You will see the Exercise 2\Data folder listed. Setting the folder as a favorite allows you to quickly navigate to your working folder.

Figure 2.2: Refresh button

6. You will see 5 shapefiles in the exercise data folder:

- Canada.shp

- Land_ownership.shp

- Mexico.shp

- Sage_grouse_current_distribution.shp

- States.shp

7. You can select them all by holding down the Ctrl key on your keyboard while left clicking on each shapefile. Select the five shapefiles (Figure: 2.3).

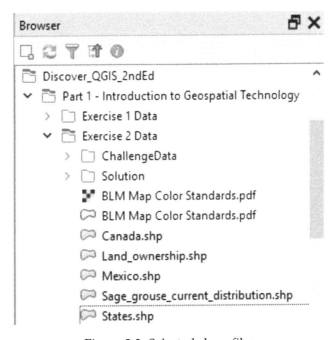

Figure 2.3: Selected shapefiles

8. Drag the five selected shapefiles onto the map canvas from the Browser Panel. You can also right-click on these layers and choose Add Selected Layers to Project. QGIS should now look like figure 2.4, on the following page. The random colors that QGIS assigns to the layers may be different than the figure below but that is fine.

Note: If you do not see anything displayed in the map canvas, you may need to zoom to full extents of the map by pressing the Zoom Full button. Alternatively, you can click View | Zoom Full.

Figure 2.4: Shapefiles Added to QGIS

9. Now you will save the QGIS project. Click on Project | Save from the menu bar (Ctrl + S). Navigate to your Exercise 2\Data folder and save your project as Exercise 2.

> A QGIS project is saved as a *.qgs file. A new feature of QGIS 3 is that a project database (*.qgd) is also saved with the project. The *.qgd file is a spatialite database. At QGIS 3.2 projects began being saved as *.qgz files. These are zipped project files that contain both the *.qgs and *.qgd files. Here your project will be saved as Exercise 2.qgz. Note that you still have the option of choosing Project | Save Project As and choosing a Save as type of *.qgs.

10. Right click on the Sage_grouse_current_distribution layer in the Layers Panel, and choose Zoom to Layer from the context menu. This will zoom you into the extent of that dataset.

The data layers are rendered on the map canvas in the order they appear in the Layers Panel. The layer that is on the top of the list in the Layers Panel will be drawn on top of the other layers in the map canvas. Notice that the the Land_ownership layer is above the Sage_grouse_current_distribution layer. This means that Land_ownership is covering up the Sage_grouse_current_distribution layer on the map.

Now you will change this drawing order.

11. Select the Sage_grouse_current_distribution data layer in the Layers Panel and drag it to the top position. You will see a line as you drag this layer up the list. Drop it when it is in the desired position. Next drag Land_ownership so that it is the second layer in the list.

12. Your map should now resemble the figure 2.5.

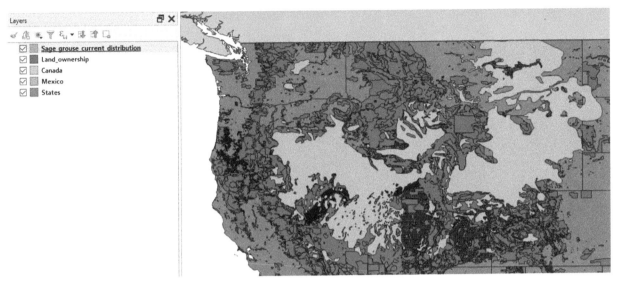

Figure 2.5: Layers Reordered and Zoomed into Sage-grouse Range

Now all the data layers should be in the correct order. Typically, data layers will be organized with point data layers on top of line layers on top of polygon layers. Raster data layers are usually placed at the bottom.

With the layers in the best drawing order, let's turn our attention to the coordinate reference system for the map.

13. Note that the lower right hand corner of QGIS displays EPSG: 4269. The number 4269 is the EPSG code for the coordinate reference system (CRS) the map is currently in (shown in figure 2.6).

Figure 2.6: Project CRS

> EPSG codes are id numbers for different coordinate reference systems. They can be searched for from this website: http://spatialreference.org/ref/epsg/.

14. Click on Project | Project Properties from the menu bar to open the Project Properties window.

15. Select the CRS tab.

> You can also simply click on the EPSG code in the lower right hand corner to open the Project Properties window to the CRS tab. This is a handy shortcut

The CRS for the current QGIS map project is highlighted in the Coordinate systems of the world section. The well known text version is displayed in the Selected CRS section. This is a detailed explanation of the CRS which is a geographic coordinate system using the NAD83 datum. This section also shows a map with the valid bounds of the CRS. This CRS makes the lower 48 look stretched out and distorted, so you'll want to change the maps CRS into something that makes the lower 48 "look correct".

16. Click OK to close the Project Properties window.

Since the Sage_grouse_current_distribution layer is in an Albers projection, and the QGIS map is in a geographic CRS, that means that the Sage_grouse_current_distribution layer is being projected on-the-fly into the geographic projection of the map. This happens automatically in QGIS 3.

17. Right-click on the Sage_grouse_current_distribution layer and choose Set CRS | Set Project CRS from Layer option from the context menu (Figure 2.7). This will put the map into the same Albers CRS of the Sage grouse layer. Note that the EPSG code in the lower right corner now reads 5070 for the Albers CRS. This CRS gives the western U.S. an appearance we are more used to. Any other map layers not in Albers, will now be projected on the fly into Albers.

Figure 2.7: Setting the Project CRS to that of a layer

Now you will change the layer names in the Layers Panel. The layer names match the names of the shapefiles by default. However, these names will appear on the legend. So you will always want to change these to proper names that your map reading audience will understand.

18. Right-click on the Sage_grouse_current_distribution layer, and choose Properties from the context menu, to open the Layer Properties window. Choose the Source tab on the left. Click in the box next to Layer name and change the name to *Sage-grouse Habitat* (shown in figure 2.8, on the facing page). Click OK to close the Layer Properties window.

> Alternatively, you can right-click on a layer in the Layers Panel and choose Rename from the context menu to make the layer name editable directly in the Layers panel.

19. Change the other layers names as follows:

- Change Land ownership to Federal Land Ownership
- Change States to State Boundaries

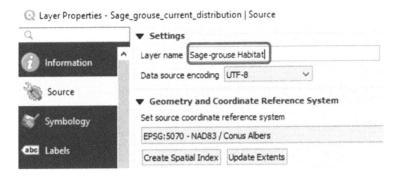

Figure 2.8: Changing the Layer Name

Notice that the Layer Properties window has a *Search* box in the upper left corner. If you cannot remember where a layer parameter is found within Layer Properties, you can use this to search for keywords. The Layer Properties tabs will be filtered based on your search term. For example, try typing *Coordinate* into the *Search* box too find information about the coordinate reference system for the layer. These search boxes are found throughout the QGIS interface.

20. Press `Ctrl + S` or choose `Project | Save` to save the changes you have made to your project.

2.4 Task 2 - Style Data Layers

Now that you have set up your map, you will symbolize your layers and begin to craft a well-designed map.

Visually you will want the land ownership and sage-grouse habitat to have the most weight. Canada and Mexico are there for reference but should fall to the background. You will make them both light gray.

1. Double-click on the Canada layer to open the Layer Properties window (this is a short cut to open Layer Properties).

2. Click on the Symbology tab.

3. Select Simple fill (reference figure 2.9).

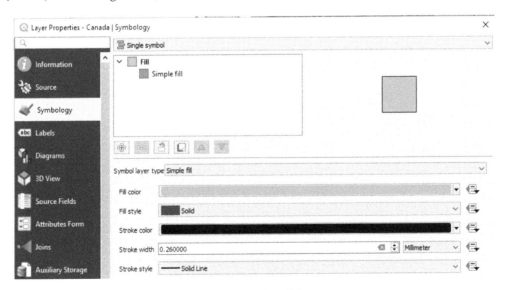

Figure 2.9: Simple Fill Settings

4. Below Symbol layer type are settings for both the fill and stroke for this polygon layer. Click on the color bar to the right of Fill color (shown in figure 2.10) to open the Select Fill Color window.

Figure 2.10: Changing the Fill Color

With the Select Fill Color window you can pick existing colors in a multitude of ways (shown in figure 2.11). To the left are four tabs that let you choose colors (from left to right) A) Color Ramp, B) a Color Wheel, C) Color Swatches, or a D) Color Picker. To the right you can define colors based on E) hue, saturation and value (HSV), F) red blue and green (RGB) values or G) HTML notation. There is also an Opacity slider.

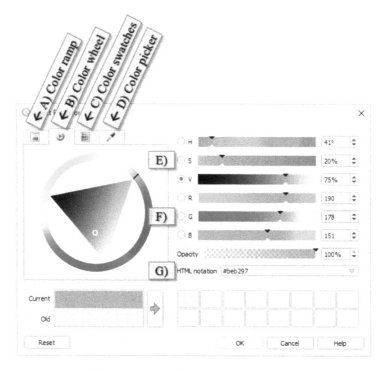

Figure 2.11: Color Picker Fill Settings

5. Set the color to Hue: 0 Sat: 0% and Val: 90%.

6. Click OK to close the Select Fill Color window.

7. Back in the Layer Properties window, keep the default Stroke style of Solid Line but note the other options from the dropdown menu.

8. Click OK on the Layer Properties window to close and accept the symbology settings for the Canada layer.

9. You will symbolize Mexico with the same symbol as Canada. Instead of going through the same steps you will use a short cut. Right-click on the Canada layer and choose Styles | Copy Styles | All Style Categories. Then right-click on Mexico and choose Styles | Paste Styles | All Style Categories.

Your map should now look like figure 2.12, on the facing page.

10. Using the same workflow, give the State Boundaries a white fill. You will be able to find white in the Color

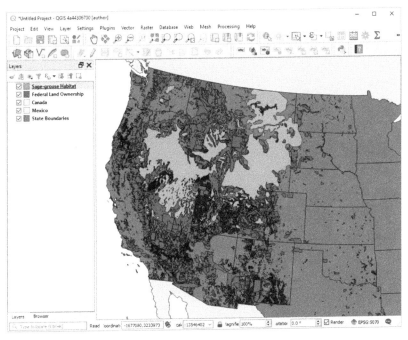

Figure 2.12: Mexico and Canada changed to a gray fill

swatches | Standard colors palette.

Now you will style the Land Ownership layer. Instead of making the entire layer one color as you have done thus far, you will assign a unique color to each land managing agency. You will also learn how to symbolize the layer using the Layer Styling Panel. How do you know which agency is managing each parcel? This will be information contained in the attribute table.

11. Right-click on Federal Land Ownership layer in the Layers Panel, and choose Open the Attribute Table from the context menu.

There are thirteen columns of information. Can you find the one that contains the land manager?

12. Close the Attribute table when done.

13. Find the row of buttons atop the Layers Panel. To open the Layer Styling Panel, click the left most button which looks like a paint brush (See figure 2.13, on the next page). You can also use the keyboard shortcut F7 to open this pane. The panel will open on the right side of the QGIS map canvas. Like all panels this can be undocked to a free floating panel or moved to a different docking position. In a dual monitor environment it can be nice to have the Styling Panel in a different monitor. At the top of the panel is a drop down menu that allows you to choose the target layer.

14. Set the target layer to Federal Land Ownership. Below the target layer is a dropdown for render type. So far you have used the default Single Symbol renderer. Now you will switch to Categorized renderer.

15. Click the drop down menu and change from Single Symbol to Categorized (Figure 2.14, on the following page). Next you need to choose the attribute column to symbolize the layer by. The column AGBUR is the one that contains the managing agency values.

16. Click the drop down arrow and choose AGBUR as the Column.

17. Click the Classify button (shown in figure 2.14, on the next page). This tells QGIS to sort through all the records in the table and identify all the unique values in that column. Now you will be able to assign a specific color to

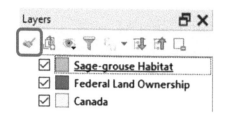

Figure 2.13: Opening the Layer Styling Panel

each class by double clicking on the color square.

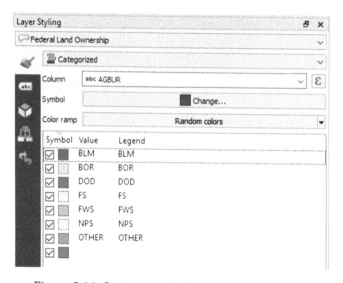

Figure 2.14: Setting up the Categorical Renderer

Notice that there is a symbol with no values. These are parcels with no values (NULL) in the AGBUR field. They represent private and state inholdings within federal lands. Since you are just interested in depicting federal land ownership you'll delete that symbol class.

18. Select that bottom symbol by clicking on it, and then click the Delete button ⊟ to remove that symbol. Now those parcels will not be included on the map.

For the remaining federal land ownership symbols you will use the BLM Standards Manual for land ownership maps https://www.ntc.blm.gov/krc/uploads/223/Ownership_Map_Color_Reference_Sheet.pdf

> Note: A PDF of the BLM Map Color Standards is also available in your exercise folder and is named BLM Map Color Standards.pdf.

The BLM has designated colors for each type of land ownership. When composing a map it is important to pay attention to industry specific standards. Following them will make the map more intuitive to the target audience. For example, people are used to seeing Forest Service land depicted in a certain shade of green.

19. To color BLM lands, double-click on the color patch left of BLM in the Layer Styling Panel. The Symbol selector for BLM lands will open.

20. Select Simple fill.

21. Click on the Fill color patch to open the Symbol Selector > Select Fill Color window.

22. In the Symbol Select Fill Color window, change the Red, Green, and Blue values to 254, 230, and 121 respectively (shown in figure 2.15). This will change the color to a specific shade of tan representing BLM lands. Click the Go back ◀ button twice to return to the main layer in the Layer Styling Panel.

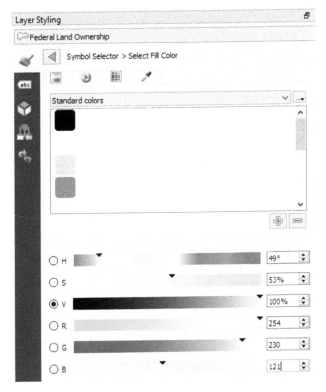

Figure 2.15: Setting the Fill Color for BLM Lands

> Notice as you make changes with the Layer Styling Panel, that those changes appear instantly on the Map Canvas, without having to click an Apply button! This becomes even more powerful when using tools like the Color wheel to find just the right color interactively. All symbology and Labeling options are available from the Panel. So there are two places to make Symbology changes in QGIS: Layer Properties | Symbology and the Layer Styling Panel. Many users find making changes from the Panel to be so efficient that they rarely use Layer Properties | Symbology.

23. Use the values below to change the RGB colors for the remaining six land ownership classes.

- BOR -- 255, 255, 179
- DOD -- 251, 180, 206
- FS -- 179, 222, 105
- FWS -- 127, 204, 167
- NPS -- 177, 137, 193
- OTHER -- 150, 150, 150

Finally you do not want any border lines on these polygons. They are too visually distracting on such a complicated thematic polygon layer.

24. Make sure you are back at the main layer styling with all land ownership classes visible in the Layer Styling Panel.

25. Unselect all the layers by clicking in the white space outside of the land ownership symbol classes.

26. Just below where the Column is specified locate the Symbol -- Change... button. Click the Change... button.

27. Select Simple fill and change the Stroke Style to No Pen. This will remove the outline for all polygons.

28. Click the Go back ◀ button to return to the main layer. Again using this setting provides a way to make a change to all symbol classes, or all selected Symbol classes, in one operation.

29. Turn off Sage-grouse Habitat by clicking the check box next to the name in the Layers Panel.

Your map should now resemble figure 2.16.

Figure 2.16: Federal Lands Symbolized

Now you will set a background color for the map. Since states are filled with white, setting a background color of light blue will serve to represent the Pacific Ocean.

30. From the menu bar choose Project | Project Properties.

31. On the General tab, click the white color patch next to Background color to open the Select Color window.

32. Set the RGB value to: 224, 254, 254.

33. Click OK on the Select Color window and OK on Project Properties to save the setting.

The states are white with a black border and serve to show non-federal land as white which is great. However, the Sage-grouse_Habitat_styling34 are obscured since they are below Federal Land Ownership.

34. Right-click on the State Boundaries layer and choose Duplicate from the context menu. You can have multiple copies of layers for cartographic purposes.

35. Drag the Duplicated layer (State Boundaries copy) to the top of the Layers Panel and turn it on.

36. Set State Boundaries copy as the target layer in the Layer Styling Panel.

37. Click on Simple fill.

38. Give the layer a Fill style of No Brush (see figure below). It will now just be the state outlines above Federal Land Ownership.

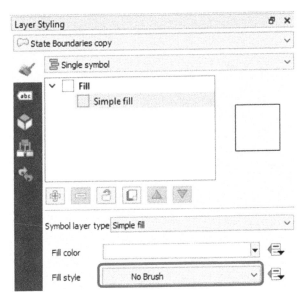

Figure 2.17: Duplicated State Boundaries Set to No Brush

The last layer to work with is the Sage-grouse Habitat. You will make the Sage-grouse Habitat polygons have a crosshatch pattern. This will allow the map reader to see the land ownership data beneath.

39. Turn on the visibility for the Sage-grouse Habitat layer.

40. Set the Sage-grouse Habitat as the target layer in the Layer Styling Panel.

41. Click on Simple fill.

42. Change the Symbol layer type to Line pattern fill. This fills the polygons with a line pattern and allows you to adjust line width, color, angle and spacing.

43. Click on Simple line. Change the Color to RGB 170, 0, 255.

44. Click on Line pattern fill. Change the Spacing to 1.5.

45. Now you will add an outline to this symbol. To do this you will add a new symbol element. Select the Fill and click the Add symbol layer ⊞ button.

46. A Simple fill symbol layer is added. Change the Fill style to No Brush.

47. To set the Stroke color you choose the purple you just chose for the Line pattern fill from the set of recently used colors. Click the drop down arrow to the right of the Stroke color. Find the Recently Used Colors, locate the purple, and click on it. See Figure 2.18, on the following page.

48. Set the Stroke width to 0.46.

49. Now you will zoom in tighter to the Sage-grouse Habitat data.

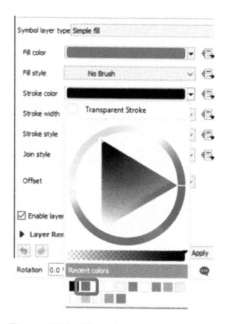

Figure 2.18: Choosing a Recent Color

50. Right-click on the Sage-grouse Habitat layer and choose Zoom to Layer from the context menu. (see figure 2.19).

As it turns out, the data for Mexico is not needed. Sometimes you are given data that does not end up being used, but is nice to have in case you do need it.

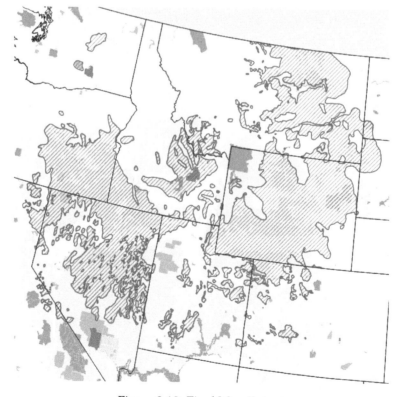

Figure 2.19: Final Map Extent

51. Save 💾 your project!

2.5 Task 3 - Compose Map Deliverable

Now that all the data is well styled you can compose the map deliverable.

> Note that this task incorporates some changes to the layout new to QGIS 3.6. There is nothing that will prevent you from completing it in 3.4 however. If using 3.4 you will just see different options for setting the map extent in the Print Composer.

1. First you will open a New Print Layout. From the menu bar choose Project | New Print Layout, click the New Print Layout 🗐 button or use the keyboard shortcut Ctrl + P.

2. Name the Layout *"Exercise 2 - Sage-grouse Habitat"* (shown in figure 2.20).

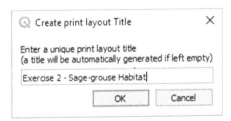

Figure 2.20: Beginning a New Print Layout by Entering a Title

3. Click OK. A new Print Layout will open. This is where you craft your map.

The Print Layout is an application window with many tools that allow you to craft a map. For detailed information about the Print Layout, refer to the QGIS manual: https://docs.qgis.org/testing/en/docs/user_manual/print_composer/overview_composer.html The main window of the Print Layout displays the piece of paper upon which the map will be designed. There are buttons along the left side of the window that allow you to add various map elements: map, scale bar, photo, text, shapes, attribute tables, etc. Each item added to the map canvas becomes a graphic object that can be further manipulated (if selected) by the Item Properties tab on the right side of the layout. Across the top are buttons for exporting the composition, navigating within the composition and some other graphic tools (grouping/ungrouping etc.)

4. Your first task will be to set the paper size. The default paper size is A4. The requirements document specified a letter sized map. To change the sheet size right-click on the blank page and choose Page properties from the context menu. The Item Properties tab changes to display Page properties (figure 2.21, on the next page).

> QGIS Print Layouts allow you to add as many pages to a Layout as you wish. These can also be of differing page sizes and orientations. You need to right-click on a given page to access the page dimensions.

5. Here you can specify details about the overall composition. Set the Size to Letter.

6. Next set the Orientation to Landscape.

7. Using the Add new map to layout 🗖 button, drag a box on the map sheet where you'd like the map to go. Remember that you'll need room for a title at the top of the page and a legend to the right of the map (reference figure 2.22, on page 49).

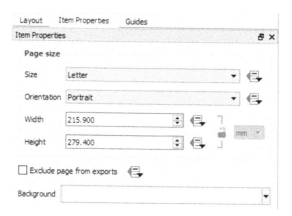

Figure 2.21: Page Properties

The map object can be resized after it's added by selecting it and using the handles around the perimeter to resize with the Select/Move item tool. This tool lets you select map features such as the map, a text block, legend etc. Remember when an object is selected, the Item Properties tab will show properties specific to that object.

8. With the map selected click on the Item Properties tab. New to QGIS 3.6 are a series of buttons across the top of the panel for controlling the map extent. Click the Set Map Extent to Match Main Canvas Extent button. That will help orient the map on the sheet of paper as it appears in QGIS Desktop. (*There is a fuller explanation for this button series in Part 4 - Exercise 1.*)

If you need to make adjustments to the scale in the Main properties section you can adjust the Scale value. Map scale is a ratio of Map Distance/Ground Distance. Here the number is roughly 8400000 which can be read as a scale of 1:8,400,000. To zoom out you increase this number. To zoom in you reduce this number. Clicking the Update Map Preview button forces the map view to refresh.

9. Set the Scale value to 9000000

10. If you need to pan the map you can use the Move Item Content button. This allows you to pan the map content in the map frame without changing the scale. It is normal to have to make adjustments to get the map extent just right. Try to make your figure match the figure 2.22, on the next page.

Now you will add the title to your map.

11. Use the Add new label tool to drag a box all the way across the top of the composition. The text box can be resized after the fact by using the graphic handles.

12. By default the text box will be populated with the placeholder text *Lorem ipsum*. Using the Item Properties tab Main Properties section, replace the holder text with the title: '*Greater sage-grouse Current Distribution*'.

13. In the Appearance section you can change the font. Click the Font button to open the Text Format window. Change the font to : Times New Roman, Bold, Size 36. You can use the search box above the font list to search for Times New Roman.

14. Below the font settings are some alignment settings. Set the Horizontal and Vertical alignment to center.

15. Now you will add a legend. Use the Add new legend tool to drag a box on the right side of the map (shown in figure 2.24, on page 50).

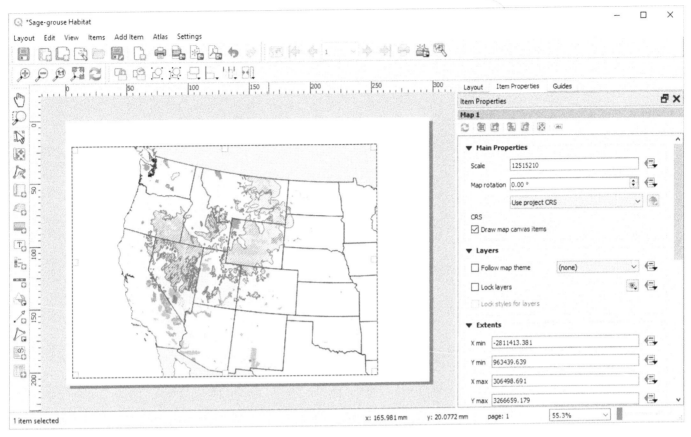

Figure 2.22: Print Layout Extent

Figure 2.23: Title Font Settings

The upper most State boundaries copy layer does not need to appear in the legend, nor does Mexico. State boundaries copy is there purely for cartographic reasons and Mexico does not appear on the map. The Item Properties tab will be used to configure the legend (see figure 2.25, on the next page).

16. Uncheck Auto update. This will enable you to modify the legend, however, updates to the map will no longer be reflected in the legend unless you re-enable Auto update.

17. Select the State Boundaries copy layer and click the Remove item button  to remove it. Do the same for Mexico.

18. Now you will work with the Federal Land Ownership layer. The land ownership classes are abbreviations. Here you will edit them to be more clear to the map readers. Click on the BLM class and click the Edit button.

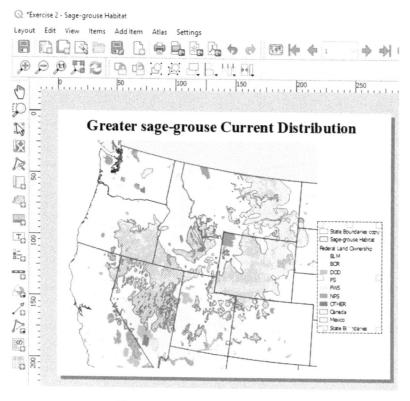

Figure 2.24: Adding A Legend

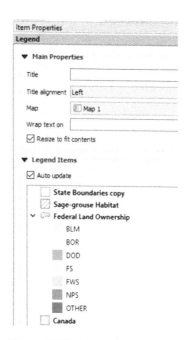

Figure 2.25: Legend Properties

19. In the Legend item properties window change the name to "Bureau of Land Management". Go through each remaining land ownership class and edit them to match the figure 2.26, on the facing page.

Now you will add a neatline around our map.

Figure 2.26: Legend Labels

20. From the set of toolbar click the Add Shape 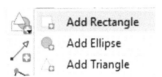 tool. It is an expandable tool with three options. Choose rectangle as shown in figure 2.27.

Figure 2.27: Add Shape -> Add Rectangle Tool

21. Drag a box around the map object and legend.

22. On the Item Properties tab, click the Style button.

23. Click Simple fill and give it a Fill style of No Brush.

24. Give it a Stroke width of 1.

25. Adjust the box so that it aligns with the map boundary.

You may find it necessary to send the neatline to the back so you can still select the map object or legends. Technically these are underneath the neatline object since it was added last. Across the top the Layout has a series of graphic tools on the Actions Toolbar. These allow you to control: object locking, grouping/ungrouping objects, raising/lowering objects, aligning objects, distributing objects and resizing objects.

Figure 2.28: Actions Toolbar

26. Select the neatline rectangle and choose Send to back as shown in the figure 2.29, on the following page.

The last items to add to the map are the data sources and date.

27. Click the Add new label T tool.

Figure 2.29: Send to Back

28. Drag a box in the lower right hand corner of the composition. Using the Item Properties type:

- Data Sources: The National Atlas & USFWS

- Cartographer: <your name>

- Date: Month, Day, Year

29. You can manually enter the date. However, as an additional challenge, it is also possible to use an expression to automate the date. To do this click on the Insert an expression button.

30. The Insert expression window opens.

31. Use the search box to find the String | concat() function.

- Double click on the function to enter it into the expression. This functions concatenates different blocks of text together.

- Inside the parenthesis type: 'Created on: '

- As you form your expression you will see a small red triangle indicating an issue with your expression. This is to be expected since you haven't completed it yet. It is designed to be a helpful indicator of an invalid expression

Figure 2.30: Concat Function

- Enter a comma after this first text block (after the single quote).

- Now search for the Conversions | to_date() function.

- Double-click it to add it to your expression after the comma.

- Enter the variable $now after the opening parenthesis.

- End your expression with two closing parentheses.

- Your expression should now look like: `concat('Created on:  ', to_date($now))`

- Click OK to insert your expression.

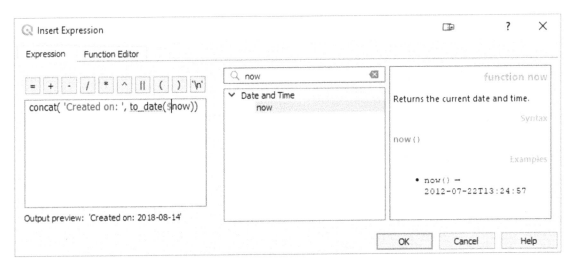

Figure 2.31: Date Expression in the Expression Window

32. Format the expression so that it is just after the Cartographer line.

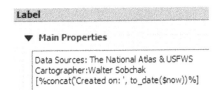

Figure 2.32: Final Text with Expression

33. To finish set to font for the text as Times New Roman with a font size of 8.

34. Congratulations your map is finished! The final step is to export it to a high-resolution jpg image.

35. Click the Export as image button.

36. The Save Layout As window opens.

- Choose the `Exercise 2\Data` folder.

- Choose JPG as the Save as type

- Name the file `exercise2_Map.jpg` and click Save.

- The Image Export Options window will open. Since the requirements document specified 300 dpi keep this default setting and click Save.

37. The final map should look like the figure below.

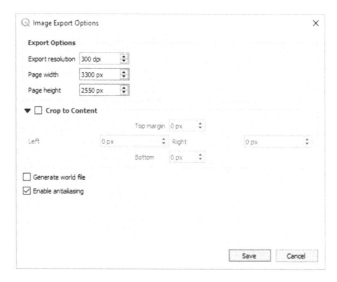

Figure 2.33: Image Export Options

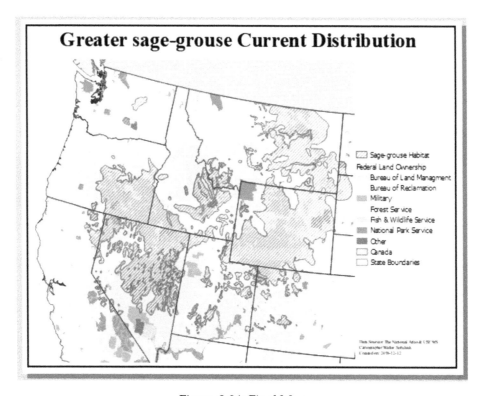

Figure 2.34: Final Map

2.6 Conclusion

In this exercise you created a well-designed map using some of the cartography tools available in QGIS Desktop. You created a nice map highlighting federal land ownership within sage-grouse habitat for a client. This involved styling layers, styling layers by categorical attributes and crafting a map composition.

2.7   Discussion Questions

1. Export the final map as a high-resolution jpg for your instructor to grade.

2. What are two ways to add vector data to QGIS Desktop?

3. How would a portrait orientation change the composition of the map? Describe how you would arrange the map elements.

4. No map is perfect. Critique this map. What do you like about it? What do you dislike about it? How would you change this map to improve it? Would you add other data layers or add labels? One of the best ways to evaluate a map is to judge how it delivers the desired message to the target audience.

2.8   Challenge Assignment

1. Another biologist working with black bears on the east coast heard about your great work on the sage-grouse map. She would like you to create a similar map for her. The data she is providing is in the Exercise 2 Data/Challenge folder.

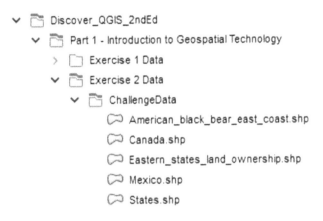

Figure 2.35: Challenge Data

2. She also needs a letter sized, color, map figure that shows the relationship between black bear habitat and federal land ownership along the eastern seaboard. She is interested in seeing how much habitat is under federal versus non-federal ownership.

3. She is providing data from the US Fish and Wildlife Service depicting current occupied range for black bear on the east coast. She is also providing federal land ownership, state boundaries and country boundaries from the US National Atlas. The land ownership data has an attribute column describing which federal agency manages the land (AGBUR). This land ownership dataset has another category in the AGBUR field for Wilderness Areas called "Wild". These should be styled with a dark green.

4. She wants to have the habitat data shown so that the federal land ownership data is visible beneath. She would like each different type of federal land styled with standard Bureau of Land Management colors. The map should also include a title ("Black Bear Current Distribution"), a legend, data sources and the date. The map should be a high-resolution (300 dpi) jpg image. Perhaps you can incorporate some improvements to this map!

5. There are several features of QGIS that can greatly speed up map production once you've already built a similar map with similar data. You don't need to start from the beginning on the new map. You can:

   a. Save a copy of the current QGIS project. (Project | Save As... or Ctrl + Shift + S). Then bring the other set of data in and Copy/Paste the symbology as you did with copying the Canada symbology to Mexico. Then remove the original Sage-grouse related data.

b. Save the symbols for these layers as QML files. Open Layer Properties | Symbology. At the bottom of the window in the Layer Rendering section find the Style drop-down menu and choose Save Style... In the Save Layer Style window save the QML file to the exercise folder. Add the new layer and open Layer Properties | Symbology and choose Style | Load Style and select the QML file. This is more steps, but is useful if you think you will use a style repeatedly for different map projects.

c. You can save map templates which helps with time spent on the Print Layout. Templates store all the map elements. You can then load a map template into a new Print Layout. To save your Sage-grouse map as a template open the Print Layout. Then choose Layout | `Save as template`. You can then choose Layout | `Add Items from Template` to load this template into Print Layouts in other projects. All map elements will be imported. This can save considerable time. Organizations often use this strategy because it allows them to create a create a consistent look. For example, which logo is used and where it is placed. Plus the template can include all required map elements, so organizational maps have a consistent style. Once a template has been imported, you will still need to tweak the positions of map elements to accommodate the new geography.

d. You can also Duplicate Print Layouts (Layout | `Duplicate Layout`) for quick duplication of a map.

6. Experiment with these techniques during this challenge to learn which workflow is best for you in this situation.

Exercise 3

Creating Geospatial Data

Objective - Digitize Information from a Scanned Hardcopy Source

3.1 Introduction

In this exercise, you will learn how to georeference a scanned map. Georeferencing is the process of transforming the coordinate system of the scanned map, from the coordinate system produced by the scanning process, into a real world projected coordinate reference system. You will then learn how to digitize information contained in the scanned map into a shapefile. The first task will be to create the empty shapefile to digitize features into. In addition, you will learn how to edit existing vector datasets.

This exercise will continue to introduce you to the QGIS interface. It is important to learn the concepts in this exercise, as later exercises in this workbook will require the skills covered here.

This exercise includes the following tasks:

- Task 1 - Create a new shapefile.

- Task 2 - Georeferencing an Image.

- Task 3 - Digitizing From Georeferenced Data.

- Task 4 - Editing Existing Geospatial Data.

3.2 Objective: Digitize Information from a Scanned Hard Copy Source

While there is a large amount of digital information readily available to users of GIS, there's still a large amount of information that has not been converted to digital format. For hundreds of years of hard copy paper maps contained all geospatial data. Many historic, and even newer, hard copy maps have never been digitized. It is possible to extract the information from hardcopy sources through a process called digitizing. In this exercise, you will use heads-up digitizing to digitize parcels in a portion of Albuquerque, New Mexico from a scanned map. This will be accomplished through a five-step digitizing process:

1. Create a shapefile to store the data that will be digitized.

2. Load the scanned map source data into QGIS

3. Georeference the source map

4. Digitize parcels

5. Save

3.3   Task 1 - Create a New Shapefile

In Task 3, you will be digitizing parcels from a georeferenced data source. In this first task you will learn how to create the new shapefile you will eventually digitize into.

1. Open QGIS.

2. On the Data Source Manager toolbar click the New Shapefile Layer ⩔ button. This will open the New Shapefile Layer window. This tool can also be found from the menu bar by clicking Layer | Create Layer.

3. Click the Browse button to the right of File name.

Figure 3.1: Browse for File name

4. Navigate to the Exercise_3_Data folder and name the new layer parcels.shp.

5. Set the Geometry type to Polygon.

6. Click the Select CRS 🌐 button to open the Coordinate Reference System Selector window.

The City of Albuquerque, like most American municipalities, uses the State Plane Coordinate System (SPCS) for their data. You will use the same CRS for your new shapefile.

7. In the Coordinate Reference System Selector window type *New Mexico* into the Filter. This will limit the list below to just those with New Mexico in their name. You will see the different SPRC CRSs for New Mexico. New Mexico has 3 zones and Albuquerque is in the Central zone. Notice that the window gives a preview of the valid extents of the CRS (see figure 3.2, on the next page).

8. Select the NAD83(HARN) / New Mexico Central (ftUS) with an EPSG code of 2903. Click OK once you have selected this CRS to be returned to the New Shapefile Layer window.

While creating your new shapefile you have the option of adding attribute columns. It is possible to add them later, but if you know of some attribute columns you will need in the layer, it makes the most sense to define them here. The ID attribute is automatically added to every shapefile you create.

For this exercise, you will need an attribute column to hold the zoning code.

9. In the New field section of the New Shapefile Layer window, define a new field named zonecode as Type Text data with a Length of 5.

This means the new zonecode attribute column will store data as text and will only be able to accommodate five characters of data. Since the longest zoning code is 4 digits this is more than enough.

10. Click Add to fields list and you will see the new zonecode attribute added.

11. Now that you have completed specifying all the criteria for your new shapefile layer click OK to approve the new shapefile options. The new empty layer will be added to the Layer Panel with default symbology.

12. Open Layer Properties for the new parcels layer and choose the Information tab. You will see that it has 0 features and has the Spatial Reference System you specified. Switch to the Source fields tab to review the attributes

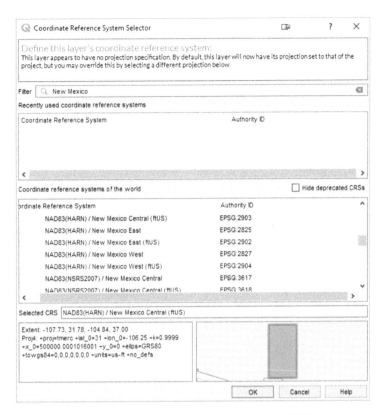

Figure 3.2: Browsing for the Correct CRS

for this new layer. When you have finished reviewing the information click OK to dismiss Layer Properties.

3.4 Task 2 - Georeferencing an Image

Now that you have created an empty shapefile to store the digitized information, you will perform a coordinate transformation (also known as georeferencing) on the source data set so that it is in an Earth-based coordinate system. In this case, the coordinate system will match your parcel shapefile (NAD83(HARN) / New Mexico Central (ftUS)).

In this next section you will be introduced to Plugins. These are add-ons to QGIS which which add specific functionality which is otherwise missing from QGIS. They are authored in Python and can be found in the QGIS Plugins Repository (https://plugins.qgis.org/). Some plugins are developed by the core QGIS developers. However, Plugins can be developed by anyone so most are developed by independent organizations and developers. You will use numerous plugins in this workbook (See Appendix B for a list of the most useful plugins by type).

To perform this task you will be using the GeoReferencing plugin.

1. Now you will check the CRS of your QGIS project.

2. Look at the lower right hand corner of QGIS Desktop and ensure that EPSG: 2903 is listed. If not right click on the parcels layer and from the context menu choose Set CRS | Set Project CRS from Layer.

3. Save the project to the `Exercise_3_Data` folder and name it `exercise3.qgz`.

4. Now you will enable the Georeferencer GDAL plugin. From the menu bar choose `Plugins | Manage and Install Plugins`

5. The Plugins manager will open. Options along the left side allow you to switch between: All, Installed, Not Installed, New, Installed from ZIP, and Settings. The plugin you will use is a core QGIS Plugin named *Georeferencer GDAL*.

6. Since it is a core plugin it will already be installed. You just need to enable it. Click on Installed plugins tab and check the box next to Georeferencer GDAL (shown in figure 3.3).

Figure 3.3: Enabling the Georeferencer Plugin

7. Click Close to close the Plugins window.

8. To open the Georeferencer plugin go to the menu bar and choose `Raster | Georeferencer`.

9. The Georeferencer window opens. Click the Open Raster button at the upper left hand side (see figure 3.4).

Figure 3.4: Open Raster Button in the Georeferencer

10. Navigate to the `Exercise_3_Data` folder and select the `zone_map.bmp` and click Open (shown in figure 3.5, on the facing page). If the Coordinate Reference System Selector window opens click Cancel to close. This dataset does not yet have an Earth-based coordinate system. The source data will now be loaded in the Georeferencer.

The image is a parcel map from the county assessor. On the map, there are 5 points with their associated names (for example, one point's name is: I25 27). These are geodetic benchmarks maintained by the U.S. National Geodetic Survey. To georeference this scanned map, you will create control points at these five locations. The plugin will then develop a georeferencing equation based off the set of source and target coordinates at these five locations. QGIS will obtain the source coordinates from your mouse click on those points. You will look up the target coordinates for these benchmarks from the NGS website.

11. The NGS website is at `https://www.ngs.noaa.gov/cgi-bin/ds_desig.prl`. Open the site.

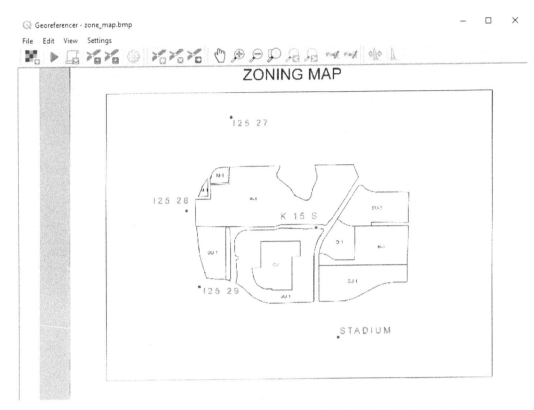

Figure 3.5: Georeferencer Window with the Raster Data Loaded

Note: If you are unable to access the internet, the NGS Data Sheets have been downloaded and saved in the Exercise_3_Data/NGS_Data_Sheets folder. Please read the next few steps to learn how the NGS Data Sheets were acquired.

You will search for each of the benchmarks that appear on the map by searching for each benchmark's datasheet. You will use the Station Name option to do the search.

12. To find the first station, enter the station name of I25 27 (include the space), and then choose *NEW MEXICO* for the state. The search is shown in the figure 3.6, on the next page. Note: the station name is I25 27 with a capitalized letter i.

The search should return the page shown in figure 3.7, on the following page.

13. Highlight the station name and click the Get Datasheets button and you will get something that looks like the figure 3.8, on page 63.

This is an NGS Data Sheet. It gives measurement parameters for NGS benchmarks located throughout the United States. One piece of information it includes are coordinates for benchmarks in State Plane feet (highlighted in the figure 3.8, on page 63 above). There are two sets of State Plane coordinates on the NGS Data Sheet; one is in meters (MT) and one is in feet (sFT). Be sure to use the set in feet. *Important Note*: There is a dash before the North coordinate. It is *not* a negative number.

14. Find the data sheet for each benchmark shown in the map and fill in the coordinates in the table below. The coordinates for the first station have already been entered.

Simple table:

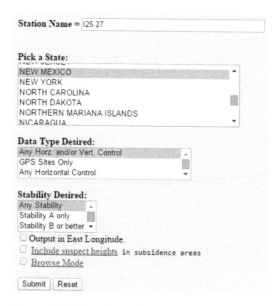

Figure 3.6: Searching for the I25 27 Datasheet

Station List Results for: NM-I25 27*

```
Help
 Dist PID... Set. Set_By H V Vert_Source Latitude..... Longitude..... Stab C Designation
 ---- ------ ---- ------ - - ---------- -------------- -------------- ---- - ----------
 |....|FO1302|1969|NMHC..|2 3|29/LEVELING|N350445.73582|W1063813.49687|C...|G|I25 27
```

Figure 3.7: NGS Datasheet Search Result

Benchmark	Northing	Easting
I25 27	1,484,404.48	1,524,608.32
I25 28		
I25 29		
K 15 S		
STADIUM		

15. The next step is to enter the control points in the Georeferencer. Click on the Add point ⚑ button.

When adding a control point is important to be precise and click directly on the intended location. To help make your selection more precise, you can zoom and pan by using tools in the View toolbar (shown in figure 3.9, on the next page). If you want to redo a control point you can either use the Move point ⚑ button or click the Delete point ⚑ button then click on the point to delete, then re-add it.

16. Zoom in to point I25 27. With the Add point button selected, click on the center of point I25 27.

17. The Enter map coordinates window opens. Enter the easting and northing State Plane Coordinates that you retrieved from the NGS Data Sheet into the two boxes. Make sure you enter them correctly, and do not use thousands separators. The correct coordinates are entered for I25 27 in the figure 3.10, on page 64.

18. Click OK and a red control point will appear on the map where you clicked. The source (Source X, Source Y) and destination (Dest. X, Dest. Y) X,Y coordinates will display in a table at the bottom of the window.

The NGS Data Sheet

See file dsdata.pdf for more information about the datasheet.

```
PROGRAM = datasheet95, VERSION = 8.12.5.2
1         National Geodetic Survey,    Retrieval Date = NOVEMBER  3, 2018
 FO1302 ************************************************************************
 FO1302  DESIGNATION -  I25 27
 FO1302  PID         -  FO1302
 FO1302  STATE/COUNTY-  NM/BERNALILLO
 FO1302  COUNTRY     -  US
 FO1302  USGS QUAD   -  ALBUQUERQUE WEST (1990)
 FO1302
 FO1302                      *CURRENT SURVEY CONTROL
 FO1302  _____
 FO1302* NAD 83(1992) POSITION- 35 04 45.73582(N) 106 38 13.49687(W)   ADJUSTED
 FO1302* NAVD 88 ORTHO HEIGHT -  1545.38  (+/-2cm)     5070.1   (feet) VERTCON
 FO1302  _____
 FO1302  GEOID HEIGHT    -        -21.349 (meters)                   GEOID12B
 FO1302  LAPLACE CORR    -          7.34  (seconds)                  DEFLEC12B
 FO1302  HORZ ORDER      -  SECOND
 FO1302  VERT ORDER      -  THIRD ? (See Below)
 FO1302
 FO1302.The horizontal coordinates were established by classical geodetic methods
 FO1302.and adjusted by the National Geodetic Survey in December 1993.
 FO1302.
 FO1302.The NAVD 88 height was computed by applying the VERTCON shift value to
 FO1302.the NGVD 29 height (displayed under SUPERSEDED SURVEY CONTROL.)
 FO1302
 FO1302.Significant digits in the geoid height do not necessarily reflect accuracy
 FO1302.GEOID12B height accuracy estimate available here.
 FO1302
 FO1302.The vertical order pertains to the NGVD 29 superseded value.
 FO1302
 FO1302.The Laplace correction was computed from DEFLEC12B derived deflections.
 FO1302
 FO1302. The following values were computed from the NAD 83(1992) position.
 FO1302
 FO1302;               North       East     Units Scale Factor Converg.
 FO1302;SPC NM C   -   452,447.391  464,701.544  MT  0.99991535  -0 13 20.9
 FO1302;SPC NM C   - 1,484,404.48 1,524,608.32  sFT 0.99991535  -0 13 20.9
 FO1302;UTM  13    - 3,883,070.670  350,750.959  MT  0.99987453  -0 56 27.7
```

Figure 3.8: NGS Datasheet

Figure 3.9: View toolbar

> Often the source dataset will not include survey monuments with known coordinates. This is typical if you are georeferencing a scanned aerial photograph. In those situations you need to use features such as cities, geographical features, historic buildings or road intersections as the control points. In that case you would choose the *From map canvas* option. Then simply click on the corresponding location on the QGIS map canvas to select the Destination X and Y coordinates.

19. Repeat this procedure for points I25 28, I25 29, K 15 S and STADIUM. After the five control points have been entered your Georeferencer window should look like the figure 3.11, on the next page.

20. Now you will set up the transformation. Click the Transformation Settings button.

21. Choose the Polynomial 1 as the Transformation type. The Transformation type determines how the image will be transformed from source to destination coordinates. Polynomial 1, Polynomial 2, and Polynomial 3 are

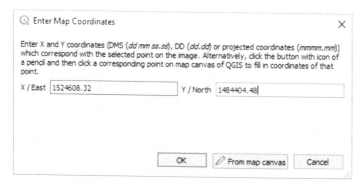

Figure 3.10: Adding a Control Point for 'I25 27'

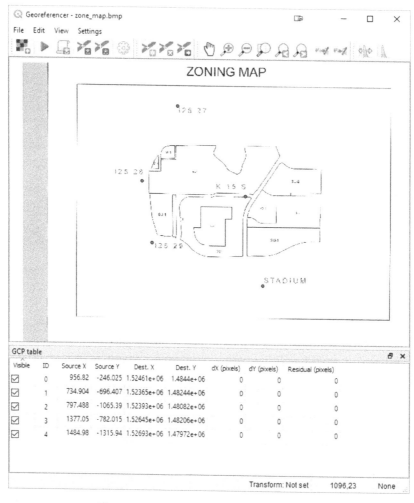

Figure 3.11: All Control Points Entered

all commonly used. They are also sometimes referred to as first (affine), second and third order transformations. Polynomial 1 requires only three control points whereas Polynomial 2 requires 6, and Polynomial 3 requires 10. Linear and Helmert are more simple and are only suited for rasters which are already in a projected coordinate reference system. Thin Plate Spline is similar to Polynomial 3. Projective is used for transforming oblique imagery such as satellite images.

22. Choose Nearest neighbor as the Resampling method. This is the standard raster resampling method for discrete

data such as a scanned map.

23. Click the browse button to the right of Target SRS. Type *2903* into the Filter. Select the NAD83(HARN) / New Mexico Central (ftUS):EPSG 2903 CRS then click OK.

24. Click the browse button to the right of Output raster. Navigate to your `Exercise_3_Data` folder and name the file `zone_map_modified_spcs.tif` and click Save.

25. Check Load in QGIS when done.

26. Leave the remaining parameters as is.

27. Click OK to close the Transformation settings window and perform the transformation.

Figure 3.12: Transformation Settings

28. Click the Start georeferencing ▷ button to run the transformation.

29. Once the transformation is complete, the layer will be added to QGIS desktop.

30. Before closing the Georeferencer click the Save GCP Points as ⬇ button. Navigate to your exercise data folder and save them as a .points file. This will preserve the data used in the transformation. You could replicate your work in the future by loading these points into the Georeferencer with the Load GCP Points ⬆ button.

31. Close the Georeferencer window.

32. Right-click on the `zone_map_modified_spcs.tif` and choose Zoom to layer to see the georeferenced image.

33. Using the Data Source Manager or the Browser panel add the `netcurr.shp` shapefile from the `Exercise 3 Data` folder to QGIS. This is a shapefile representing city streets produced by the City of Albuquerque. If the transformation was done correctly, the streets will line up with the georeferenced parcel map image (shown in

figure 3.13).

34. Save your QGIS map document.

Figure 3.13: Georeferenced Parcel Map

3.5   Task 3 - Digitizing From Georeferenced Data

Now you will digitize the parcels off the georeferenced image into the parcels shapefile.

1. Drag the parcels layer above the zone_map_modified_spcs layer in the Layers panel. Right-click on parcels and choose Toggle editing. This puts the parcels layer into edit mode. Notice that a pencil appears next to the layer in the Layers panel indicating that layer is in edit mode.

2. Turn off the netcurr layer's visibility.

3. Using the Zoom in ⊕ tool, drag a box around the M-1 parcels in the northwest corner of the image. You will digitize these first.

There is an Editing toolbar for editing vector datasets (see figure 3.14). If it's not visible, go to the menu bar to View | Toolbars and turn it on. The tools available change slightly depending on the geometry of the data you are editing (polygon, line, point). For example, when editing a polygon layer you will have a tool for adding polygon features. Hover over each tool to get pop-up descriptions for what each does.

Figure 3.14: Editing Toolbar

4. Click on the Add Polygon Feature tool ⬡ Your cursor will change to an editing cursor that looks like a set of cross hairs.

Polygons are constructed of a series of nodes which define their shape. Here you will trace the outline of the first parcel clicking to create each node on the polygons boundary.

5. Put your cursor over a corner of one of the polygons. Left click to add the first point, left click again to add the second, and continue to click around the perimeter of the parcel. After you have added the final node finish the polygon with a right-click.

6. An Attributes window will open asking you to populate the two attributes for this layer: id and zonecode. Give the parcel an id of 0 and the zonecode is M-1 (shown in figure 3.15). Each parcel feature will receive a unique id starting here with zero. The next parcel you digitize will be id 1, the one after that id 2 etc.

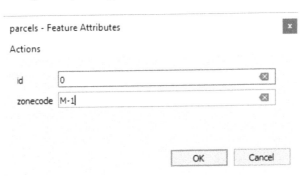

Figure 3.15: Attributes Window

7. Click OK to close the Attributes window and complete the polygon. As you experienced, adding single isolated polygons is pretty straightforward.

If you want to delete the polygon you have just added there are several ways to do this: A) Click the Current Edits tool dropdown menu and choose Roll Back for Selected Layer(s). B) Go to the menu bar and choose Edit |Undo. C) Select the feature using the Select features tool and click the Delete selected features button on the Digitizing Toolbar.

8. To work on the next polygon, zoom back to the extent of the image. You can do this by clicking the Zoom Last button.

9. Find the big parcel in the south central area. There is a parcel with zoning code SU-1 that wraps around O-1. Zoom to that area.

10. Open the Layer Styling Panel and set the Parcels layer as the target layer. Near the bottom of the Styling Panel is a Layer Rendering section. Expand this section and find the Opacity slider. Set the Opacity to 50%. This will allow you to see the source data underneath your parcels as you digitize.

11. Digitize the outer boundary of the SU-1 parcel ignoring the O-1 parcel for the moment. Fill in the attributes when prompted (id=0, zonecode=SU-1). The SU-1 polygon will be a ring when completed but for now it covers the O-1 parcel.

12. To finish SU-1 you will use a tool on the Advanced Digitizing toolbar. Turn that toolbar once from the menu bar by choosing View | Toolbars, and checking Advanced Digitizing. Toolbars and Panels can also be accessed by right-clicking on the menu bar or tool bars. This will open a context menu with all available toolbars and plugins. Dock the Advanced Digitizing toolbar where you would like, as shown in figure 3.16, on the next page (All toolbars in the QGIS interface can be moved by grabbing the stippled left side and dragging them to different parts of the interface.) Again hover over each tool to become familiar with what each does.

Figure 3.16: Advanced Digitizing Toolbar

13. Now you'll use the Add Ring ⬡ tool. Select it and click around the perimeter of the O-1 parcel. Right click to finish. This creates a ring polygon (shown in figure 3.17).

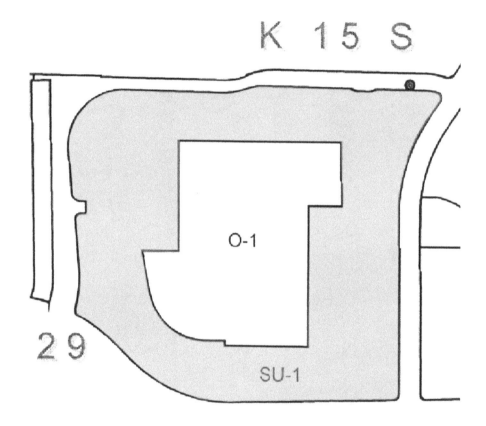

Figure 3.17: SU-1 Ring Polygon Completed

14. To digitize O-1 you will use a tool that is part of the Digitizing Tools plugin. First open the Plugin Manager and switch to the All tab. Use the search box to find the *Digitizing Tools* plugin. Select the Plugin and click the Install Plugin button. You should get the message Plugin Installed Successfully. Close the Plugin manager and make sure the Digitizing Tools toolbar is visible. Dock the toolbar where you'd like and familiarize yourself with the available tools.

Figure 3.18: Digitizing Tools Toolbar

15. On the Attributes toolbar, click the Select Features by area or single click 🔲 tool and select the SU-1 polygon.

16. On the Digitizing toolbar, select the dropdown next to the Fill ring with a new feature (interactive mode) tool and select Fill all rings in selected polygons with new features tool (selection shown in figure 3.19, on the next page).

Figure 3.19: Fill All Rings with New Features Tool

17. You will immediately be prompted to enter the attributes for the new O-1 polygon (id=2, zonecode=O-1).

18. Click OK when done and the new polygon will appear. It automatically fills the space leaving no gaps.

19. Use the Identify Features tool to click on O-1 and SU-1 and verify that they are attributed correctly.

Note: If you end up needing to move one or two misplaced vertices on a finished polygon you can do that. Use the Node Tool ▼. With the Node tool selected when you hover over a feature the vertices will become visible. To move one click once on one you want to move and again where you want it to be repositioned.

To digitize the remaining polygons, you will first turn on snapping options to make it easier to have adjacent polygons share vertices and/or segments.

20. To configure snapping options go to the menu bar and choose View | Toolbars | Snapping Toolbar. Dock the Snapping Toolbar where you would like.

Figure 3.20: Snapping Toolbar

This is a toolbar that lets you configure what layers you can snap to while editing. You can also set the snapping tolerance.

21. Click the Enable Snapping button.

22. Click on the Setting drop down button menu and choose Open Snapping Options

Figure 3.21: Snapping Options

23. The Project Snapping Settings window opens. Where it reads All Layers click the drop down and choose Advanced Configuration.

24. Here you can set snapping options for each layer in a map document. Check the box next to Parcels since you want to snap your parcels to that layer. Set the Tolerance for parcels to 10, the Units to pixels and choose a Type of *vertex*.

The Snapping mode lets you control what portions of a feature are being snapped to: - To vertex will snap to vertices - To segment will snap to any part of another layers edge - To vertex and segment will snap to both.

The Tolerance determines how close your cursor needs to be to another layer before it snaps to it. It can be set in screen pixels or map units.

25. Check the box under Avoid intersections to the right of Units (shown in the figure 3.22). This enables topological editing. When digitizing a shared boundary with this option checked you can begin with one of the vertices at one end of the shared boundary. Then continue digitizing the boundary of the new polygon and end at a vertex at the other end of the shared boundary. The shared boundary will be created automatically eliminating digitizing errors.

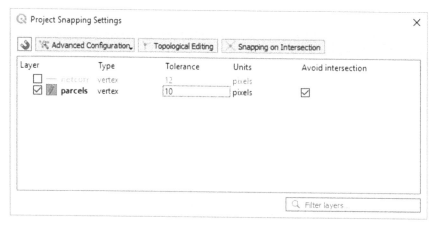

Figure 3.22: Snapping Options

26. Close the Project Snapping Options window when done.

If snapping is interfering with digitizing a parcel polygon you can go to the Snapping Toolbar and adjust your settings. Clicking the Enable Snapping button will toggle snapping on and off.

27. Finish digitizing the polygons. Anytime you have a parcel that shares a boundary with another, use snapping to make sure you create two parcels without a gap in between.

Remember, you can adjust the snapping tolerance and what features are being snapped to vertex, segment, and vertex and segment.

28. When finished, click the Toggle Editing button to exit out of editing mode. You will be prompted to save your changes. Click Save to save the edits.

29. Turn off the zone_map_modified_spcs raster---you're done with that now. It was an intermediate step necessary to get the parcel boundaries digitized.

30. Save your QGIS project.

3.6   Task 4 - Editing Existing Geospatial Data

Now that you have digitized data into the empty shapefile you created, you will learn how to modify existing shapefiles.

1. Open the Data Source Manager. Switch to the Raster tab. Click the browse button on the right side of the Source section. The Open GDAL Supported Raster Dataset(s) window opens. Find the filter drop down that is set by

default to All files. Set the filter to Multi-resolution Seamless Image Database (*.sid, *.SID). Navigate to the `Exercise 3 Data` folder. Select all four SID images. Click Open and then Add to add them to QGIS.

2. Drag the parcels layer above the images in the Layers panel.

3. Turn off the parcels layer.

4. Now you will make an edit to a line layer. Turn on the netcurr layer.

5. Zoom into the location highlighted in figure 3.23.

Figure 3.23: Zoom Into This Area

You will digitize the missing main road, shown in yellow in the figure 3.24, on the following page.

6. Toggle on editing for netcurr.

7. Set your Snapping options so that only netcurr is being snapped to, with a Mode of *To vertex* and a Tolerance of 10 pixels.

8. Using the Add Line Feature tool on the Digitizing Toolbar digitize the new road. Make sure to snap to the roads at the northern and southern ends. Use the centerline of the road while digitizing.

9. There are many attributes for this layer. You will just enter a few. Enter the STREETNAME as *Park*, the STREETDESI as *Place*, the STREETQUAD as *SE* and the COMMENTS as *Exercise 3*. Click OK.

10. Toggle off editing and Save.

3.7 Conclusion

In this exercise, you have successfully digitized information using the five-step digitizing process. Additionally, you have recreated the original source data (scanned as a raster) in the vector format. Digitizing can be a time-consuming and tedious process, but can yield useful geographic information.

Figure 3.24: Road to Digitize

3.8 Discussion Questions

1. What can contribute to errors in the georeferencing process?

2. What other vector geometries (point/line/polygon) could be appropriate for digitizing a road? In which instances would you use one vector geometry type over another?

3. When you created the parcels shapefile you added a text field to hold the zoning codes. What are the possible field types? Explain what each field type contains, and provide an example of a valid entry in the field.

4. Aerial photography has a lot of information in it. What other features could you digitize from the imagery in this exercise? Explain what vector geometry you would use for each.

3.9 Challenge Assignment

You have successfully created the parcel data from a scanned map. You have also fixed the roads data in this part of town. There are some sports facilities visible: two football fields and a baseball field. Create a new layer and digitize those three facilities (include the grassy field areas at a minimum).

Create a simple page sized color map composition using the QGIS Desktop Print Composer showing your results. Show the parcels, sports facilities, parks, roads and aerial photography. Use Categorized styling to give a unique color to each zone code in the parcel data. Include:

- Title

- Legend (be sure to rename your layers so that the legend will be meaningful.)

- Date and Data Sources

You can credit the data sources as the City of Albuquerque and yourself. If you need to refresh your memory on creating a map layout, review Exercise 2.

Exercise 4

Understanding Remote Sensing and Analysis

Objective – Explore and Understand How to Display and Analyze Remotely Sensed Imagery

4.1 Introduction

In this exercise, you'll learn how to display and inspect multiband imagery in QGIS, then use QGIS data processing tools to conduct an unsupervised classification of multispectral imagery. This exercise includes the following tasks:

- Task 1 – Display and Inspection of Image Data

- Task 2 – Performing an Unsupervised Classification

4.2 Objective: Learn the Basics of using QGIS for Image Analysis

Image analysis is one of the largest uses of remote sensing imagery, especially with imagery that has recorded wavelengths beyond the visible spectrum. Here you will learn how QGIS can be be used in combination with the FOSS application SAGA (http://www.saga-gis.org/) to also conduct image analysis. SAGA is a standalone software package that can be installed separately. However, the main analysis tools are bundled with QGIS. This means that QGIS can be used as a front-end for accessing the SAGA analysis tools.

4.3 Task 1 - Display and Inspection of Image Data

There are many ways to view multiband image data. Here you will explore some display options for a multiband image in QGIS.

1. Open QGIS and open the `Exercise_4_MultiSpectral_Imagery.qgz` project file.

2. The project contains is an aerial photograph covering a portion of the Davis Purdue Agriculture Center in Randolph County, Indiana.

3. Double click on the layer name in the Layers Panel to open the Layer Properties, then click on the Information tab.

The Information tab shows you the source file Name and the Path where the data are stored on your computer. Notice that the Path is hyperlinked. This is a handy new feature. Clicking on this will open up the source folder in your file browser. It also provides information about the dataset. For example, the Width (1,501) and Height (709) of the image in pixels and the CRS. The file format is also given via the GDAL Driver line. Remember that GDAL is a FOSS library for reading and writing raster data files.

What is the file format for this image?

Figure 4.1: Multi-band Image in QGIS

4. Switch to the Source tab. Here you will find Layer name, and this is one of the places where you can change the name that appears in the Layers Panel. There is also a setting named Set source coordinate system which allows to correctly define the CRS if it is missing or wrong. This dataset has a correctly defined CRS so no action is needed here.

5. Switch to the Symbology tab.

This image has three bands. Each band represents a segment of the electromagnetic spectrum. In this case, band 1 represents the red portion, band 2 the green portion, and band 3 the near-infrared portion. Therefore, in this image, we are able to see characteristics of the landscape that you cannot see with your naked eyes, as they only detect visible light.

When an image has multiple color bands, QGIS defaults to a Multiband color rendering of that image. Colors on your computer monitor are created by combining three color channels: red, green and blue (RGB). By selecting three bands from a multiband image, and illuminating them with either red, green or blue light we create a color image. The multiband color renderer defaults to displaying Band 1 through the red channel, Band 2 through the green channel and Band 3 through the blue channel. However, we can change which bands are displayed through which channels. These are known as band combinations. Different aspects of the landscape can be seen via different band combinations.

6. In the Band Rendering section click the drop-down arrow for the Red band and change it to Band 3. Change the Blue band to Band 1 (see figure 4.2, on the next page).

7. Click Apply and move the Layer Properties window so you can see the changes in the raster rendering.

> What is the difference between using Apply versus OK? Clicking OK saves the changes and closes the dialog window. Clicking Apply saves the changes and leaves the window open. Use Apply if you want to change a setting and leave the dialog window open to make other changes. Use OK if you want to make a change and close the window.

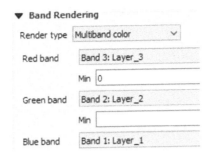

Figure 4.2: Changing the Band Combinations

8. The image should now look like figure 4.3. This band combination creates what is known as a false color composite. Vegetation reflects a lot of near-infrared energy. You are now looking at the near-infrared through the red channel so vegetation shows up as red tones. The brighter the red, the more vigorous and healthy the vegetation.

Figure 4.3: False Color Composite

The Symbology tab also allows you to adjust the Min/Max Value Settings along with Contrast enhancement. Expand the Min/Max Value Settings. Each band has values from 0-255. This section allows you to control how that range of values is used in rendering the image. The default is Min/Max which uses the full range of values. Change this setting to Cumulative count cut with the default values of 2% and 98%. This setting eliminates the bottom and top 2% of the values.

9. Next change the Accuracy setting to Actual(slower). This setting lets you either estimate the range of values from a sample or get the full range of values. Obtaining actual values can take longer since QGIS has to scan all the values in the image. This image is so small that you are not incurring much overhead by scanning the dataset for the full range of values. Notice that you can also set the Statisics extent to either Whole raster, Current canvas or Updated canvas. Leave this setting at the default of Whole Raster.

10. Change the Contrast enhancement to Stretch to MinMax. This will stretch the colors from the minimum and maximum values minus those outlying values. Click Apply. You will see the Min Max values for each band change in the Band Rendering section. Now look at the image on the map canvas. It is brightened up a bit. (see figure 4.4, on the next page.) You are both applying a stretch and eliminating the bottom and top 2% of the values via the

Cumulative count cut setting.

Figure 4.4: Resulting Image Rendering

11. Now choose a Min/Max Value Setting of Mean +/- standard deviation. Click Apply to see the image change.

These are the values within one standard deviation of the mean value. This is useful when you have one or two cells with abnormally high values in a raster grid that are having a negative impact on the rendering of the raster.

12. You can also look at one individual band. Change the Render type to Singleband gray. Choose Band 3 as the Gray band. Set the Contrast enhancement to Stretch MinMax. Click Apply (see figure 4.5.).

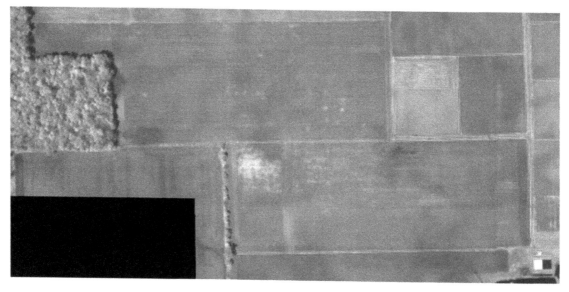

Figure 4.5: Near-infrared Shown Alone

13. Change the Gray band setting to each of the other two bands and see how different they look.

14. Change back to a false color composite view:

- Render type: Multiband color

- Red band = Layer 3

- Green band = Layer 2

- Blue band = Layer 1

- Contrast enhancement = Stretch to MinMax

- Click Apply

15. In the Layer Properties, click on the Transparency tab.

16. With the Global Opacity setting you can control the transparency of the entire image.

17. You can also define image values that you want to be transparent. Notice that in the southwest corner there is a black rectangle with no image data. No are known as *No Data* cells. On the Transparency tab click the Add values from display button then click on the black rectangle on the map. QGIS will measure the values for all three bands where you clicked and enter them into the Transparent pixel list.

18. Click Apply. The black rectangle of no data pixels disappears.

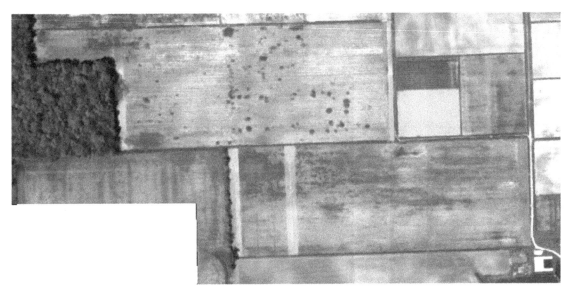

Figure 4.6: Raster with Transparent No Data Cells

19. Click on the Pyramids tab.

Raster data sets can get very large. Pyramids help render large images more quickly. Without them, QGIS will try to render each pixel in an image even though your monitor may not have enough resolution to display each pixel. Pyramids are lower resolution versions of the image that will increase performance. This particular image is small so you will not build any now.

20. Click on the Histogram tab.

Here you can view the distribution of data values in your raster. If it is a multiband image, you can view data for each band. The histogram is generated automatically when you open this tab (see figure 4.7, on the next page). Note that you can save the histogram as an image with the Save plot button.

21. Save your QGIS project.

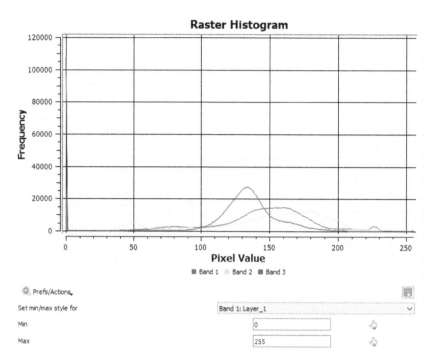

Figure 4.7: Image Histogram

4.4   Task 2 - Performing an Unsupervised Classification

In an unsupervised classification, the software automatically classifies the image into homogeneous areas. Pixels are automatically grouped based on the reflectance values. This is opposed to a supervised classification where you train the software based on locations with known features. An unsupervised classification is much simpler and quicker to perform but will likely be less accurate.

1. Open QGIS and then open the `Exercise_4_Data/Exercise_4_Landsat.qgz` file.

2. This project contains a subset of a Landsat 8 scene covering Rome. There are separate rasters for bands 2, 3, 4, 5, 6, and 7. The image was acquired on June 12, 2014.

3. You will be using a Processing tool to conduct the unsupervised classification. From the menu bar, choose `Processing | Toolbox` to open the Processing Toolbox panel.

4. Type *cluster* into the Search box at the top of the panel to help locate the tool. (figure 4.8, on the facing page)

5. Double-click on the SAGA - Image Analysis K-means clustering for grids tool.

6. Fill out the tool as follows (see reference figure 4.9, on the next page):

7. Click the ellipsis button to the right of Grids to open the Multiple selection window. Click Select all and OK.

8. Choose a Method of Combined Minimum Distance/Hillclimbing.

9. Change the number of Clusters to 7.

10. Select Normalise. This setting normalizes the input grids before clustering.

11. Uncheck the Statistics output so you will only output the Clusters.

12. Click Run to run the cluster analysis. The result will be a temporary file.

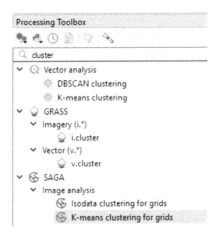

Figure 4.8: Searching Toolbox

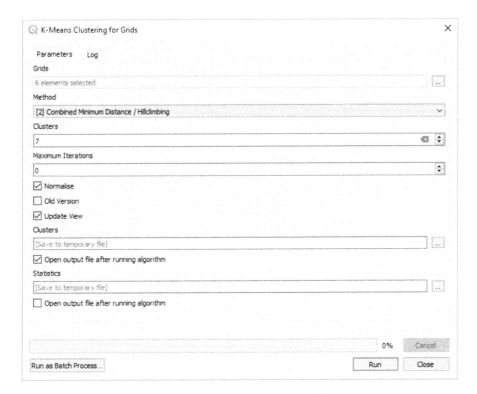

Figure 4.9: K-Means Clustering Tool Settings

13. The temporary grid and a Statistics table are added to the Layers Panel. The *Clusters* grid will appear in the map canvas styled on a black to white color ramp.

> By default QGIS names output layers by the name of the processing algorithm. Here this is fine, since you used a temporary file as the output. However, when saving the output to a permanent file you can change this behavior. From the menu bar choose Settings | Options then switch to the Processing tab. Expand the General section. There is a setting which reads: Use filename as layer name, which you can set as appropriate.

Now you will style the data.

14. Open Layer Styling Panel with the target layer being the new layer.

15. Change from a Singleband gray renderer to a Paletted/Unique values render. This renderer gives a different color to each unique value in the raster.

16. Set the Color ramp to Spectral.

17. Click the Classify button Your image should resemble figure 4.10 below. The tool has classified or grouped the pixels into categories based on common reflectance characteristics.

> Using this tool on another set of imagery will require you to experiment with different numbers of clusters and clustering methods to ensure that the resulting classification represents meaningful categories on the ground.

Figure 4.10: Unsupervised Classification Symbolized

The data now shows the seven classes of data. You will be able to identify those representing vegetated areas, barren soil, built up areas and water. At this point you could refine your symbology to represent these features.

4.5 Conclusion

In this exercise, you have learned the basics of working with multispectral imagery in QGIS. You learned how to access data processing tools in QGIS and how to do an Unsupervised Classification. You will learn how to perform a supervised classification in Part 5 - Remote Sensing, on page ??.

4.6 Challenge Assignment

You have used QGIS to perform an Unsupervised Classification of the multispectral imagery. Create a simple page sized color map composition using the QGIS Print Layout composer to show your results. Include:

- Title

- Legend (be sure to rename your layers so that the legend will be meaningful.)

- Date and Data Sources

You can credit the data sources as the U.S. Geologic Survey and yourself. If you need to refresh your memory, review Exercise 2.

Exercise 5

Basic Geospatial Analysis Techniques

Objective – Use Basic Spatial Analysis Techniques to Solve a Problem

5.1 Introduction

In this exercise, the you'll explore some of the basic analysis tools available in QGIS to conduct a spatial analysis for a team of surveyors visiting National Geodetic Survey Monuments in Albuquerque, New Mexico. You will then create a map of the results. The surveyors wish to have a map showing monuments within the Albuquerque city limits. They will use this map to plan their fieldwork for the week.

This exercise includes the following tasks:

- Task 1 – Data Preparation

- Task 2 – Querying and Extracting Subsets of Data

- Task 3 – Buffering and Clipping Data

- Task 4 – Preparing a Map

5.2 Objective: Use Basic Spatial Analysis Techniques to Solve a Problem

Conducting effective spatial analysis in a GIS does not necessarily require the use of extremely complex algorithms and methods. By combining multiple simple spatial analysis operations, you can answer many questions and provide useful results. Determining the order in which these simple spatial analysis operations are executed is often the hardest part of conducting spatial analysis. Additionally, data is rarely available in exactly the format and subset that you require. A large part of almost all GIS projects is simply obtaining and preparing data for use.

In this exercise, the you'll utilize four basic geospatial analysis techniques: selection, buffer, clip, and dissolve.

- Selection uses set algebra and Boolean algebra to select records of interest.

- Buffer is the definition of a region that is less than or equal to a distance from one or more features.

- Clip defines the areas for which features will be output based on a 'clipping' polygon.

- Dissolve combines similar features within a data layer based on an attribute.

5.3   Task 1 - Data Preparation

In this task, you will obtain GIS data for this exercise by visiting several online GIS data portals, A) the National Geodetic Survey (NGS) website, B) City of Albuquerque GIS Department, C) the New Mexico Resource Geographic Information System (RGIS) and D) the Bernalillo County GIS Department. All of these websites provide free geospatial information.

Note: Copies of this data have already been obtained and are available in the `Exercise_5_Data/RawData` folder. If you are unable to obtain the data yourself, you may skip to Task 2 and use the Raw Data.

5.4   Task 1.1 - Obtain Shapefiles of NGS Monuments

We first want to go to the same National Geodetic Survey (NGS) website you visited in Exercise 3. This time you will download a shapefile of the monuments in the Bernalillo County, New Mexico. This is the county in which Albuquerque is situated.

1. In a web browser, navigate to `http://www.ngs.noaa.gov`

2. Click on the Survey Mark Datasheets link of the left side of the page.

3. Click the Shapefiles button.

4. Use the COUNTY retrieval method:

5. Pick a State = New Mexico then click Get County List

6. Pick a County = Bernalillo

7. Data Type Desired = Any Vertical Control

8. Stability Desired = Any Stability

9. Compression Options = Send me all the Shapefiles compressed into one ZIP file...

10. File Prefix = Bern

11. (Leave all other options as the default values)

12. Click the Submit button

13. Click the Select All button

14. Click Get Shapefile

15. When the dialog box appears to save the ZIP file, save it into the `Exercise_5_Data/MyData` directory.

16. Extract the ZIP file into the `MyData` directory.

5.5   Task 1.2 - Obtain the Municipal Boundaries

Since you will identify monuments within the Albuquerque City limits, you'll need an Albuquerque City limit dataset. You will download the data from the City of Albuquerque GIS Department.

1. In a web browser, navigate to `http://www.cabq.gov/gis/geographic-information-systems-data`

2. Scroll down until you find the Municipal Limits data.

3. Download the Boundaries shapefile to your folder.

4. Save the ZIP file into your `Exercise_5_Data/MyData` directory.

5. Extract this ZIP file into the exercise directory.

5.6 Task 1.3 - Obtain the Census Tract Boundaries

You will visit the RGIS clearinghouse. This is the main source for geospatial data for New Mexico. You will download census tract boundaries for Bernalillo County.

1. In a web browser, navigate to `http://rgis.unm.edu`

2. Click the Get Data button

3. In the folder tree underneath Filter data by Theme, expand Census Data

4. Expand 2010 Census

5. Click on 2010 Census Tracts

6. Download the Bernalillo County 2010 Census Tracts shapefile to your folder.

7. Save the ZIP file into your `Exercise_5_Data/MyData` directory.

8. Extract this ZIP file into the exercise directory.

5.7 Task 1.4 - Obtain Road Data

Finally, you will visit the Bernalillo County GIS Program to download a roads data set. This is the main source for geospatial data for New Mexico. You will download census tract boundaries for Bernalillo County.

1. In a web browser, navigate to `http://www.bernco.gov/Download-GIS-Data/`

2. Find the Download GIS data section

3. Find Road Inventory

4. Download the Road Inventory Zip file to your folder.

5. Save the ZIP file into your `Exercise_5_Data/MyData` directory.

6. Extract this ZIP file into the exercise directory.

5.8 Task 2 - Querying and Extracting Subsets of Data

Now that you have collected the necessary data, you will add it to a blank QGIS map document. Take a moment to familiarize yourself with the data and what information it contains. As with any project, you will have to do some data preparation to make it useful for the analysis.

5.9 Task 2.1 - Working with coordinate reference systems

1. Open QGIS.

2. Using the Data Source Manager or the Browser panel, add all four shapefiles to QGIS (see figure 5.1, on the following page).

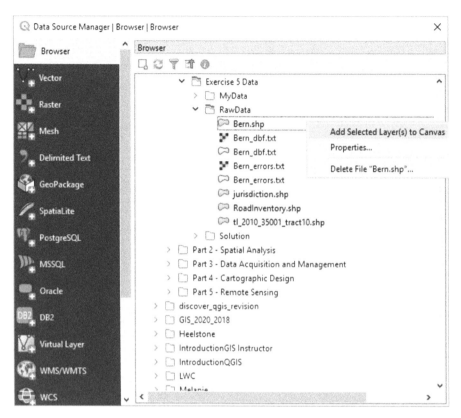

Figure 5.1: Adding Data via the Data Source Manager

3. Organize the layers in the Layers Panel so that the Bern monuments layer is on top, followed by the RoadInventory, tl_2010_35001_tract10 (tracts), and jurisdiction.

4. Save your project to the Exercise_5_Data folder as exercise5.qgz.

Does it look like all the layers are lining up together?

5. Hover over each layer in layer properties and you will see some pop up information including the file path and the EPSG code for the layers' CRS. Note that the Census Tracts (tl_2010_35001_tract10) and Monuments (Bern) are in geographic coordinates and the Road Inventory and jurisdiction are in the State Plane Coordinate System (SPCS).

6. Right-click on the Road Inventory layer and choose Set CRS | Set Project CRS from Layer from the context menu. This can be done from Project Properties | CRS but this is a quick way to set the project CRS to the CRS of a particular layer.

The project is now in NAD83(HARN)/New Mexico Central(ftUS)(EPSG: 2903). This means that the Census Tracts and Monuments are being projected on the fly into EPSG:2903. Projecting on the fly is fine for cartographic purposes. However, when conducting a geospatial analysis, the data layers involved should be in the same CRS. Typically, data layers will also be clipped to the extent of the study area to reduce rendering and data processing time. These procedures are often referred to as normalizing your data. For the typical analysis, a majority of your time is spent obtaining data and normalizing it. Once all the data is organized and normalized, the analysis can proceed quickly.

You will want to put all four layers into the same CRS for this analysis. You will put them all into the SPCS CRS of the project.

7. Right-click on the Bern layer in the Layers panel and choose Export | Save Features As from the context menu. This will open the Save Vector Layer as... window (shown in the figure 5.2).

You will save these layers into a GeoPackage which is the default vector file format in QGIS 3.x. This will be a handy data database container to store all the derived project layers. This type of workflow also has the advantage of preserving all the input shapefiles as backups of the original raw downloaded data.

8. Use the default Format of GeoPackage.

9. Click the Browse button to the right of File name and navigate to the Exercise_5_Data/MyData folder and name the GeoPackage BernalilloCounty after the county you are working in for your analysis.

10. Type in a Layer name of Monuments_spcs. It is helpful to employ some sort of naming convention to your files and layer names. Here you are including the CRS in the layer name.

11. Click the Browse button for the CRS. The Coordinate Reference System Selector window will open.

12. From the Recently used coordinate reference systems choose NAD83(HARN)/New Mexico Central (ftUS) EPSG:2903. Note the valid extents preview for this State Plane zone. The valid extent for this CRS is limited to just the central section of the State of New Mexico. In order to use this CRS, your study area needs to fit within the highlighted area. State Plane zones are designed so that each U.S. county fits entirely within in a zone. This is a great choice of CRS for this project. Click OK.

13. The Add saved file to map should be checked (this is the default setting). You will want the layer added after it has been created.

14. Click OK and the layer will both be projected into a new CRS and saved into a new file format (GeoPackage). You should also receive the message that the Layer Exported: Successfully saved vector layer....

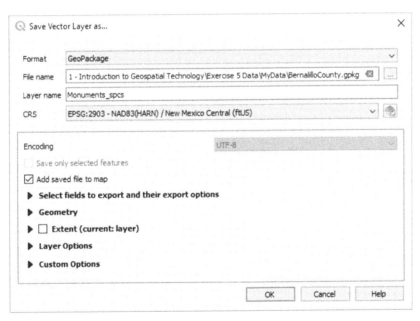

Figure 5.2: Reprojecting the Bern Layer into a GeoPackage

15. The output is named in the Layer Panel with the GeoPackage name followed by the layer name. Rename this layer to just *Monuments*.

16. You no longer need the original Bern layer in your map. Right-click on the original Bern layer and choose Remove from the context menu. Click OK on the Remove layers and groups window.

17. Repeat the above steps to export the Census Tracts (tl_2010_35001_tract10) layer into EPSG:2903. Save it into the same GeoPackage. You will navigate to the `Exercise_5_Data/MyData` folder and just select the existing *BernalilloCounty* GeoPackage. Then name the new layer `CensusTracts_spcs`. Remove the original tl_2010_35001_tract10 layer from your project.

18. Rename the new layer in the Layers Panel as *Census Tracts*.

19. Save your project.

5.10   Task 2.2 - Dissolving Tract Boundaries into a County boundary

For the map, you will need a polygon that represents the county boundary. The Census Tracts collectively define the county, so you will use the dissolve tool to create a county boundary from the Census Tracts. This tool merges adjacent polygons into a single polygon.

1. First you will change a default setting. Recall that by default QGIS names output layers by the name of the processing algorithm. Now you will change this behavior. From the menu bar choose `Settings | Options` then switch to the Processing tab. Expand the General settings. There is a setting which reads: Use filename as layer name. Check this box. Click OK to dismiss the Options window.

2. From the menu bar choose `Vector | Geoprocessing Tools | Dissolve` (see reference figure 5.3).

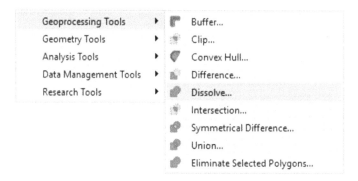

Figure 5.3: Locating the Dissolve Tool

3. Set Input layer to `Census Tracts`.

You can use this tool to dissolve adjacent polygon features based on attributes. For example, if you had counties of the United States you could dissolve them based on the State name attribute and create a state boundaries layer. Here you will not need to use attributes. You will dissolve all the tract polygons into one to create the county boundary.

4. Leave the Dissolve field(s) [optional] alone since you won't be using attributes in this operation.

5. You will save the output to the project BernalilloCounty GeoPackage. Click the browse button to the right of the Dissolved option and choose Save to GeoPackage. Browse to the `Exercise_5_Data/MyData` folder, select the `BernalilloCounty.gpkg` and choose Save.

6. The Save to GeoPackage window will open. Name the Layer name `Bernalillo_county`.

7. Make sure Open output file after running algorithm is checked.

8. Click Run to run the Dissolve tool. Once the tool has executed, click Close. The `Bernalillo_county` layer will appear in the Layers Panel.

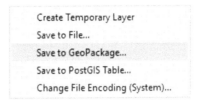

Figure 5.4: Saving the Dissolve Output to a GeoPackage

Figure 5.5: Dissolve Tool Settings

9. Remove the Census Tracts layer from the Layers Panel. It was an intermediate dataset. All you need is the Bernalillo County Boundary.

10. Save your project.

5.11 Task 2.3 - Select Monuments

You will want to filter the monuments so that you only have the ones with the orders and classes you're interested in. Here you only want monuments that meet the following requirements:

- Elevation Order = 1

- Last recovered on or after 1995

- Satellite Observations were used for monument coordinate determination.

- Information relating to these requirements can be found in these attribute columns:

  - ELEV_ORDER

  - LAST_RECV

  - SAT_USE

(For information on what an elevation order and class is, visit http://www.ngs.noaa.gov/heightmod/Leveling/)

1. Double-click the Monuments layer to open the Layer Properties.

2. Select the Source tab.

3. Find the Provider Feature Filter area. This is where you can define the contents of a layer based on the attributes. It is a way to filter a layer.

4. Click the Query Builder button to open the Query Builder window. Here you can write a SQL query to filter your data.

All the attribute fields are listed on the left. Below the fields are operators you can use to build your SQL expression. The expression is built in the blank window at the bottom. When building the expression, it is best to double-click fields and field values instead of manually typing them in so that you avoid syntax errors.

5. Double-click on the field ELEV_ORDER and it will appear in the expression window surrounded by double quotes. Attribute columns are always surrounded by double quotes in QGIS.

6. Click the = sign under Operators to add it to the expression.

7. In the right side Values section click the All button to see a list of all the values contained in that field.

8. Double-click the 1 value so that your expression reads "ELEV_ORDER" = '1'.

Since you want monuments that have both an elevation order of 1 and were last recovered on or after 1995 you will now use the AND operator. The AND operator selects records where both conditions evaluate to TRUE.

9. Double-click the AND button under Operators to add it to the expression.

10. After the AND operator you will create the portion of the expression dealing with LAST_RECV.

11. Once you have done that, add another AND operator and create the third portion of the expression dealing with the SAT_USE.

12. The final expression should look like the figure 5.6.

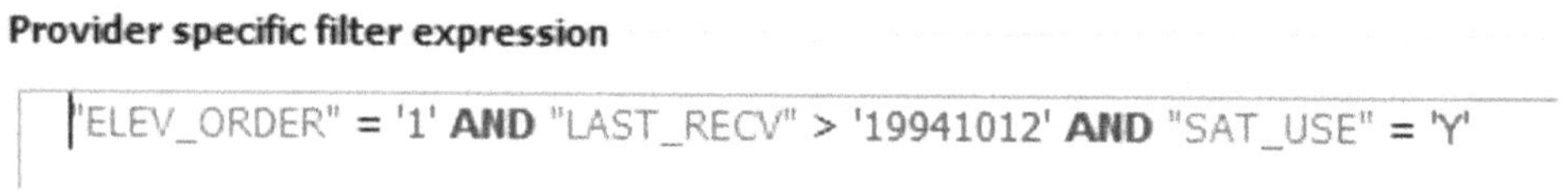

Provider specific filter expression

"ELEV_ORDER" = '1' **AND** "LAST_RECV" > '19941012' **AND** "SAT_USE" = 'Y'

Figure 5.6: Filter SQL Expression

13. Click the Test button. You should get a Query Result of 47 rows. If you have a syntax error you will be notified and you'll have to figure out where the error lies. Any extra tics ' or quotes " will throw an error. Click OK to dismiss the query result dialog.

14. Click OK to set the Query and close the Query Builder window.

15. Click OK again to close the Layer Properties.

16. There is an indicator space to the right of each layer in the Layers Panel. After you have created a filter on a layer you will see the filter icon ▽ there. This is a reminder that this layer has a filter in place. Hovering over the icon with your cursor will produce a pop-up with the expression used (see figure 5.7, on the facing page). Double-clicking on the icon will re-open the Query Builder window.

It is always a good idea to open the attribute table to ensure that the layer has been filtered the way you needed.

17. Open the attribute table for the Monuments layer and verify that the table only includes 47 filtered features.

```
Filter:
"ELEV_ORDER" = '1' AND
"LAST_RECV" > '19941012'
AND "SAT_USE" = 'Y'
```

Figure 5.7: Filter SQL Expression

This will be reported on the attribute table's title bar at the top.

18. With the data properly filtered, the map should now resemble the figure 5.8.

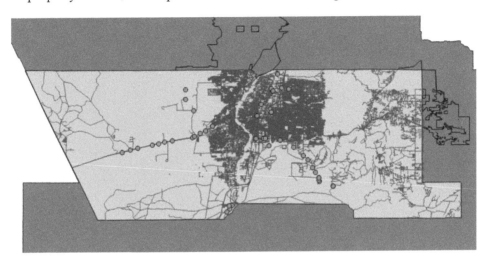

Figure 5.8: QGIS with the Filtered Monuments

19. Save your project.

5.12   Task 3 - Buffering and Clipping Data

Now that you have prepared the county boundary and the monuments layers, you will identify just the monuments within the Albuquerque City limits. First, you will create a filter on the jurisdiction layer and the RoadInventory layer as you did for monuments.

The jurisdiction layer covers much more than Bernalillo County. Albuquerque covers just a portion of the county and jurisdiction extends north and south of the county boundary.

1. Open the attribute table for jurisdiction. The first field JURISDICTI has the city names. Notice that the majority consists of unincorporated areas. You can left click on the field header and you will see a small arrow appear. Subsequent clicks allow you to toggle back and forth between an ascending and descending sort of the record, making it easier to find certain values. Close the Table.

2. Open the Layer Properties for the jurisdiction layer and select the Source tab.

3. As you did with the Monuments layer use the Query Builder to create a feature filter expression. The expression you create should select only the polygons where JURISDICTI equals *Albuquerque*.

4. When done click OK on the Query Builder and close the Layer Properties window.

5. In the Layers Panel, drag jurisdiction above the Bernalillo County layer and turn off RoadInventory. Your map should resemble the figure 5.9, on the following page.

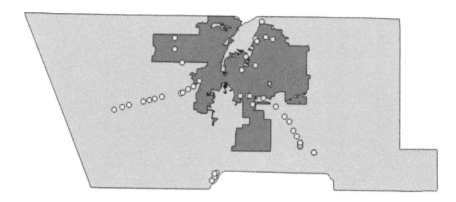

Figure 5.9: QGIS with the Filtered Jurisdiction Layer

6. Open the attribute table for RoadInventory.

There is a lot of information in the RoadInventory shapefile. So far you have filtered a layer within QGIS, but left the data on disk the same. Now you will select the major roads and save them to a new layer in the GeoPackage. Considering the attribute table, what field would you use to select out major roads?

7. Select (highlight) the RoadInventory layer in the Layers Panel and click on the Select Features By Value button dropdown menu and choose the Select Features by Value option (figure 5.10).

Figure 5.10: Select Features by Value Button Menu

You can also open this tool by pressing *F3*. See Appendix A for more keyboard shortcuts.

The Select Features by Value window opens. This is a new tool that allows you to interactively search for data by attribute. Once selected you can Flash features, Zoom to Features and Select Features. The fields are listed down the left side. The middle boxes can be used to enter values. When doing so they autocomplete. To the right you can choose from a series of operators and actions.

8. Scroll down until you find the Class field.

9. Begin typing the value *Major* into the box. You will see a list appear with the values in that column that match what you have typed so far (it autocompletes). Select Major and left-click to accept.

10. The operator option to the right will switch to Contains. Click the drop-down menu and change it to Equal to (=) (figure 5.11, on the facing page).

11. Click Flash Features and you will see all the major roads flash on the map canvas!

12. Click Select Features to select all major roads (figure 5.12, on the next page.

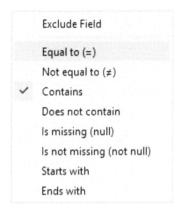

Figure 5.11: Select Features by Value Operators

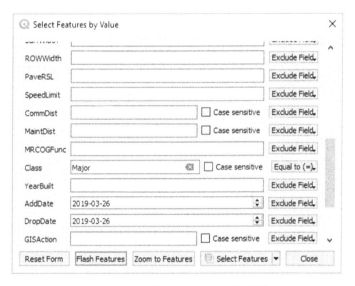

Figure 5.12: Select Features By Value

13. Click Close to dismiss the Select Features by Value window.

14. Open the attribute table for this layer.

You should see that you now have 4,593 out of 37,963 records selected. You can use the dropdown at the lower left corner of the attribute table to show just the selected set of records (see figure 5.13).

Figure 5.13: Toggling the Attribute Table View

15. Close the attribute table.

16. You will now export out the selected set of records to your GeoPackage. Right-click on the RoadInventory layer and this time choose Export | Save Selected Features As from the context menu.

17. You will navigate to the Exercise 5 Data/MyData folder and select the existing *BernalilloCounty* GeoPackage and click Save. Name the new layer :filename:'Major_Roads .

18. Since you chose Save Selected Features As the Save only selected features should be checked.

19. Verify that the dialog looks like the figure 5.14. If so, click OK.

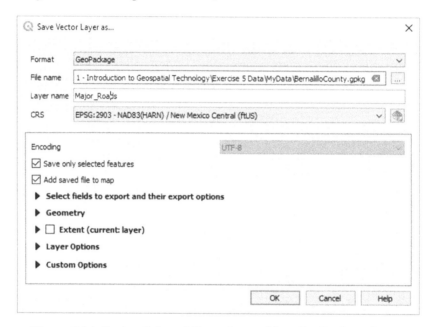

Figure 5.14: Saving Selected Records as a New GeoPackage Layer

20. Remove the RoadInventory layer from the Layers Panel. All you need for your map is Major_Roads.

Now that you have the Albuquerque City limits isolated, you will buffer Albuquerque by one mile. This will allow you to identify monuments that are either inside, or close to the city limits. Buffer is an operation that creates a new polygon layer that is a buffer distance from another layer.

21. From the menu bar choose Vector | Geoprocessing Tools | Buffer....

22. Set the Input Vector Layer to jurisdiction, which now equals the Albuquerque city boundary.

23. You will enter a Buffer distance in feet. Set the Distance to 5280 feet.

24. Save the Buffered output to a GeoPackage. You will continue working with the same project GeoPackage. Name the new layer Albuquerque_buffer.

25. Your tool should resemble the figure 5.15, on the facing page. If so, click Run and then Close.

26. Drag the new buffer layer beneath jurisdiction and you will see that it is a one-mile buffer of the boundary.

Now that you have the search area for the selected monuments, you will use the Clip tool to clip the monument layer to the buffered city limits to create a new shapefile with only the monuments the surveyors should visit. The Clip tool acts like a cookie cutter. It cuts data out that falls within the clipping layer's boundary.

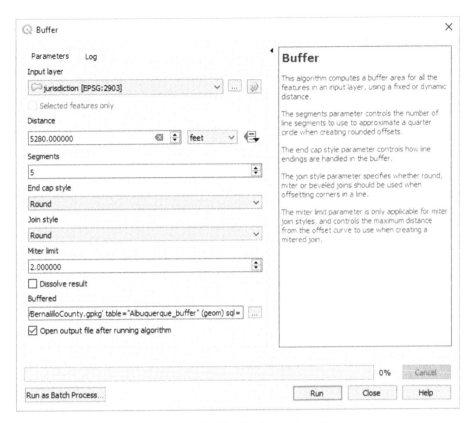

Figure 5.15: Buffer Tool Ready to Run

27. From the menu bar choose `Vector | Geoprocessing Tools | Clip....`

28. Set Input layer to Monuments.

29. Set Overlay layer to Albuquerque_buffer.

30. Name the Clipped output into your GeoPackage naming the new layer `Albuquerque_monuments`.

31. Your tool should resemble the figure 5.16, on the next page. If so, click Run and Close.

32. Remove the Monuments layer from the Layers Panel.

Finally, you will label the monuments with the FeatureID attribute.

33. Open the Layer Styling Panel ✏ with the target layer being the Albuquerque Monuments. Select the Labels ![abc] tab.

34. Click the dropdown menu where it reads No Labels, and change it to Single labels.

35. Just below where it reads Label with click the dropdown. These are all the attribute columns for this layer. Choose `FeatureId` as the field.

36. Below is a horizontal series of tabs that let you control numerous aspects of your labels. Select Buffer ![abc] tab and check Draw text buffer with the defaults (reference figure 5.17, on the following page). This will create a white halo around the labels, which can make them easier to read against a busy background.

37. Adjust the Buffer Opacity to 60% so that they are still effective but not visually dominating. Note that since

Figure 5.16: Clip Tool Ready to Run

you are using the Styling Panel all changes are visible on the map canvas immediately.

Figure 5.17: Labeling Settings in the Layer Styling Panel

38. Click the Placement  tab and set an Distance of 2. This will offset the label from the point a bit giving more room for a bigger point symbol. Note that there are many options for label placement!

39. Using what you know label the major roads using the StreetName field.

40. Select the Text abc tab. This is where you can specify font parameters. Set the font size of 5.25.

41. On the Rendering tab, in the Feature options section, choose Merge connected lines to avoid duplicate labels. This will clean up duplicate labels.

42. Change the style of the layers to make the map more attractive. Choose whatever colors you prefer. As an example, reference the map in the figure 5.18, on the next page.

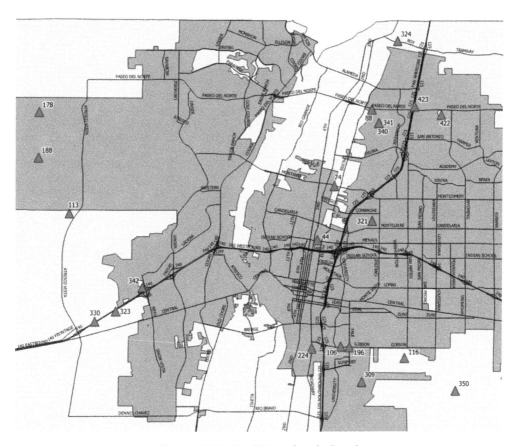

Figure 5.18: Final Data Symbolized

43. Save your project.

5.13   Task 4 - Preparing a Map

Now that you have identified the locations of the monuments that the surveyors should visit, you will make a map of the result of your analysis. You should show the major roads to give them a general idea of how to access the monuments.

1. Rename the layers in the Layers panel to:

2. Albuquerque Monuments

3. Major Roads

4. City of Albuquerque

5. Bernalillo County

You do not necessarily have to show the buffer layer. It was just a means of identifying the monuments to map. However, you have cartographers license on that choice!

6. Zoom in   to the monuments layer so that you can show as much detail as possible.

7. Use the Print Layout Composer to create a map layout.

8. Include the following map elements:

9. Title: Albuquerque Vertical Control Monuments

10. Legend

11. Your Name

12. Sources of Data

13. Scale Bar: Use the Add Scale Bar 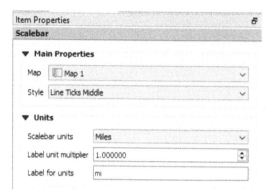 button. Set the scalebar to read in miles (See figure 5.19).

Figure 5.19: Scale Bar Parameters

Here is a sample of a completed map: 5.20, on the next page .

5.14 Conclusion

In this exercise, you used several basic spatial analysis techniques to prepare data for analysis and conduct the analysis. You reprojected data, queried and extracted data, conducted a dissolve operation and used buffer and clip to identify the final set of monuments. While none of these individual operations are necessarily complex, the sequence in which they were combined allowed you to answer spatial questions quickly and easily.

5.15 Discussion Questions

1. Export the final map for your instructor to grade.

2. Think of another use of a clip operation with the exercise data.

3. Could you use the dissolve tool to create a municipal boundary data set whereby all the unincorporated areas were merged together? If so describe how you would set up the tool.

5.16 Challenge Assignment

The surveyors' work was streamlined and efficient due to your GIS analysis. They now have extra time to visit The Village of Tijeras while they are in town. Generate the same analysis and accompanying map for monuments meeting the same criteria for Tijeras. You can use all the same data so you will not have to download anything else. For this map try to incorporate some of the Live Layer Effects. These can be found on the Layer Properties | Style tab under Layer rendering. Effects include: inner and outer glows and drop shadows. Visit Nyall Dawson's blog entry for more details: `http://nyalldawson.net/2015/04/introducing-qgis-live-layer-effects/`. You will learn more about these in Part 5.

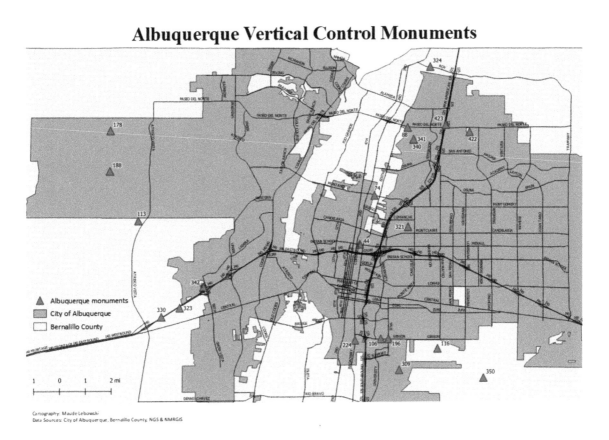

Figure 5.20: Sample Final Map

Part II

Spatial Analysis

Exercise 1

Explore Data Models, Structures, Attributes and GeoDatabases

Objective – Explore data structures, file types, coordinate systems and attributes

1.1 Introduction

This exercise features questions and activities designed to review some basic GIS and geospatial concepts. Throughout the exercise, questions will be asked for you to answer. Create a new document to write your answers and refer back using the question number.

This exercise includes the following tasks:

- Task 1 – GIS Data – Vector

- Task 2 – GIS Data – Raster

- Task 3 – Introduction to Geodatabases (SpatiaLite)

- Task 4 – Exploring Coordinate Systems

- Task 5 – GIS Data Attributes and Attribute Tables

1.2 Objective: Use Basic Spatial Analysis Techniques to Solve a Problem

Spatial Analysis is a crucial aspect of GIS—the tools allow the user to analyze the patterns and relationships of various data. Understanding the concepts of data structures, the variety of file formats, coordinates systems, and attributes are necessary in the design and the function of spatial analysis.

Discrete and Continuous objects:

- **Discrete** – Data that represents phenomena with distinct boundaries. Property lines and streets are examples of discrete data. Discrete data can be stored via vector or raster data models.

- **Continuous** – Data such as elevation or temperature that varies without discrete steps. Continuous data is usually represented by raster data.

There are two main data models within the GIS realm: Vector and Raster

- **Vector** – a representation of the world using points, lines and polygons. Vector data is useful for storing data that has discrete boundaries.

  - Points – use a single coordinate pair to define a location.
  - Lines – uses an ordered set of coordinates to define a linear feature.
  - Polygons – an area feature formed by a connected set of lines.

- **Raster** – a representation of the world as a surface divided into a regular grid of cells. Raster models are useful for storing data that varies continuously such as an aerial photograph.

Common Data Storage Formats:

- Shapefile (.shp) – a GIS file format for vector data.

- GeoTIFF (.tif/.tiff) – a GIS file format for raster data.

- ERDAS Imagine (.img) – a GIS file format for raster data

- Geodatabases (GeoPackage/PostGIS/SpatiaLite/Esri File Geodatabase) – a relational database capable of storing GIS data layers.

1.3   Task 1 - GIS Data – Vector

Examine the vector exercise exercise data using the Browser panel.

1. Open QGIS.

2. In the Browser Panel navigate to and expand the Exercise 1 Data folder.

3. You should see eight shapefiles, an ERDAS Imagine file, a GeoTIFF file, and several XML metadata files.

4. To study the properties of each file, right-click on each and choose Properties from the context menu. An abbreviated form of the Layer Properties window will open. Notice that it also includes tabs for previewing the features and attributes. (see figure 1.1).

Figure 1.1: Browser Panel Layer Properties Window

Question # 1: Studying the properties of each of the shapefiles listed below, write down the geometry type (point, line, polygon) and the number of features in the space provided below.

- BTS_Airport.shp

    - Geometry:
    - Number of Features:

- St48_d00.shp

    - Geometry:
    - Number of Features:

- TX_PRECIP_01_JAN.shp

    - Geometry:
    - Number of Features:

- TX_PRECIP_ANNUAL.shp

    - Geometry:
    - Number of Features:

- TxDOT_ARPRT_SMALL.shp

    - Geometry:
    - Number of Features:

1.4 Task 2 - GIS Data - Raster

Examine the raster datasets provided with this exercise.

1. Open QGIS.

2. In the Browser Panel navigate to and expand the Exercise 1 Data folder.

3. Along with the shapefiles you will see an ERDAS Imagine raster file and a GeoTIFF raster file along with several XML metadata files.

4. To study the properties of each raster file right-click on each and choose Properties from the context menu. The abbreviated form of the Layer Properties window will open.

Question # 2: Record the file format for each. This will be listed under the GDAL Driver Metadata section. You will also record the pixel dimensions which are stored in the Width and Height items. Use the space provided below.

- Texasdem_tsms.img

    - File format:
    - Dimensions:

- tx_terrain_hillshade_tsms.tif

    - File format:
    - Dimensions:

Question # 3: Do these look to be discrete or continuous raster datasets?

1.5   Task 3 - Introduction to Geodatabases (SpatiaLite)

This task will introduce you to another file format, the geodatabase which allow you to store spatial data in a relational database. Specifically you will use QGIS Desktop to connect to and explore the data contained in a SpatiaLite database (https://www.gaia-gis.it/fossil/libspatialite/index). SpatiaLite based on the FOSS SQLite database engine. SpatiaLite spatially enables SQLite allowing spatial data to be stored within it. This is very similar to the relationship between PostGIS and a PostgreSQL database which you will explore in Part 3 Exercise 2. SpatiaLite also adds spatial SQL functions.

A SpatiaLite database neat and tidy, being contained in a single *.sqlite file. QGIS has complete support for SpatiaLite databases. In this task, you will learn how to add layers from a SpatiaLite database to QGIS. You will then learn how to import a layer into the SpatiaLite database.

1. Open QGIS.

2. Click the Open Data Source Manager button.

3. Click the Add SpatiaLite Layer tab.

4. Click the New button to establish a new connection to an existing SpatiaLite database.

5. Select the `Exercise_1_Data\Geodatabase\NDG.sqlite` file and click Open.

6. Click Connect button to connect to the database and see the contents (see figure 1.2).

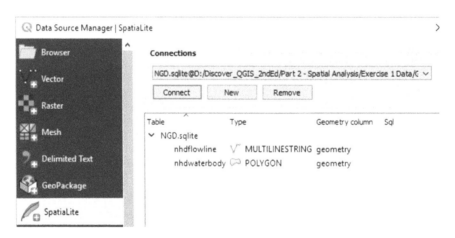

Figure 1.2: Connect to a SpatiaLite GeoDatabase

7. You will see two layers: `nhdflowline` and `nhdwaterbody`. Select both by clicking on them with the Ctrl key held down.

8. Click Add to add them to the map canvas in QGIS. Click Close to dismiss the Data Source Manager. (see figure 1.3, on the facing page).

9. Now you will import a shapefile into the NDB SpatiaLite geodatabase. From the menu bar choose Database | DB Manager to open the DB Manager window.

10. Expand the SpatiaLite section. You will see the `NGD.sqlite` geodatabase. Expand that as well. You will see the two layers (see figure 1.4, on the next page).

11. Click the Import Layer/File ![Import Layer/File icon] Import Layer/File... button to open the Import vector layer window.

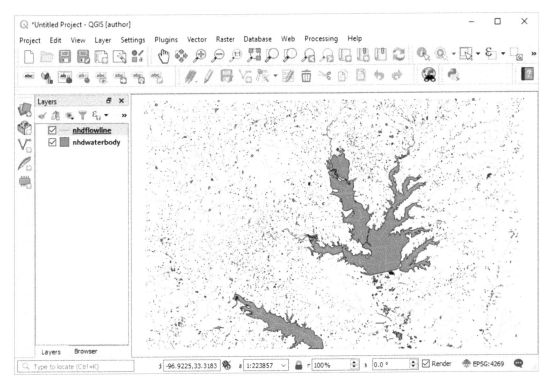

Figure 1.3: SpatiaLite Layers Added to QGIS

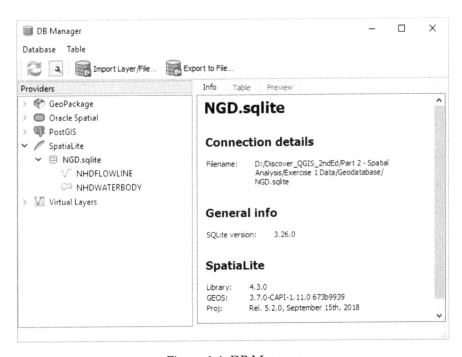

Figure 1.4: DB Manager

12. Click the ellipsis [...] button to the right of the Input section to open the Choose the file to import window.

13. Navigate to `Exercise 1 DataGeodatabase` folder and select `NHDPOINT.shp`. Click Open.

14. Name the Table `nhdpoint`.

15. In the Options section check Source SRID and ensure it is set to EPSG:4269 - NAD83. QGIS should have read this information and set it by default. This is the EPSG code for the geographic coordinate system NAD83.

16. Check Create spatial index.

17. Check your options again in the figure 1.5. If they match, click OK to import the shapefile into the database.

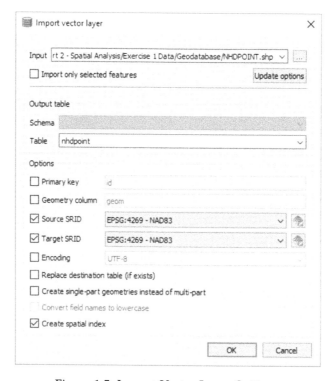

Figure 1.5: Import Vector Layer Settings

18. You should get a message that the Import was successful. Click OK.

19. You should now see `nhdpoint` listed as a new table in the database with a point icon (shown in figure 1.6, on the next page). If you do not see it click the Refresh button on the DB Manager.

20. Right-click on the `nhdpoint` layer in the DB Manager and choose Add to Canvas. Close the DB Manager.

21. You should now see the new point data added to QGIS (shown in figure 1.7, on the facing page). You have successfully connected to a geodatabase and imported a shapefile into the database!

22. Open the Browser Panel. Navigate to the `Exercise 1 DataGeodatabase` folder. Expand the `NGD.sqlite` database and you can see the imported shapefile in the database (see figure 1.8, on the next page).

Question # 4:
What is a reason to import source data into a geodatabase?

1.6   Task 4 - Exploring Coordinate Systems

Explore the coordinate reference systems of the exercise data.

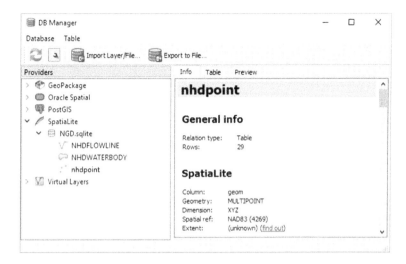

Figure 1.6: New Layer Imported into SpatiaLite

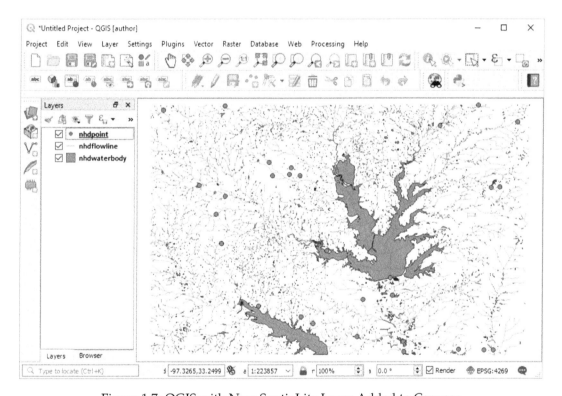

Figure 1.7: QGIS with New SpatiaLite Layer Added to Canvase

Figure 1.8: SpatiaLite Database in the Browser Panel

1. Open QGIS.

2. Open the Browser Panel

3. By right-clicking and selecting Properties from the context menu, identify the coordinate reference system for the following datasets in the `Exercise 1 Data` folder. Record your answers below:

Question #5:

- `St48_d00.shp`:

- `texasdem_tsms.img`:

- `TxDOT_ARPRT_SMALL.shp`:

4. Add the `BTS_AIRPORT.shp` shapefile to QGIS by right-clicking on the layer in the Browser Panel and choosing Add Selected Layer(s) to Canvas.

5. To identify the coordinate system of loaded layer `BTS_AIRPORT.shp` right-click on the layer in the Layers Panel and choose Properties from the context menu.

6. Click on the Information tab in the Layer Properties window. You will see the coordinate reference system of the layer next to CRS section.

> The Source tab also displays the CRS for the layer and allows you to define the CRS of the layer, within the map document. You would need to do this if it has been incorrectly defined or if the CRS is undefined. To permanently define the CRS of a layer you can use the Assign Projection tool in the Vector general section of the Processing Toolbox.

Question #6: What is the current coordinate system of this data?

Let us say for purposes of our analysis that we would like to change the coordinate system of the `BTS_Airport.shp` layer.

7. Click on the `Processing | Toolbox` or click the Toolbox button ⚙ on the Attributes toolbar to open the Processing Toolbox panel. Use the search box to search for the keyword **CRS**. Find the Reproject Layer tool. Double-click on the tool to open it.

8. Set the Input layer as `BTS_AIRPORT.shp`.

9. Set the Target CRS as UTM Zone 14, NAD83. To do this click the Select CRS 🌐 button and use the Filter in the Coordinate Reference System Selector window to search for the EPSG code. For this CRS it is **26914**. Note that you could also use the Filter to search for **UTM Zone 14**.

10. Save the Reprojected output to a shapefile named `BTS_Airport_utm.shp`

> There are usually more than one way to accomplish a task in QGIS. You have already seen that a layer can also be reprojected by right-clicking on it and choosing Export | Save Features As... There is no best way. You can use whichever method suits your workflow.

1.7 Task 5 - GIS Data Attributes and Attribute Tables

1. Open QGIS and start a new empty project.

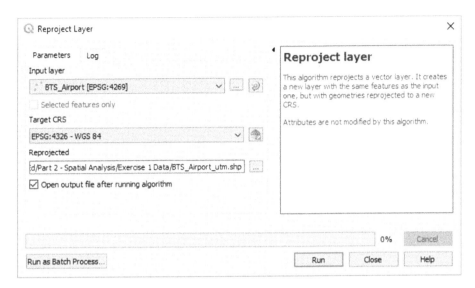

Figure 1.9: Reproject Layer Tool

2. Add `State_of_Texas.shp` and `TxDOT_ARPRT_SMALL.shp` to the map canvas.

3. Open the attribute table for the `TxDOT_ARPRT_SMALL.shp` shapefile by right-clicking on it in the Layers Panel then choosing Open Attribute Table from the context menu.

Question #7: How many records are in this table?

Question #8: How many attributes does this shapefile have?

4. Open the attribute table for the `State_of_Texas.shp` shapefile.

Question #9: How many records are in this table?

Question #10: How many attributes does this shapefile have?

Question #11: If you wanted to identify all Regional airports from the State_of_Texas.shp shapefile on the map how would you do that?

1.8 Conclusion

In this exercise, you were able to identify the data models, geometry, and number of features for several exercise data sets. You connected to a SpatiaLite geodatabase and imported a shapefile into it. You identified the coordinate reference systems of data and reprojected a dataset. Finally, you reviewed working with attribute tables. Knowing how to determine the characteristics of datasets is a necessary step in spatial analysis.

1.9 Discussion Questions

1. What is the importance of coordinate reference systems? Why are there so many different coordinate systems and map projections?

2. Describe the pros and cons of rasters and vectors.

Exercise 2

Introduction to Table Joins and Classification

Objective – Understand Attribute Table Joins and Data Classification

2.1 Introduction

GIS data comes in many formats. As you collect data from various sources on the internet, you will realize that the data you acquire will not always be spatially enabled. There may be a spatial component to the data, but it is not yet a GIS dataset. For example, you may have an Excel spreadsheet with county population statistics. The data has a spatial component, county designation, however, it is not data that is ready to be mapped. In this exercise you will learn how to perform a table join to attach data to the attribute table of an existing GIS dataset. You will then learn how to classify the data.

This exercise includes the following tasks:

- Task 1 – Data Exploration and Attribute Joins
- Task 2 – Data Classification

2.2 Objective: Explore and Understand Geospatial Data Models

In this exercise we will look at some tabular data and determine how to join it to an existing dataset. This is a common data preparation step before beginning an analysis.

Join – Appending the fields of one table, to those of another table, based on a common attribute. Typically, joins are performed to attach more attributes to the attribute table of a geographic layer.

Classification – the process of grouping a series of data values into meaningful categories.

2.3 Task 1 - Data Exploration and Attribute Joins

The data for this exercise includes one shapefile: U.S. County boundaries (countyp010.shp). The layer only covers the contiguous lower 48 states. There is also one tabular dataset: U.S. Census data (ce2000t.dbf) for counties.

In order to map the data in the table, we will need to join it to the county shapefile. In order to perform such a join there needs to be a common attribute between the table and the shapefile.

1. Open QGIS and add the county shapefile.

2. Open the countyp010 attribute table and examine the contents (shown in figure 2.1, on the following page).

113

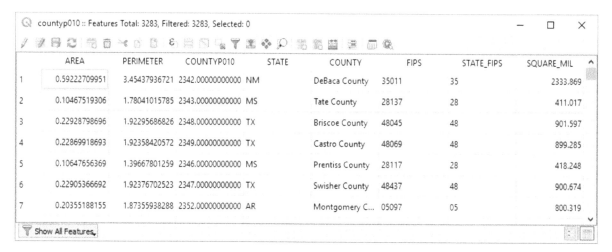

Figure 2.1: Counties Attribute Table

You can see that there are 3,283 records in the table. What kind of attributes does this data set have? The Area and Perimeter fields are created as part of the file format (shapefile). These represent the area and perimeter of each feature in map units. Since this dataset is in the Geographic Coordinate System these units are in decimal degrees. This is a difficult unit to work with so these values do not provide much information. The Square_Mil field at the far right is much more useful. This holds the area of each polygon in square miles. CountyP010 is a unique ID. There are also fields for State abbreviation, county name and FIPS codes.

FIPS stands for Federal Information Processing Standards. They are unique codes for census designations. Each state has a FIPS code and each county has a FIPS code. This dataset has a column for the State_FIPS but not the county FIPS alone. The first two digits in the FIPS column are the State FIPS code. The last three digits in the FIPS column are the County FIPS code. Combining both State and County FIPS codes provides a unique ID for each county in the U.S.

With this data, you can identify the state and county names and the size of each county. Now you will examine one of the standalone tables.

3. Close the county attribute table.

4. Use the Data Source Manager to add the (ce2000t.dbf) table.

5. Right-click on the table in the Layers Panel and choose Open Attribute Table from the context menu. Examine the attributes.

6. This table contains many fields of socioeconomic data such as total population, population by age, population by gender etc.

What field can be used to join this to the Counties attribute table? At first you might think the County column would work. Click the County column header so that an upward facing arrow appears. (Remember that this allows you to toggle back and forth between an ascending and descending sort of the data.)

Notice that there are numerous Adams County entries from several states (shown in figure 2.2, on the next page). Therefore, County name is not a unique ID. However, the FIPS column is a unique ID that will be used to join to the FIPS column in the shapefile.

7. Close the attribute table.

8. Right-click on the countyp010 layer and choose Properties from the context menu to open the Layer Properties window.

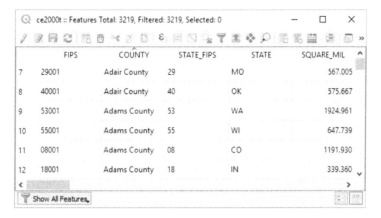

Figure 2.2: Census Data Table Sorted by County

9. Click on the ◀ Joins tab. This is where you configure joins for the layer.

10. Click the Add new join 🔁 button. The Add Vector Join window opens.

The Join layer is the table you will join to the attribute table of the shapefile. Since you only have one table in your Layers Panel there is only one choice: ce2000t. Since you've previewed both the county layer attribute table and ce2000t you know that the Join field is FIPS and the Target field is also FIPS.

11. Set the Join field to FIPS.

12. Set the Target field to FIPS.

13. Check the box for Custom Field Name Prefix and expand that section. By default each joined column will include *cd2000t_* as a prefix. Replace that with *j_* to indicate joined columns with a shorter prefix.

> In this example both join fields have the same name. However, this is not a requirement. What is required is that both fields have the same data type. For example, they need to both be text fields or both integer fields. Also note that the Add Vector Join window has options for specifying which columns will be included with the join. You won't use this options here, but it is good to know it exists.

Figure 2.3: Adding a Join

14. Click OK.

15. You will see the join show up in the Join window (shown in figure 2.4). The join has now been created.

Figure 2.4: Join Established with Details Exposed

16. Click OK on the Layer Properties window to close it.

17. Reopen the countyp010 attribute table. You will see all the additional fields appended to the right side.

This join exists only within this QGIS map document. In other words, the data have not been physically added to the shapefile. However, within this map document the new fields will act as all the others. Next you will learn how to make the join permanent.

18. Right-click on the county layer in the Layers Panel and choose Export | Save Features as... from the context menu. This will allow you to save a new copy of the countyp010 shapefile with the new attributes included.

19. Set the Format to *ESRI Shapefile*.

20. Name the new shapefile countyp010_census.shp in your exercise directory and add it to the map canvas (options shown in figure 2.5). You should get a message in the message bar atop the map that the *Layer Exported: Successfully....*

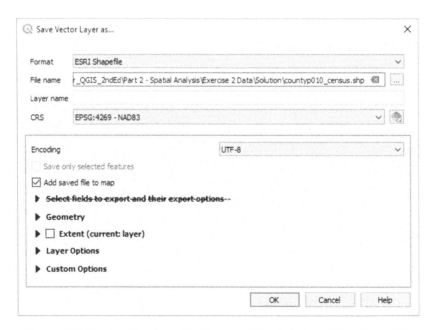

Figure 2.5: Saving the Counties Layer with a Join to a New Shapefile

21. You can now remove both the original county layer and the ce2000t table from the Layers Panel by right-clicking on each and choosing Remove from the context menu.

22. Save the QGIS map project as `exercise2.qgz` in your exercise directory.

2.4 Task 2 - Data Classification

Now that you have joined data to the counties layer, you will explore different ways to symbolize the data based on the new attributes.

1. Open QGIS and open `exercise2.qgz` if it is not already open.

2. Click on the Current CRS ◉ EPSG:4269 button in the lower right corner of QGIS. This is a shortcut to opening the CRS tab of Project Properties.

3. In the Filter box type *5070*. This is the EPSG code for the Albers Equal Area projection for the continental U.S.

4. Select the NAD83/Conus Albers coordinate systems for the map and click OK.

5. The data should now resemble the figure 2.6.

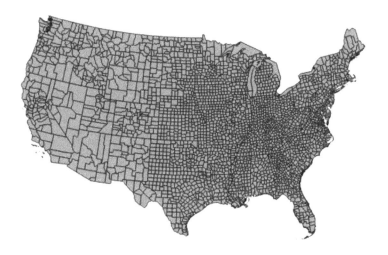

Figure 2.6: Map in Albers Equal Area Conic (EPSG 5070)

6. Open the Layer Styling Panel and set the Counties layer as the target layer.

7. Instead of the default Single Symbol renderer, choose the Graduated renderer. This allows you to choose a numeric field and classify the data into categories.

8. Choose j_POP2000 as the Column. This field has the total population in 2000.

9. Set the Color ramp to *Blues*.

10. Click the Classify button. QGIS breaks the data into five classes and assigns a color to each.

11. Keep all of the other options as their default value (shown in the figure 2.7, on the next page).

Your map should resemble the figure below. QGIS has divided the data values into five groupings and applied a color ramp across the categories. This first classification does not tell much of a story.

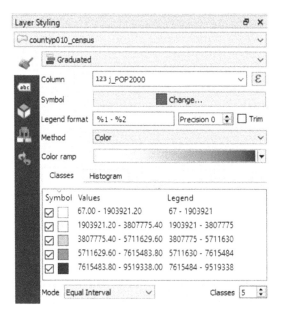

Figure 2.7: Graduated Styling Settings

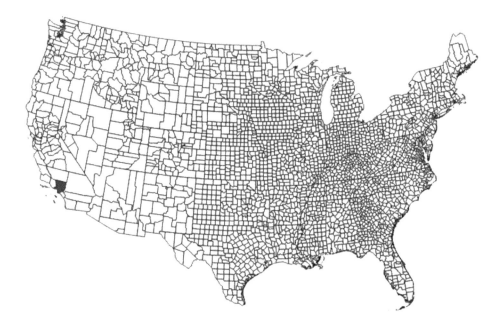

Figure 2.8: Equal Interval Classification

12. The default classification Mode used was Equal Interval. With this default mode the software attempts to create classes with the equal data value intervals.

13. Continuing with the Layer Styling Panel, switch the classification Mode to Natural Breaks (Jenks). Notice the data values change. This is an algorithm that calculates natural groupings of a series of data values.

This is a more informative portrayal of the data. There large population centers are more visible now (shown in the figure 2.9, on the facing page).

14. Change the Mode to Quantile (Equal Count). Notice the data values change. This is an algorithm that attempts

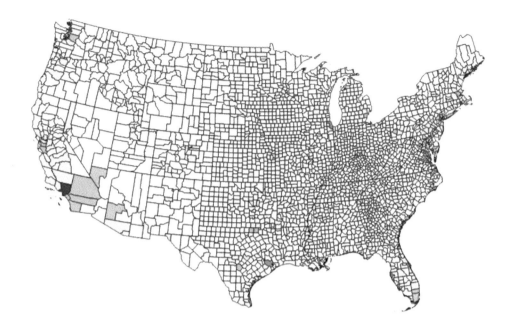

Figure 2.9: Natural Breaks (Jenks) Classification

to put the same number of features into each class. This is a much more informative depiction of total population (shown in the figure 2.10).

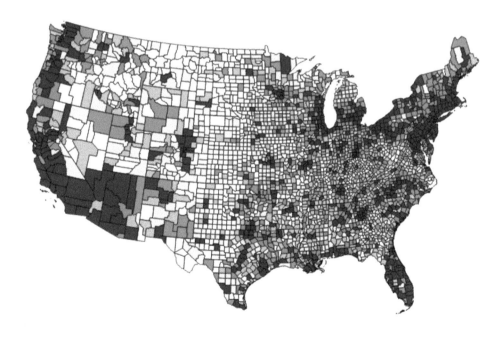

Figure 2.10: Quantile Classification

15. In addition to changing the mode, you can change the number of classes. Change the number of Classes to 4.

16. You can also change the Color ramp. Right-click on the Color ramp and choose RdBu. You will need to choose All Color Ramps from the color ramp drop down menu to find RdBu.

17. This highlights rural counties with a red color (shown in the figure 2.11).

> This is a good example of how much more efficient it is to use the Layer Styling Panel than Layer Properties | Symbology to make changes to a layers appearance.

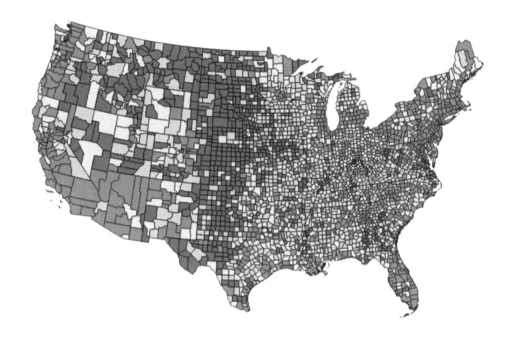

Figure 2.11: Quantile Classification with a Red-Blue Color Ramp

Tip: You can also right-click the Color Ramp and choose Invert Color Ramp option to reverse the colors.

Final Note: You can change the Legend for each class. Instead of the bottom class having values of 67-11566.75, you can double click on the Legend text for a class and change it. For example, you could change the least populated class label to 'Rural'. This is shown in the figure 2.12 below.

Classes	Histogram	
Symbol	**Values**	**Legend**
☑ ▨	67.00 - 11566.75	Rural
☑ ▨	11566.75 - 25366.00	11567 - 25366
☑ ☐	25366.00 - 61098.75	25366 - 61099
☑ ▨	61098.75 - 9519338.00	61099 - 9519338

Figure 2.12: Changing the Legend Names For Classes

2.5   Conclusion

In this exercise, you learned to join tabular data to a shapefile. Once that was complete, you were able to classify the data and produce different renderings of that data. Between the various classification modes, choosing the number of classes and the color ramp you have endless possibilities for displaying numeric data. The key is to remember what data pattern you are trying to share with the map reader. Then the challenge becomes finding the classification that will tell the story. The modes shown in this exercise are commonly used when dealing with numeric data on maps.

2.6 Discussion Questions

1. Describe the use of a join in GIS?

2. Why might you want to preserve a join outside of a QGIS map document by exporting the joined layer, versus just working with the join in the map document?

3. Why would you classify data?

2.7 Challenge Assignment

There are several more datasets in the `Exercise_2_Data/ChallengeData` folder. There is a `World_Countries` shapefile and two tabular datasets: `CO2_Readings_World.xls` and `RenewableEnergy_Percentages.dbf`. Both of these tabular formats can be brought into QGIS Desktop as tables. Identify the fields by which these two tables can be joined to the `World_Countries` shapefile.

> Note that you can add additional joins to a layer by just repeating the process in Task 1.

Once you have joined the data, make two maps: 1) Showing CO2 readings by country and 2) RenewableEnergy_Percentages by country.

Exercise 3

Working with Attributes and Spatial Queries

Objective – Understanding Attribute Queries and Spatial Queries

3.1 Introduction

In this exercise you will learn numerous skills related to working with attribute tables. You will learn how to select records using an expression. You will then learn how to add new attribute columns, calculate field values and use QGIS variables. You will also learn how to get basic statistics from an attribute column and do conditional formatting of attribute tables. In the final task you will create a buffer and learn the importance of buffering in combination with spatial queries.

This exercise includes the following tasks:

- Task 1 – Selecting Records

- Task 2 – Calculating Values

- Task 3 – Using Variables

- Task 4 – More Practice

- Task 5 – Getting Statistics

- Task 6 – Conditional Formatting of Attribute Tables

- Task 7 – Buffering and Spatial Queries

3.2 Objective: Understanding Attribute Queries and Spatial Queries

The objective of this exercise is to learn how to query attribute data, calculate values and derive statistical information from attribute data. You will learn how to perform both attribute queries and spatial queries.

3.3 Task 1 - Selecting Records

1. Open QGIS.

2. Using what you know add the usa.gpkg/counties GeoPackage layer to QGIS.

3. In Part 1 - Exercise 5 you learned how to select records using the Select Features by Value 🗐 tool. Here you will use the Select by expression window.

4. Open the attribute table 📋 and click the Select features using an expression ℇ button to open the Select by expression window. In this next section you will learn how to create more sophisticated queries.

The expression area is on the left, the central portion contains functions and all of the attribute columns (in the Fields and Values section). The right is for help and values. The Selection mode button is in the lower right.

> Note that there is a *Search* box for the *Functions* section. You will begin to notice that QGIS has search boxes in many locations! You can use this to filter the list of functions based on what you type. This makes finding specific operators and functions quick and easy!

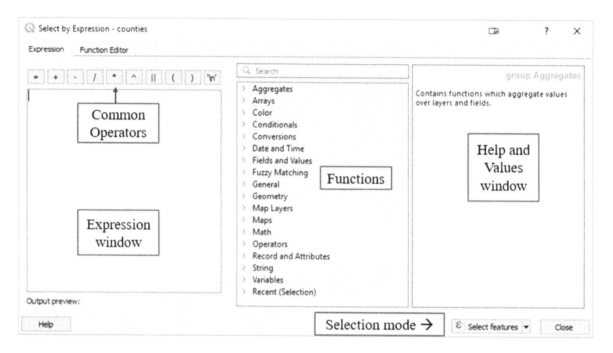

Figure 3.1: Select By Expression Window

5. First you will create an expression to select all counties in Minnesota with a population (POP2000) greater than 20,000. This expression will involve creating the portion that selects counties in Minnesota and the part that selects based on population. These two separate clauses will be joined with the AND operator. The AND operator means that both conditions need to evaluate to TRUE in order for a record to be selected.

6. Expand Fields and Values and find the STATE_NAME field. Double-click it to begin the expression. It appears in the Expression window with double quotes around it since it is a field name.

7. Click the equals operator from the common operators above the expression area.

> Note that as you create the expression you see a small red triangle pointing out an error in the expression. At this point this is simply because you are not finished. There will be an accompanying *Expression is invalid* message where it reads *Output Preview*. This feature can help you deduce where an expression is incorrectly formed.

8. On the right side Values area click the All Unique button to generate a list of all the unique values in the STATE_NAME field.

9. Then use the Search box to begin searching for *Minnesota*. The Search box autocompletes, so just typing the letters *Min* should be sufficient to locate the value 'Minnesota'. Double click Minnesota to complete the first portion of the expression.

10. In the central functions section scroll down to find the Operators section. Expand it and double click on the AND operator to add it to the expression.

11. Return to the Fields and Values section and double click on the POP2000 column. Type in the greater than symbol '>'. Complete the expression by entering 20000 without a thousands separator.

12. Your expression should now be like figure 3.2, on page 59.

Figure 3.2: Expression Using the AND Operator

Question # 1: How many records were selected?

13. You can also form queries comparing one field to another. Next form a query that will identify all U.S. counties with more males than females. It should look like: "MALES" > "FEMALES"

Question # 2: How many records are selected?

14. Next create a query that identifies just those counties in New York state with a population in 2000 greater than the 1990 population.

Question # 3: How many records were selected with that query?

15. It is also possible to search for occurrences of text in a text column. The operator LIKE can be used to search for pieces of text in a column. Let's say you wanted to identify counties with 'bull' in the name. You would use the LIKE operator, and the value would be the text you want to search for surrounded by single tics. You can then use percentage signs as wildcards. For example if you searched for '%bull', you are telling QGIS to select records with *bull* no matter what precedes it. If you search for 'bull%' you will select records with *bull* no matter what follows. You can also do both '%bull%'.

16. Compose a query where you select counties with 'land' in the name no matter what precedes or follows.

Question # 4: How many records were selected with that query?

17. The LIKE operator is case sensitive. ILIKE is not case sensitive. Change the query to use the ILIKE operator to search for *Land*.

Question # 5: How many selected records are there?

18. In the attribute table click the Deselect all ⬚ button to clear the selected set.

19. The NOT operator can be used in combination with any SQL statement to select the opposite. Create the following query shown in figure 3.3, on the next page.

20. There is also a button with the same functionality. Click the Invert selection ⬚ button and now just counties in New Mexico will be selected.

21. Export out the New Mexico counties into a new GeoPackage named nm.gpkg and name the layer nm_counties. Change the CRS of the new layer to UTM Zone 13 NAD83 (EPSG: 26913).

Figure 3.3: Expression Using the NOT Operator

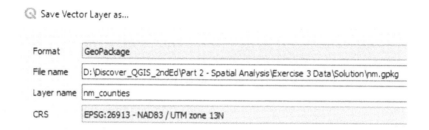

Figure 3.4: Saving Selected Counties to a New GeoPackage

22. Turn off the counties layer. Right-click on the nm_counties layer and choose Set CRS | Set Project CRS from Layer from the context menu.

23. Right-click on the nm_counties layer and choose Zoom to Layer from the context menu.

24. Save the project file as new_mexico.qgz.

3.4   Task 2 - Calculating Values

You can add new attribute columns and calculate the values for them. Values in new attribute columns can be based on attributes that already exist in the table, or they might be new. Population density is an example of an attribute that you can calculate based on values that already exist in an attribute table. To calculate population density, you take the number of people living in a geographic area (county, state, etc.) and divide by the area in square units (e.g., square kilometers, miles, hectares or acres). Here you will learn how to do this.

1. Open the new_mexico.qgz QGIS project if it is not open already.

2. Open the attribute table for the nm_counties layer.

3. Click the Toggle editing mode ✏ button which puts the table into edit mode. Notice that many of the buttons became active when the table was put into edit mode.

4. The first step in creating a population density figure is having a field with the square miles of each county. Click the New field 🔢 button and the Add field window opens.

5. Name the new field sqmi and make it Type of Decimal number(real). Click OK and the new column will be added to the far right side of the table.

6. Now you will use the Field calculator to generate the square mileage data. Click the Open field calculator 🧮 button. The Field calculator allows you to populate attribute columns with data based on an expression.

Figure 3.5: Adding a New Field

7. Since you have already created the sqmi column, click the Update existing field check box. Note that you also have the option of Create a new field within this dialog!

8. From the dropdown below, scroll down and select the sqmi column.

9. Now you will create an expression to populate the new column. In the functions area in the middle of the window expand the Geometry section. Double-click the $area operator. This alone would calculate the area in square meters. This is because your data is in UTM meters. You now need to multiply square meters by the conversion factor to square miles which is 0.000000386102159. See figure 3.6.

10. With the expression entered click OK. You now have square miles calculated for the county polygons.

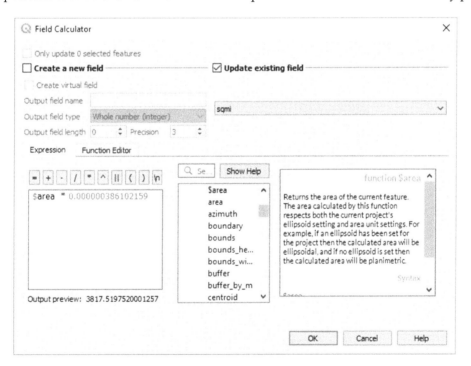

Figure 3.6: Calculating Square Mileage

11. Next you need a field to store the population density. Again click the New field button.

12. Name the new field PopDensity and make it a Type of Decimal number(real). Click OK to add the new field.

13. This time you will use the field calculator widget instead of the full Field calculator window. Notice that when you put the table into edit mode this widget appears below the toolbars(see figure 3.7, on the next page).

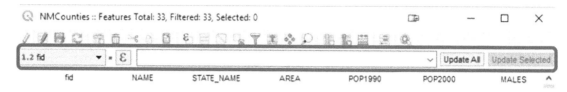

Figure 3.7: Field Editor Widget

14. Click the left side dropdown field selector so that the target field is PopDensity

15. Click the Expression $\mathcal{E}$ button.

16. In the Expression Dialog create the expression "POP2000" / "sqmi" and click OK.

17. With the expression set click Update All (see figure 3.8).

Figure 3.8: Population Density Expression

18. Click the Toggle editing mode button again to toggle out of editing mode and save your edits. Close the attribute table. Using what you know symbolize the counties by population density using a Mode of Quantile (Equal Count). (see figure 3.9)

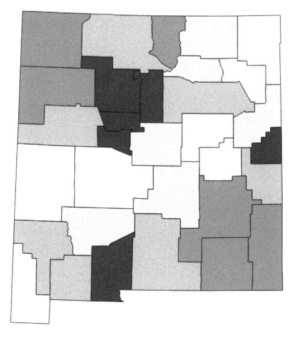

Figure 3.9: Population Density for New Mexico Counties

19. Save your project.

3.5 Task 3 - Using Variables in Field Calculations

A powerful feature of QGIS is custom variables. Variables can be set at several different scopes or levels:

- Global
- Project
- Layer

They are a way to store any constant numeric or text values. Global variables are available at the desktop application level in any QGIS instance. These can be managed from Settings | Options | Variables. Project variables are available throughout a given project. These can be set from the Project Properties window on the Variables tab. Layer level variables are available from Layer Properties on the Variables tab and are available only for that layer. The other important aspect of these variables is that they cascade from most specific scope to least specific scope. In other words, a @my_var set at the Global level will be overwritten by a @my_var set at the Project level.

1. Open the `new_mexico.qgz` QGIS project if it is not open already.

2. Open the Settings | Options and click the Variables tab.

3. This is where you can set global variables.

4. Here you will create a variable for the square meters to square miles conversion factor and one for square meters to acres.

5. Click the Add Variable ⊞ button. Enter the variable name as SqMt2SqMi and enter the conversion factor 0.000000386102159.

6. Repeat to add one named SqMt2Acres with the value 0.000247105. These variables can now be used in calculations in the Field Calculator and make your work easier.

SqMt2Acres	0.000247105
SqMt2SqMi	0.000000386102159

Figure 3.10: Both Variables Created

7. Click OK to close.

8. Open the attribute table for the nm_counties layer again and put the table into edit mode.

9. Add an `acreage` column as a Decimal number(real) column.

10. Use the table editing widget to calculate the acres column.

- Set the field to update as `acreage`.
- Click the Expression button
- Using the Search box above all the functions, search for $area. Double-click it to add it to your expression.
- Click the * operator.
- Expand the Variables section and choose the @SqMt2Acres variable you just created.
- Click OK and Update All and your `acreage` will be populated with acreage values!

> This is just one use of Variables. They can also be used to store your name as Cartographer when working in a layout. For this particular use of calculating specific geometries there is also a useful plugin named Calculate Geometry.

3.6   Task 4 - Calculating Values Challenge

Here you will create more fields and calculate them with values using all the skills you've just learned.

1. Open the `new_mexico.qgz` QGIS project if it is not open already.

2. Below is information outlining three additional fields you will add to your table. Included in the table are the new field name, the data type of the field, and what kind of data to populate the field with. Add the following fields to your NM_counties shapefile and calculate them with the correct values.

Column 1

- Name: `pop_change`
- Field Type: Whole number(integer)
- Existing attributes to use: `POP1990` and `POP2000`
- Description: Change in population from 1990 to 2000

Column 2

- Name: `sep_div`
- Field Type: Whole number(integer)
- Existing attributes to use: `SEPARATED` and `DIVORCED`
- Description: Total separated and divorced

Column 3

- Name: `sale_class`
- Field Type: Text(string) of length 4
- Existing attributes to use: `AVG_SALE87`

3. Description for column 3: You will calculate this last column with the text string *Low* for records where the `AVG_SALE87` values are <50,000, *Med* for records where the values are between 50,001-200,000 and *High* for records where the values are greater than 200,001. Note: the most basic method is to do this in two steps. First select the records with the Select features by expression tool, then calculate the selected set with the Field Calculator or widget with the Update Selected option.

Challenge The most efficient and sophisticated method for calculating column 3 is to use CASE statements which allow you to calculate these values for `sale_class` all in one operation. Use the Search function in the Expression Dialog to find CASE among the functions. CASE statements allow you to use IF/THEN/ELSE logic in SQL statements. A CASE statement is followed by at least one pair of WHEN and THEN statements. See figure 3.11, on the facing page for an example.

4. Using what you know symbolize the counties by `sale_class` using a Categorized renderer.

5. Save your map document.

Figure 3.11: Using CASE Statements in a Field Calculation

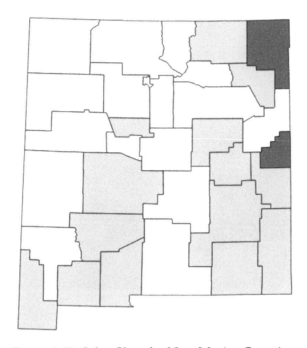

Figure 3.12: Sales Class for New Mexico Counties

3.7 Task 5 - Getting Statistics

In this task we will look at creating summaries and generating histograms.

3.8 Task 5.1 - Creating Statistical Summaries

1. Open the new_mexico.qgz QGIS project if it is not open already.

2. Click on the Show statistical summary $\sum$ button to open the Statistics Panel.

3. Remember that all panels can be undocked and placed where you need them. This means they can also be free floating on a second monitor.

4. Choose nm_counties as the target layer

5. Choose POP2000 as the column. The basic statistics for that column are displayed.

Question # 6: What is the mean value of the POP2000 column?

3.9   Task 5.2 - Generating Histograms

1. Open the `Processing | Toolbox`.

2. Search for *Histogram*

3. Find and open the Vector Layer Histogram tool.

4. Set the Input layer to nm_counties. Set the Attribute to `AVG_SALE87`. Set the number of bins to 20. Click Run.

5. A link to an HTML page with the result appears in the Results Viewer panel. Click the link to view the histogram in your default web browser. See figure 3.13.

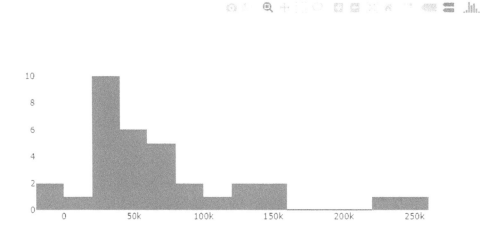

Figure 3.13: Vector Layer Histogram

6. Close the Results panel and Processing toolbox when done.

There are often more than one way to accomplish a task. Here you will see how to install and use a plugin named Data Plotly to generate a histogram. It adds a panel to QGIS which can be used to create numerous types of charts and graphs. It uses the Plotly graphing library (`https://github.com/plotly`), thus the name.

1. From the menu bar choose `Plugins | Plugin manager`. Search the All tab for the Data Plotly plugin. Select it and install it. Close the Plugin Manager when it has been installed. This plugin allows you to generate a histogram of values in a column along with 8 other chart types.

2. Click the Data Plotly ⟋ button to open the Data Plotly panel (or find it via the Plugins menu).

3. Set the Plot Type to Histogram.

4. Set the Layer to nm_counties.

5. Set the X Field to `AVG_SALE87`.

6. Change colors if you like.

7. Click Create Plot.

This very short task touched on one basic Plot type found in Data Plotly. You are encouraged to explore the other plot types on your own. Note that as of this writing there is a crowd funding campaign (https://north-road.com/qgis-data-plotly-campaign/) to add Data Plotly charts directly into a Print Layout. QGIS is continually growing, so watch for this in a future QGIS release. Also remember to support new features like this when you find them useful to your work.

3.10   Task 6 - Conditional Formatting of Attribute Tables

QGIS also allows you to color the attribute table based on SQL statements and cell values. You can choose cell colors as well as colors and fonts for cell content. This is basically MS Excel functionality in the GIS.

1. Open the `new_mexico.qgz` QGIS project if it is not open already.

2. Open the attribute table for the nm_counties layer.

3. Click the Conditional Formatting 🔲 button. A panel opens to the right of the attribute table.

4. You have the option of formatting just the cells in a specific column or entire rows. Select the Full row option.

5. Click the New Rule ⊕ New Rule button.

6. Name the rule *Low Sales Class*.

7. For the Condition click the Expression button to open the Conditional Style Rule Expression window. Create the expression `"Sale_class" = 'Low'` and click OK.

8. Your conditional rule panel now looks like the figure 3.14.

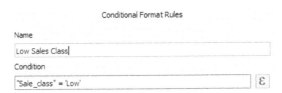

Figure 3.14: Conditional Rules Panel

9. Below this section click the drop down for Background and choose Pick color.

10. This gives you the ability to pick a color from anywhere on your screen. Click on one of the *Low* counties on the map to choose the same color for the cells (NOTE: You likely chose different colors for your map than I did which is fine).

11. Click Done. The table now has those records colored the same in the attribute table as they are on the map! A potentially convenient feature!

12. Set up the other sales class values with the correct expressions the corresponding map colors. See figure 3.15, on the next page.

3.11   Task 7 - Buffering and Spatial Queries

So far you have worked with tabular queries. You will now learn about spatial queries and how to employ them in a simple analysis. Buffering is a key vector analysis tool in GIS. It gives us the ability to create a new GIS layer representing a buffer distance from some map feature(s).

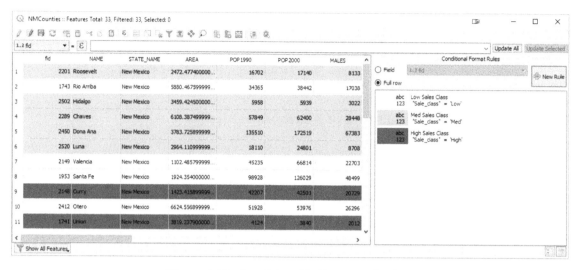

Figure 3.15: Conditionally Formatted Table

Task 7.1 - Running the Buffer Tool

1. Open QGIS and open `Exercise_3_Data/Tornado/Tornado.qgz`.

2. The red line represents a tornado's path through a residential area. The approximate area of damage was 300 meters around the path. The green polygons represent schools in the area, the parcels are in yellow and the roads black lines. To identify the area impacted by the tornado, you will create a 300 meter buffer around the path.

3. From the menu bar choose `Vector | Geoprocessing Tools | Buffer`. Fill out the Buffer tool with the parameters seen in the figure 3.16.

Figure 3.16: Buffer Tool

4. Click Run, and Close when it has finished.

A new polygon layer is created that covers all the land 900 meters from the tornado's path. You will need to employ a Blending Mode to the buffer layer so that you can see what parcels, schools, and roads were affected.

> Blending modes allow for more elegant rendering between GIS layers. They can be much more powerful than simply adjusting layer Opacity. Blending modes allow for effects where the full intensity an underlying layer is still visible through the layer above. There are 13 blending modes available. You will use these in several additional exercises. In Part 5 Exercise 2 you will learn specific use cases for different Blending modes.

5. Open the Layer Styling Panel with the target layer set to the buffer layer. Scroll down and locate the Layer Rendering section and expand it. Find Blending mode and set the Layer Blending mode to Multiply (shown in figure 3.17).

Figure 3.17: Tornado Buffer with a Multiply Blending Mode

Looking at the result we can immediately see the areas affected by the tornado.

6. Save the QGIS project.

Task 7.2 Performing Spatial Queries

In this task, you will learn how to identify exactly which parcels were affected by the tornado.

1. Begin with the QGIS map as you saved it at the conclusion of the previous task.

2. From the menu bar choose Vector | Research Tools| Select by Location....

Using Select by Location, you can conduct spatial queries. In this case, we can determine which parcels overlap with the tornado buffer.

Fill out the Select by Location tool as in the figure 3.18, on the following page. Click Run to perform the selection then click Close.

3. The parcels that intersect the tornado buffer are now selected. However, the default yellow selection color is very close to the yellow color of the parcels. To change the selection color go to the menu bar choose Project | Properties and click on the General tab.

4. Change the Selection color to a blue color so the selected parcels stand out better (shown in figure 3.19, on the next page).

From here, you could save out the selected parcels as a new shapefile. To do this you would right-click on the parcel layer and choose Export | Save Selected Features As.... You could also open the parcel attribute table and Show Selected Features to examine the attributes of those affected parcels.

5. Finally you will examine the total value of the affected parcels. Click on the Show statistical summary Σ button to open the Statistics Panel.

6. Select parcels as the target layer.

7. Set the target field to TOTALVAL.

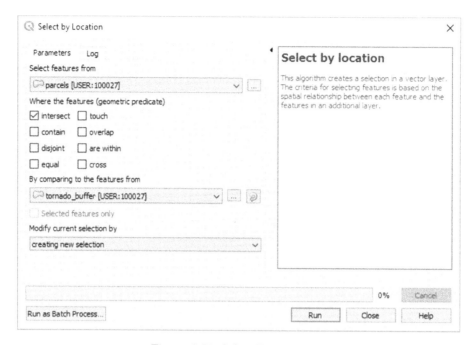

Figure 3.18: Select By Location

Figure 3.19: Affected Parcels Selected

8. Check Selected features only.

The results are shown in the figure 3.20, on the facing page. Now you know the total value of the affected parcels! This great example of how you can generate information from GIS data.

3.12 Conclusion

In this exercise, you explored how to work with attribute tables in a variety of ways. You used a buffer operation combined with the select by location operation and basic statistics tools to determine to total value of parcels

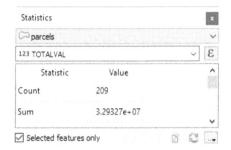

Figure 3.20: Statistics On the Affected Parcels

impacted by a tornado.

3.13 Discussion Questions

1. Why do we need data dictionaries?

2. How are Attribute selections useful in a GIS?

3. Why are buffering and spatial selections important to us?

3.14 Challenge Assignment

Repeat the steps in the second task to determine the roads that were impacted by the tornado. Report the affected road names to your instructor. Make a map composition of both the impacted roads and parcels. Turn in the final map to your instructor.

Exercise 4

Vector Data Analysis - Overlay Techniques

Objective - Understanding Basic Vector Analysis Using Overlays

4.1 Introduction

In this exercise, you will be learn about several powerful vector analysis tools. The tools are all considered overlay tools, since they produce outputs defined by how features overlap one another. You will be working with several datasets covering the Sierra National Forest in California.

This exercise includes the following tasks:

- Task 1 - Clip

- Task 2 - Intersection

- Task 3 - Union

- Task 4 - Intersection # 2

4.2 Objective Understanding Basic Vector Analysis Using Overlays

The objective of this exercise is to understand basic use of vector overlays in a geospatial analysis.

Vector Overlays – A set of tools, which work on the spatial relationships between two input vector datasets. The output is a new dataset derived from those spatial relationships.

Clip – Outputs the features of the input dataset that fall within the features of the clip dataset. It is commonly used to cut datasets to the study area boundary.

Intersection – Takes two polygon datasets and outputs the areas common to both.

Union – A topological overlay of two polygon datasets, the output preserves the features that fall within the spatial extent of either input dataset.

4.3 Task 1 - Clip

This exercise focuses on the Sierra National Forest in California. Datasets include: the National Forest boundary, Ranger Districts, and habitat data for both spotted owl and Southwest willow flycatcher. In this first task, you will be clipping data to the study area. The spotted owl is listed as Threatened and the southwest willow flycatcher is listed as endangered by the U.S. Fish and Wildlife Service.

Figure 4.1: Southwest Willow Flycatcher - Photo credit Jim Rorabaugh/USFWS [Public domain]

Figure 4.2: Spotted Owl - Photo credit John and Karen Hollingsworth; photo by USFS Region 5 (Pacific Southwest) [Public domain]

1. Open QGIS.

2. From the exercise directory, add both the `Sierra_Natl_Forest.shp` and `CA_Spotted_Owl_HmRngCore.shp` shapefiles to QGIS.

3. Move the Sierra National Forest layer below the spotted owl layer so the map canvas resembles the figure 4.3, on the next page.

In this case, you are only interested in the data covering the Sierra National Forest. Notice that the spotted owl data covers far more territory than the forest. Therefore, you will clip the spotted owl data to the forest boundary. Clip will create a new shapefile consisting of the spotted owl polygons within the forest boundary. It is standard protocol to clip datasets to the extent of the study area. This reduces data to only that which needs to be processed, and makes processing and rendering faster.

Before conducting a spatial analysis, you need to ensure that all the involved layers are in the same coordinate reference system.

4. Open the Layer Properties for each layer, and identify the coordinate reference system.

Question # 1 – Are both layers in the same coordinate reference system? What is the coordinate reference system of each layer?

5. From the menu bar choose `Vector | Geoprocessing Tools | Clip`. This will open the Clip tool. Enter the following options:

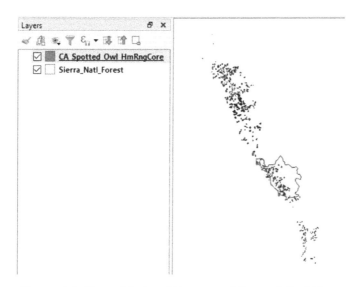

Figure 4.3: Sierra National Forest and Spotted Owl Data

   a. Input layer = CA_Spotted_Owl_HmRngCore

   b. Overlay layer = Sierra_Natl_Forest

   c. Clipped output = `Exercise_4_Data/MyData/Sierra_Spotted_Owl.shp`

   e. Click Run

   f. Click Close

NOTE that QGIS lets you save geoprocessing output into a variety of formats including File (shapefile etc.), GeoPackages, PostGIS and the default of a temporary layer. The latter can be very useful when generating intermediate datasets or for testing an algorithm.

---

6. The new layer will appear in the Layers Panel. Remove the original CA_Spotted_Owl_HmRngCore layer as you no longer need it.

7. Right-click on the Sierra_Natl_Forest layer and choose Zoom to Layer.

Your map should now resemble the figure 4.4, on the following page. Unlike selecting by location and exporting the selected set to a new layer, the Clip operation actually cuts spotted owl polygons at the forest boundary where they crossed the forest boundary.

8. Save the project as `Exercise4.qgz` in the data folder.

4.4   Task 2 - Intersection

You will now include the southwest willow flycatcher habitat data in the analysis.

1. Open QGIS and open `Exercise_4_Data/Exercise4.qgz` if it is not already.

2. Add `Sierra_WillowFlycatcher.shp` shapefile to QGIS. This data set falls completely within the forest boundary so there is no need to clip it.

3. Drag the Sierra_WillowFlycatcher layer to the top of the layers list in the Layers Panel so it draws on top of all other layers.

Figure 4.4: Spotted Owl Data Clipped to the National Forest Boundary

4. Spend a few minutes styling your data.

    a. Give the National forest a light green color and black outline.

    b. Give the spotted owl habitat an orange fill and black outline.

    c. Give the Southwest willow flycatcher habitat a red fill and red outline.

5. Your map should now resemble the figure 4.5, on the next page.

6. Use the Zoom In ⊕ tool to drag a box and zoom in to the area outlined in black in the figure 4.5, on the facing page above.

You will notice that in this area, there is some overlap between the Southwest willow flycatcher and spotted owl habitat (shown figure 4.6, on the next page). Since these are both sensitive species, areas of habitat overlap will be important areas to protect. You could certainly conduct a spatial query to select Southwest willow flycatcher polygons that overlap spotted owl polygons. However, here you will see the value of using the Intersection tool to identify these overlapping areas.

7. Open the Processing Toolbox by choosing Processing | Toolbox or by clicking the Toolbox ⚙ button.

> This tool can also be found by clicking the menu bar and choosing Vector menu | Geoprocessing Tools | Intersection.

8. Search for *Intersection* and find the Intersection tool in the Vector Overlay section.

9. Fill out the tool with the following parameters (shown in figure 4.8, on page 144):

    a. Input layer = Sierra_Spotted_Owl

    b. Overlay layer = Sierra_WillowFlycatcher

    c. Save the Intersection output as a shapefile named `Exercise_4_Data/MyData/OverlapAreas.shp`.

    d. Check Open output file after running algorithm.

Figure 4.5: All Three Layers Loaded and Symbolized

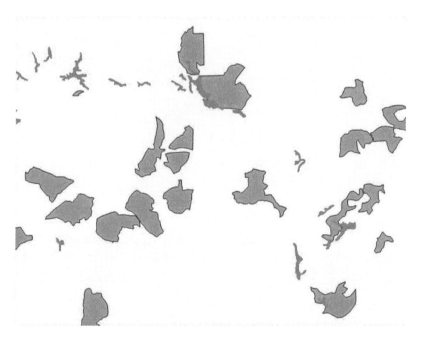

Figure 4.6: Zoomed in to Overlap Areas

  e. Click Run to perform the intersect operation and Close when it has finished.

10. Drag the OverlapAreas layer to the top of the layers list in the Layers Panel so it draws on top of all other layers.

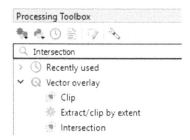

Figure 4.7: Searching the Processing Toolbox

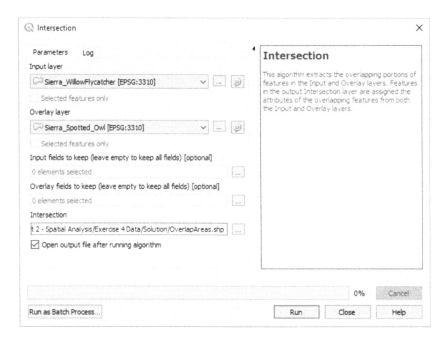

Figure 4.8: Intersection Tool

11. Style the OverlapAreas with a bright yellow Fill and Border. Your map should now resemble the figure 4.9, on the next page.

12. Save your map.

> The GEOS geometry engine used by QGIS has a high standard for feature geometries. Especially when running vector overlay operations you may recieve invalid geometry errors. In that case you can run the Vectory Geometry | Fix geometries tool.

4.5   Task 3 - Union

You will now combine both habitat layers in different ways using both the Union and Dissolve tools. Union creates a new GIS layer that combines all the geometries of both input layers. Dissolve merges all coincident polygons together.

1. Open QGIS and open `Exercise_4_Data/Exercise4.qgz` if it is not already.

2. Search the Processing Toolbox for *Union* and find the Union tool in the Vector Overlay section.

3. Fill out the Union tool as in the figure 4.10, on the facing page:

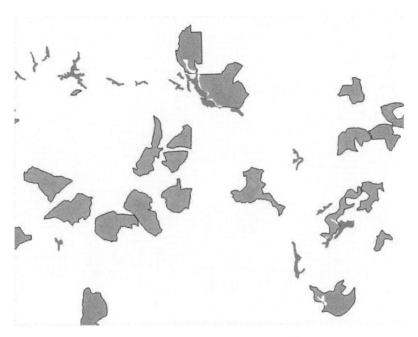

Figure 4.9: Areas of Habitat Overlap

a. Input layer = Sierra_Spotted_Owl
b. Overlay layer = Sierra_WillowFlycatcher
c. Save the Union output as a shapefile named `Exercise_4_Data/MyData/CombinedHabitat.shp`.

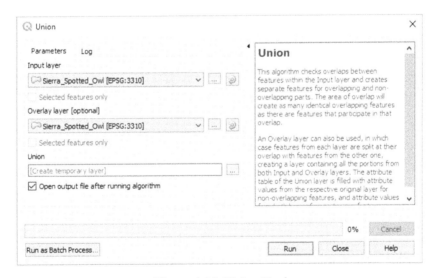

Figure 4.10: Union Tool

4. When finished click Run to perform the union operation and Close when it has finished.

Note that while a tool runs the *Log* tab is displayed with message output. If an error occurs you can switch back to the *Parameters* tab, makes some changes and re-Run the tool.

The output contains all the polygons from both layers (shown in figure 4.11, on the next page). In addition, all the polygons retain their original attributes! Overlapping areas receive attributes from the Overlap layer (Sierra_WillowFlycatcher).

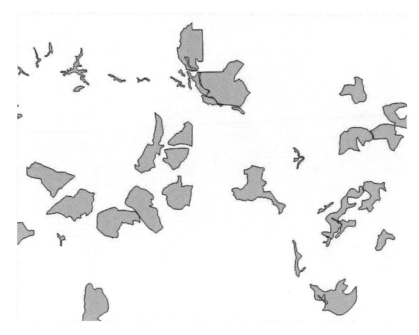

Figure 4.11: Union Output

Now you will Dissolve all the polygons into one contiguous polygon layer representing areas of habitat for both species.

5. Search the Processing Toolbox for *Dissolve* and find the Dissolve tool in the Vector Geometry section.

6. Fill out the Dissolve tool so it matches the figure 4.12:

   a. Input layer = CombinedHabitat
   b. Dissolve fields: leave this blank. If you were to dissolve based on one or more attributes you would click the ellipsis button and choose the fields that would participate.
   c. Save the Dissolved output as a shapefile named `Exercise_4_Data/MyData/CombinedHabitat_dissolved.shp`.

7. When finished click Run to perform the dissolve operation, and then click Close.

8. Figure 4.13 shows the output of the Dissolve operation.

9. Save your QGIS project.

4.6   Task 4 - Intersection # 2

In this final task, you will incorporate the Ranger District shapefile into the analysis. There are three Ranger Districts in the Sierra National Forest. You will determine the Ranger District that each spotted owl habitat polygon is situated in. To do this you will conduct another intersection. This will allow you to cut habitat polygons at the ranger district boundary and attach the attributes from the Ranger District layer onto the spotted owl layer.

1. Open QGIS and open `Exercise_4_Data/Exercise4.qgz`.

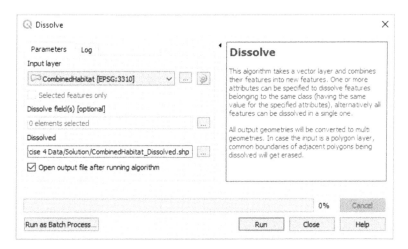

Figure 4.12: Dissolve Tool

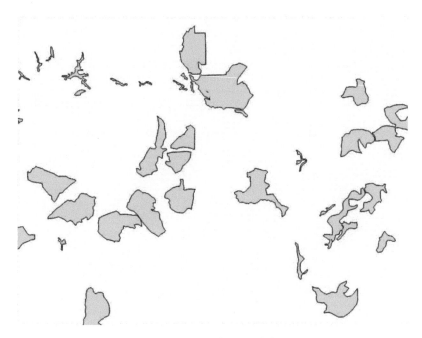

Figure 4.13: Dissolve Tool Output

2. Add the `Sierra_Ranger_Dist.shp` shapefile to the project.

Remember that data layers need to be in the same coordinate reference system when conducting a geoprocessing operation between layers.

3. Open the Layer Properties for the Ranger District layer.

Question # 2 – What is the coordinate reference system of the Ranger District layer?

4. Since it is in a different coordinate reference system than the other datasets, you will first have to save it to a new coordinate reference system.

5. Right-click on Sierra_Ranger_Dist in the Layers Panel and choose Export | Save Selected Features As. . . .

6. Fill out the Save vector layer as. . . form as shown in the figure 4.14, on the following page. You can find this

CRS by searching for the EPSG code for CA Albers: 3310.

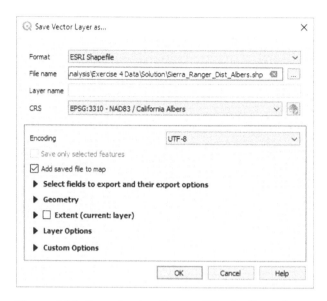

Figure 4.14: Reprojecting Ranger District Boundaries

7. Once the layer has been reprojected, remove the original Ranger District layer from the Layers Panel.

8. Style the new Albers Ranger District layer with a Transparent Fill and a Border of dark green (result shown in figure 4.15, on the next page).

Figure 4.15: Symbolized Ranger District Boundaries

9. Now you are ready to conduct the second intersection. From the Processing toolbox expand the ⏱ Recently used section and find Intersection.

10. Fill out the tool to match the figure 4.16, on the facing page. The output will be in the form of a new spotted owl habitat shapefile cut at the Ranger District boundary.

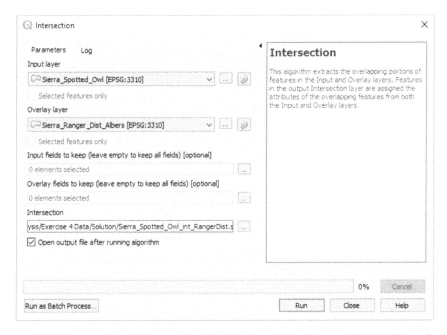

Figure 4.16: Intersection Between Spotted Owl and the Ranger District Boundaries

11. Click Run and Close when done.

12. Select the Spotted_Owl_RangDist layer in the Layers Panel by clicking on it once.

13. Now use the Identify 🔍 tool to query the individual polygons of the Spotted_Owl_RangDist shapefile. You will see the additional Ranger District attribute columns added.

14. Save your project.

4.7 Conclusion

In this exercise, you explored the use of vector overlay tools with habitat data in the Sierra National Forest. There are many similar overlay tools which, when used in combination, allow you to parse the spatial relationships of multiple data layers. These tools allow you to extract data and turn it into information by narrowing down the area of interest.

4.8 Discussion Questions

1. Describe the Clip operation.

2. Describe the Intersect operation.

3. How do Intersect and Clip compare in their output?

4. Before you run an overlay tool, what aspect of your input spatial data layers should you inspect to ensure it is the same for all layers?

4.9 Challenge Assignment

The Southwest willow flycatcher data also covers multiple Ranger Districts. Conduct a spatial join between the Southwest willow flycatcher data and the Ranger districts as you did with spotted owl in the last task. Compose a map that shows the both the spotted owl and Southwest willow flycatcher data styled by the Ranger District they are situated in.

Exercise 5

Vector Data Analysis - Creating a Site Selection Model

Objective – Using the QGIS Graphical Modeler to Perform a Site Selection Analysis

5.1 Introduction

In this exercise you will learn how to streamline a workflow with a model. Using the QGIS Graphical Modeler, you will string tools together using the output of one operation as the input to the next. You can later edit model parameters and share it with others.

This exercise includes the following tasks:

- Task 1 Exploring the Data
- Task 2 Creating the Model - Part 1
- Task 3 Creating the Model - Part 2
- Task 4 Creating the Model - Part 3

5.2 Objective: Understanding Site Selection Analysis Using the Graphical Modeler

The objective of this exercise is to learn how to conduct a site selection analysis using the QGIS Graphical Modeler.

5.3 Task 1 - Exploring the Data

1. Open QGIS.

2. Add all five layers from the `HeliportData.pgkg` GeoPackage to a new, blank, QGIS project:

- `Airports`
- `Counties`
- `CityBoundaries`
- `Roads`
- `Water_features`

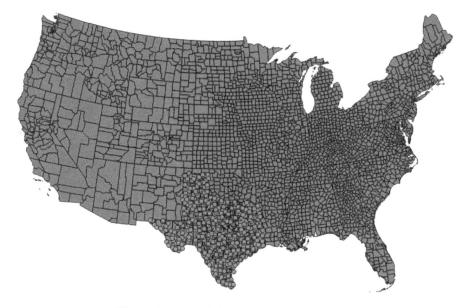

Figure 5.1: Site Selection Analysis Layers

3. Arrange the data layers so that points are on top of lines, which are on top of polygons. Move the CityBoundaries polygon layer above the Counties layer (reference figure 5.1).

Clearly the data layers cover a variety of spatial extents. One likely step will be to Clip them so that they all cover the same spatial extent.

4. One item to check right away is the coordinate reference system of each layer. This is standard practice in any analysis. Open the Layer Properties for each layer and determine the coordinate reference system for each.

Question # 1 – What is the coordinate reference system for these layers?

Since they are all in the same coordinate reference system no re-projecting will be required.

When building a site selection model, you are usually presented with a scenario. The scenario has parameters, which you will have to address to find the solution. The scenario below describes the parameters for the site selection you will do for this exercise. The best method to solve a scenario like the one below is to extract the parameters from the description and write them down into verbal descriptions. Then from your descriptions you can transcribe them into GIS operations: buffer, intersect, =, <>, etc.

Scenario

A company is looking to lease a helipad at an airport for their company helicopter. This company is situated in Nueces County, Texas and wants the helipad to be within three miles of the Corpus Christi city limits, but not in the city limits. The pilots request that the heliport be within a half mile of any source of water. It must also be within a mile from a County road. As you have some knowledge of GIS you are being asked to find the best solution.

1. Complete the descriptions below. The first two entries in Description and Extent have been entered for you. Study the data layers in QGIS and complete the table. At that point you will have a better understanding of what you have to work with.

Data Layer -- Description and Extent

Airports -- Airports, Airfields, Heliports of Texas

City Boundaries -- City Limits of Populated Areas of Texas

Water Features --

Counties --

Roads --

2. The next step is to think about the site selection analysis. Read the Scenario carefully and think about the steps required to finish it. The first two GIS Operations have been worked out for you (shown below). Complete the rest of the GIS Operations from the Scenario description. If there is a selection involved open the attribute table and determine what the field name will be and what value you will be selecting for.

Scenario Parameter -- GIS Operations

Scenario Parameter -- Select Nueces County from USA Counties and Save as a new shapefile. Attribute column = `COUNTY`. Value = `Nueces`

Airports of the USA -- Clip to Nueces County

Must be within three miles of Corpus Christi city limits but not inside city limits -- Select by Attributes Corpus Christi from CityBoundaries of Texas. The attribute column = `Name`. Value = `Corpus Christi`. Buffer three miles around the Corpus Christi City limits. Use the Difference tool to erase the Corpus Christi boundary from the buffer.

Must be within half a mile of water --

Must be within a mile of a County road --

3. Save your project as `exercise 5.qgz` in the exercise data directory.

5.4 Task 2 - Creating the Model - Part 1

Now you understand the data you have to work with. You also know that you will have to determine which airports meet the criteria laid out in the completed table above. The next task is to begin building the model.

1. Open QGIS and open `exercise 5.qgz` if it is not already.

2. From the menu bar choose `Processing | ToolBox`.

The tools are arranged according to the provider (QGIS, GDAL, GRASS, SAGA). Remember the search bar is available to help you find tools. Many tools are native QGIS tools indicated by the QGIS logo next to them. Notice that there is a section for Models . There is a default folder for models, and if saved there, they will show up as model tools in the Toolbox | Models section. You can set the location of this default folder as you will see next.

3. From the menu bar choose `Settings | Options`.

4. Click on the Processing tab and expand the Models section.

5. Double-click the folder path to the right of the Models folder and an ellipsis button will appear to the right.

6. Click on the ellipsis button to open the Multiple selection window. Click Add and navigate to the Exercise

5 Data folder. Select the MyData folder and click Select folder. Back at the Multiple selection window you should see the new folder added to the list. You can add as many folders as you need. Again QGIS will look in these locations for Model tools. Click OK to accept the changes. (shown in figure 5.2).

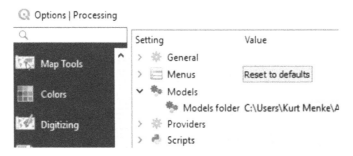

Figure 5.2: Processing - Models Options

You can also set folders containing Python Script tool locations from this Processing Options window.

7. Click OK to close the Options | Processing window.

8. From the menu bar now choose Processing | Graphical Modeler. The Processing Modeler window will open.

The Processing Modeler allows you to create complex models using an intuitive graphic interface. When working with a GIS, most analysis operations are not isolated, but rather part of a chain of operations. Using the Modeler, that chain of processes can be incorporated into a single process. This allows you to run the entire analysis as a single operation. It also allows you to execute the same model on a different set of inputs! No matter how many steps and different operations it involves, a model is executed as a single operation, thus saving time and effort, especially for larger models.

The left hand panel has two tabs: Inputs and Algorithms. The model itself will be designed in the right hand window.

9. In the Model properties panel are two text inputs: Name and Group. Name the model *Helipad Site Selection* and the Group *Discover QGIS* (shown in figure 5.3, on the next page).

10. Next you will save your model. Click the Save ![icon] button to open the Save Model. Navigate to your MyData folder and name it HelipadSelection. It will be saved as a .model3 file. Click Save. You should receive the *Model was correctly saved* message.

Both the processing environment and the modeler underwent major changes in the move from the QGIS 2.x line to to the 3.x line. Therefore, models created in QGIS 2.x are incompatible with 3.x and vice versa.

11. Return to the main QGIS window and expand the Models section of the Processing Toolbox. You will see the Group named Discover QGIS and if you expand that group you will see your model listed (shown in figure 5.4, on the facing page).

The first analysis step will be to create your study area boundary. This will involve creating a Nueces County shapefile from the USA wide Counties layer.

12. The first step in creating a model is to define the inputs. All of your data is vector data. Click on the Inputs tab to the Graphical Modeler and double-click on Vector Layer.

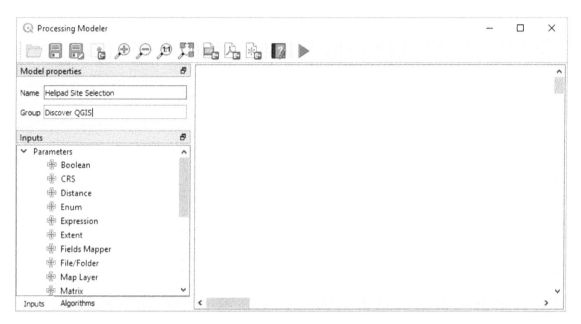

Figure 5.3: Processing Modeler with Name and Group Specified

Figure 5.4: Model Listed as a Model Tool in Toolbox

Notice that there is a Save Model in Project ⬛ button. Clicking this embeds the model in your QGIS project. You won't do that here. But remember it is an option. This can be useful if you are shipping a project and want to include the model with it.

The Parameter Definition window opens. Here you are simply defining the conceptual parameter. You will not actually connect it to the GIS data layer until you are ready to run the model.

    a. Parameter name = *Counties Layer*.

    b. Set the Geometry type to Polygon.

    c. Keep the box checked for Mandatory (default setting) indicating that the end user will need to complete this parameter in order to run the tool.

13. If your Parameter Definition window looks like the figure 5.5, on the next page, click OK.

The Counties Layer parameter will now appear on the Processing Modeler canvas (shown in figure 5.6, on the following page).

14. The next input parameter will be a Vector Field. Double-click on a Vector Field Input.

    a. Set the Parameter name to County Name Attribute

    b. Set the Parent layer to Counties Layer.

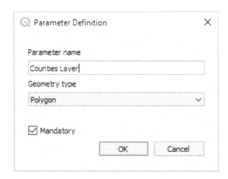

Figure 5.5: Parameters for the First Model Input

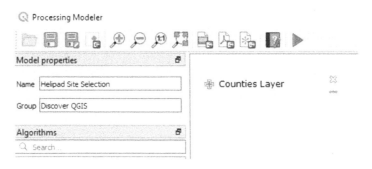

Figure 5.6: First Input Added to Model

c. Set the Allowed data type to String. When running the tool this will limit the attribute selection choice to appropriate fields.

d. Since you have familiarized yourself with your data you also know enough to set the default value for the attribute column name. Set the Default value to *COUNTY*.

15. If your Parameter Definition window looks like the figure 5.7, click OK.

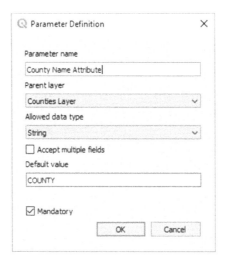

Figure 5.7: County Attribute Paremeter Definition

16. Drag the County Name Attribute input so that it is below Counties Layer (shown in figure 5.8, on the facing page). You can arrange the model elements into an attractive and intuitive flow. Since you specified a Parent layer

you will see a dashed line connecting the two inputs.

Figure 5.8: First Two Inputs Added

17. Now you will add the Extract by attribute algorithm. Click on the Algorithms tab. It is basically the Processing Toolbox, but notice there is a category for Modeler tools.

18. As you have done with the Processing Toolbox, utilize the Search window. Search for the algorithm by typing *Extract*. Double-click on the Vector selection | Extract by attribute algorithm. The Extract by attribute window opens. Fill it out as follows (reference figure 5.9, on the next page):

    a. Description - Extract Nueces County

    b. Input layer = County Layer

    c. Selection attribute = County Name Attribute

    d. Operator =

    e. Value (Refer to your notes in the table above) Note: It will not need quotes, just type it in as it appears in the attribute table.

    f. Extracted (attribute) = This is the what the end user will see for the output layer. Name this *Nueces County*.

Note: There is a slight difference here between a Graphical Modeler tool and a standard Toolbox tool. Here the output can be saved as a temporary file that will be used as input to the next algorithm, or it can be saved to a layer that you will specify when you run the model. Typing in anything in this space tells the Modeler that this output will be saved. The text you supply will be the description for the output when executing the model tool. You will choose the actual name of the output layer and its location when you execute the model. Since you may want the Nueces County boundary for cartographic reasons you will choose to save it as a layer.

19. Click OK to set the parameters for the Extract by attribute algorithm.

The first complete algorithm has been added! You can drag the parameter boxes to arrange them as you would like and the connecting arrows will follow (example in figure 5.9, on the following page). You can also double-click on any model input or algorithm at any time to open the Parameter Definition or the tool window and make changes.

20. Save the model and close the Processing Modeler window.

21. From the Processing Toolbox panel, expand Models | Discover QGIS.

Your model is obviously not yet complete. However, it is already a geoprocessing tool that you can open, set parameters for, and run. Try the model out to see what happens with its current configuration.

22. Double-click on the Helipad Site Selection model in the Processing Toolbox to open the model as a tool. You can also right-click on it and choose Execute.

23. Set Counties Layer to Counties. The County Name Attribute defaults to COUNTY. Keep Nueces County as a temporary file for now. Even though it will be saved out you still have the choice to save it as a temporary layer. This can be handy while testing the model. (reference figure 5.11, on page 159).

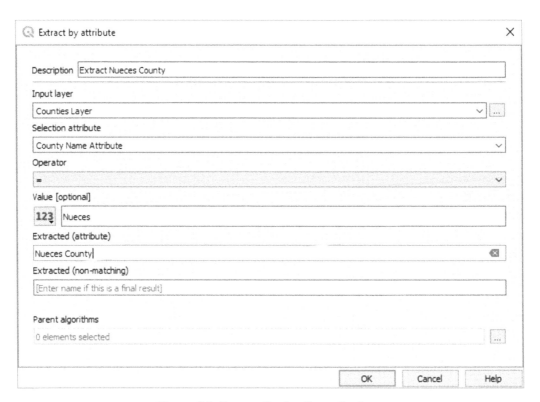

Figure 5.9: Extract By Attribute Settings

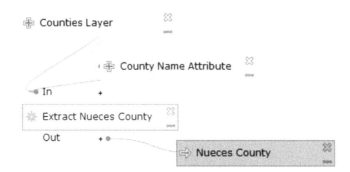

Figure 5.10: First Algorithm Added to the Model

24. Click Run. The temporary Nueces County layer will be added to QGIS. Zoom in and verify that Nueces county was correctly selected using the tool.

25. For now, remove this layer from QGIS and then save your QGIS project.

5.5   Task 3 - Creating the Model - Part 2

Now that your basic model is set up, you will add additional functionality to it. In this task you will work on geoprocessing the data for the CityBoundaries, Roads, and Water_features layers. You will also clip the airports to Nueces County.

1. Open QGIS and open `exercise 5.qgz` if it is not already.

2. From the menu bar now choose `Processing | Graphical Modeler`.

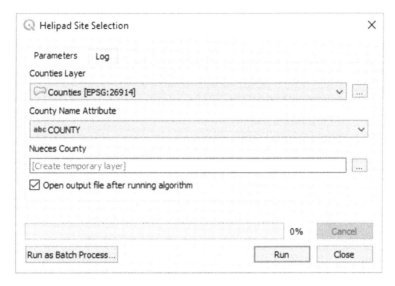

Figure 5.11: Running the Model as a Tool

3. Once the Processing Modeler opens, click the Open Model 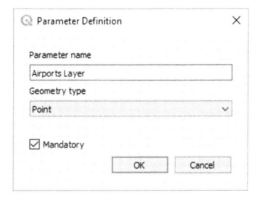 button and open the Helipad Site Selection model (if it is not already open).

4. Now you will add a parameter for Airports. Click the Vector Layer input parameter and fill out the Parameter definition as in the figure 5.11.

Figure 5.12: Airports Layer Parameters

5. You will clip Airports with the Nueces County layer. Click on the Algorithms tab and search for *Clip*. Find the Clip to in the Vector overlay section and open it. Set up the tool as follows:

    a. Description - Clipping Airports

    b. Input layer = Airports Layer

    c. Overlay layer = 'Extracted (attribute)' from algorithm 'Extract Nueces County'

    d. Clipped output = Leave blank since this will be an intermediate layer

Your model should now resemble the figure 5.13, on the next page. No output is displayed for the clipped airports because it will not be saved out as a layer.

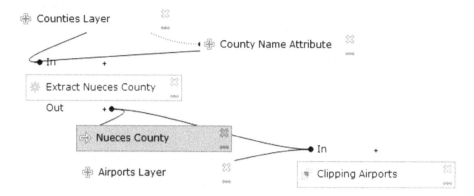

Figure 5.13: Clip Algorithm Added to Model

Now you will work with the CityBoundaries. This is the most involved parameter because the site must be both within three miles of Corpus Christi and beyond the Corpus Christi city limits.

6. Add a Vector Layer input for City Boundaries

    a. Parameter name = *City Boundaries Layer*.

    b. Set the Geometry type to Polygon.

    c. Keep the box checked for Mandatory

    d. Click OK

7. Situate it below the Airport Layer.

8. You will need to set up an Extract by attribute algorithm on City Boundaries Layer in order to extract the Corpus Christi boundary. Therefore, you will need another Vector field attribute. Click on Inputs tab and choose Vector field.

    a. Set the Parameter name to City Boundaries Attribute

    b. Set the Parent layer to City Boundaries Layer.

    c. Set the Allowed data type to String.

    d. Set the Default value to *NAME*.

    e. Click OK

9. Situate it below the City Boundaries Layer.

10. Add another Extract by attribute algorithm to the model with the following parameters:

    a. Description - Extract Corpus Christi

    b. Input layer = City Boundaries Layer

    c. Selection attribute = City Boundaries Attribute

    d. Operator =

    e. Value - Corpus Christi

    f. Extracted (attribute) = Leave blank

g. Click OK

11. The next step for processing the City Boundary site selection parameter is to buffer the Corpus Christi layer by three miles. Click on the Algorithms tab and find Buffer in the Vector geometry section. Use the following parameters:

   a. Description - Buffering Corpus Christi

   b. Input layer = Extracted (attribute) from algorithm Extract Corpus Christi

   c. Distance = 4828.03 (This equals 3 miles in meters. You are using meters since the data is in UTM meters)

   d. Segments = 5 (QGIS will not output true curves but this option allows you to control the smoothness of the output. The higher the number, the smoother the output will be, as QGIS will use that many segments to approximate the curve.)

   e. Dissolve result = Yes

   f. Buffered ouput - Leave blank

   g. Click OK

The last parameter detail related to the boundary of Corpus Christi is that the airport needs to be located outside the city limits. Therefore, you need to take the three mile buffer output, and run a Difference algorithm on it, with the Corpus Christi output as the Difference layer. This will take the buffer and erase from it the portion within the city limits, leaving a three mile ring around the city limits.

12. Click on the Algorithms tab and search for *Difference*. Find the Vector overlay | Difference tool and use the following parameters:

   a. Description - Difference

   b. Input layer = Buffered from algorithm Buffering Corpus Christi

   c. Overlay layer = Extracted (attribute) from algorithm Extract Corpus Christi

   d. Difference ouput - Leave blank

   e. Click OK

Your model should now resemble the figure 5.14, on the following page.

Now you will work on the Roads parameter. First, the County roads will be selected, then buffered by one mile.

13. Add a Vector Layer input for Roads with the following parameters:

   a. Parameter name = *Roads Layer*.

   b. Set the Geometry type to Line.

   c. Keep the box checked for Mandatory

   d. Click OK

14. Situate it below the City Boundaries Layer input

15. Add a Vector field input with the following parameters:

   a. Set the Parameter name to Roads Attribute

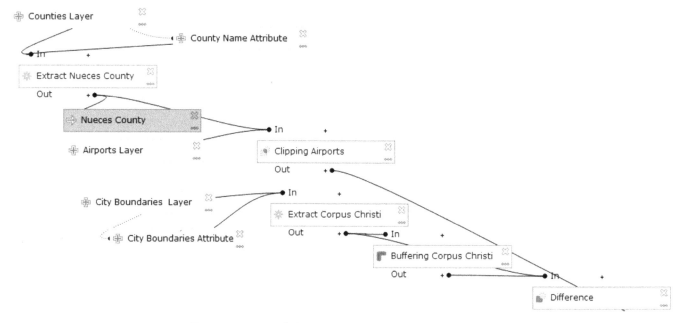

Figure 5.14: Model Incorporating Corpus Christi

    b. Set the Parent layer to Roads Layer.

    c. Set the Allowed data type to String.

    d. Set the Default value to *RTTYP*.

    e. Click OK

16. Add another Extract by attribute algorithm to the model with the following parameters:

    a. Description - Extract County Roads

    b. Input layer = Roads Layer

    c. Selection attribute = Roads Attribute

    d. Operator =

    e. Value - C

    f. Extracted (attribute) = Leave blank

    g. Click OK

17. Now you will buffer the County roads by one mile. Add another Buffer algorithm and use the following parameters:

    a. Description - Buffering County Roads

    b. Input layer = Extracted (attribute) from algorithm Extract County Roads

    c. Distance = 609.34 (1 mile in meters)

    d. Segments = 5

    e. Dissolve result = Yes

    f. Buffered ouput - Leave blank

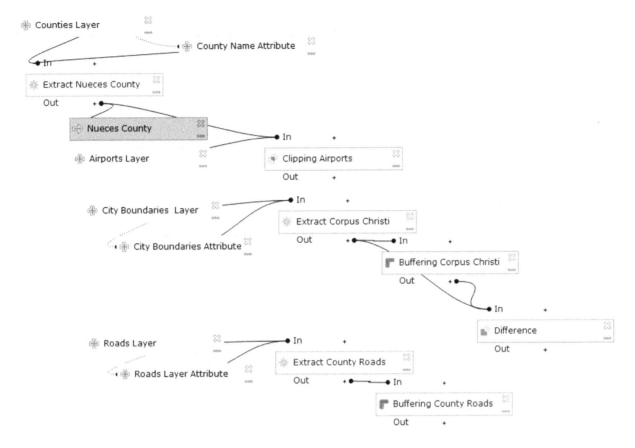

Figure 5.15: Model Incorporating Roads

g. Click OK

Your model should now resemble the figure 5.15.

The last parameter to address the distance to Water Features which be buffered by 0.5 miles.

18. Add a Vector Layer input for WaterFeatures with the following parameters:

    a. Parameter name = *Water Features Layer*.

    b. Set the Geometry type to Line.

    c. Keep the box checked for Mandatory

    d. Click OK

19. Situate it below the Roads Layer Attribute input

20. Now you will buffer the Water Features by 0.5 miles. Add another Buffer algorithm and use the following parameters:

    a. Description - Buffering Water Features

    b. Input layer = Water Features Layer

    c. Distance = 804.67 (0.5 miles in meters)

    d. Segments = 5

    e. Dissolve result = Yes

    f. Buffered ouput - Leave blank

    g. Click OK

Your model should now resemble the figure 5.16.

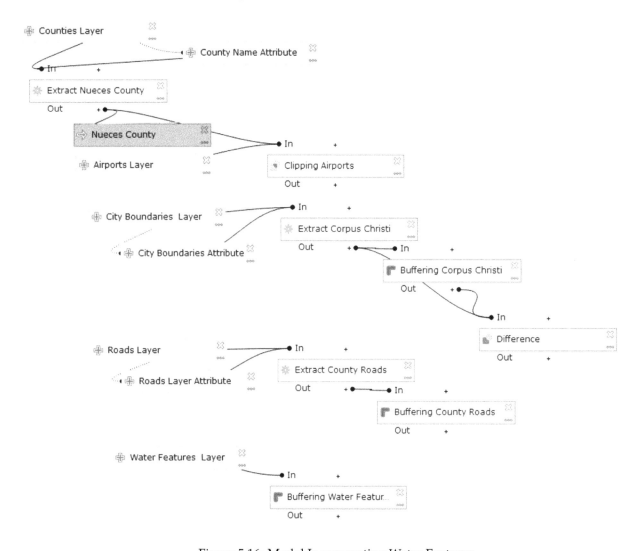

Figure 5.16: Model Incorporating Water Features

21. Save the model.

5.6 Task 4 - Creating the Model - Part 3

In this final task, you will combine all the individual parameters into one layer representing the combination of all parameters. This will represent the acceptable area for helipad locations. Then you will run a clip algorithm on airports to determine which airports meet all the criteria.

1. Open QGIS and open exercise 5.qgz if it is not already.

2. From the Processing Toolbox panel, expand Models | Discover QGIS. Right-click on the Helipad Site Selection model and choose Edit Model from the context menu. (Figure 5.17)

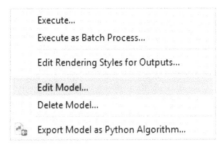

Figure 5.17: Model Context Menu

> Did you know that you can export a model as a Python script? The model context menu includes the option *Export Model as Python Algorithm*. This is a great way to begin to learn how to write python script tools.

You can combine the water buffer, county roads buffer and the three mile ring around Corpus Christi using the Intersection algorithm. This will compute the area of overlap between the three layers.

3. Click on the Algorithms tab and find the Intersection tool in the Vector overlay section. Use the following parameters:

    a. Description - Intersection

    b. Input layer = Difference from algorithm Difference

    c. Overlay layer = Buffered from algorithm Buffering County Roads

    d. Since you need to Intersect more than two layers, you need to set a Parent algorithm. Click the ellipsis button for the Parent algorithms. When the Multiple Selection window opens check the Buffering Water Features. See 5.18.

    e. Intersection ouput - Leave blank

    f. Click OK

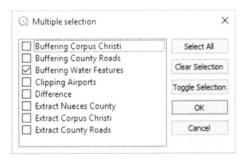

Figure 5.18: Setting A Parent Algorithm

4. Finally, you will clip the airports with the output of the Intersection giving you the final solution. Click on the Algorithms tab and find Clip. Use the following parameters:

    a. Input layer = Clipped from algorithm Clipping Airports

    b. Overlay layer = Intersection from algorithm Intersection

    c. Clipped output = *Final Solution*

The final model should resemble the figure 5.19.

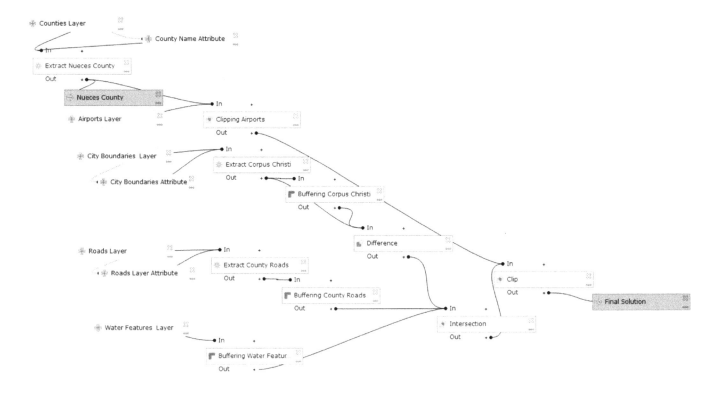

Figure 5.19: Final Model

5. Save the Model and Close it.

6. Congratulations! You have created your first geoprocessing model!

7. From the Processing Toolbox panel, expand Models | Discover QGIS. Right-click on the Helipad Site Selection model and choose Execute from the context menu.

8. Fill out all the parameters as shown in the figure 5.20, on the facing page. Notice that since you set default attribute values those are populated automatically. Click Run when ready.

If the model ran correctly, the FinalSolution layer should contain Cuddihy Field as the only selected airport (shown in figure 5.21, on the next page).

Note on Running Models: Models can also be run from the Processing Modeler interface. You can click the Run model ▶ button. You will be prompted to Save the model, then you will be presented with the same model window shown in the figure below.

Note on Debugging Models: Here we have written out the vast majority of outputs to temporary files. If you get an error or an incorrect result, it can be helpful to save out questionable intermediate datasets. For example, say you are getting an error or an unexpected result from a buffer operation. Try outputting the result of the Extract by attribute dataset that feeds into the buffer algorithm. This will let you determine if the prior step is working correctly. To do this all you have to do is enter a name for the output in question like you did for Nueces County and the Final Solution.

Figure 5.20: Helipad Site Selection Tool

Figure 5.21: Final Solution

5.7 Conclusion

In this exercise you have been exposed to both site selection modeling and the use of Graphical Modeler in building a workflow. Building the model is certainly time consuming. However, the benefits are many, especially if this is a workflow you will have to perform many times.

By clicking on the Export as image ![icon] button in the Processing Modeler you can export the model to a graphic.

This graphic can then be included in a report or a presentation. This can help you explain the technical workflow to others.

If the client changed their mind on the distance from Corpus Christi, you could simply adjust that buffer distance in the model, and rerun it to see how the solution changed. Without the model, you would be starting from scratch in this scenario.

This model can now be run against similar set of data at a different site such as Seattle or Boston. If you were to run it against another set of data, some of the parameters of the Extract by attribute would have to be edited. However, that is easily done. Models allow you to streamline big workflows.

5.8　Discussion Questions

1. How does Graphical Modeler make spatial analysis easier?

2. Export your model as a graphic and turn in with your exercise.

5.9　Challenge Assignment

The client has decided that they can expand the Corpus Christi parameter from 3 miles to 3.5 miles. Edit the buffer distance in the model for the Corpus Christi buffer and determine how that changes the number of airports meeting their needs. Make a map of each scenario to show the client. You may want to output some intermediate datasets such as the Intersection or Buffers to be able to show these criteria on your maps.

Exercise 6

Vector Data Analysis - Network Analysis

Objective – Learn the Basics of Network Analysis

6.1 Introduction

In this exercise, you will learn how to conduct analyses related to linear networks. You will learn how to determine the shortest path from origin to destination and how to allocate a linear network into service areas.

This exercise includes the following tasks:

- Task 1 Basic Network Analysis

- Task 2 Allocating Service Areas

6.2 Objective: Learn the Basics of Network Analysis

The objective of this exercise is to learn how to conduct basic network analysis. To do this you will learn to use some new native QGIS network tools along with some GRASS processing tools for allocating service areas.

6.3 Task 1 - Basic Network Analysis

In this task, you will use some new native QGIS network tools to determine the shortest distance between two points via a San Francisco streets layer. You will do this both by shortest overall distance and by time traveled.

1. Open QGIS.

2. Add the MTA_DPT_SpeedLimits layer from the SanFrancisco GeoPackage to QGIS.

3. This is a street network for the City of San Francisco. Open the attribute table to see what kind of data you have to work with. Notice that in addition to having the street name and type, there is a column populated with speed limits for each road segment. Close the attribute table.

4. Open the Layer Styling Panel 🖌 and symbolize the data by speed limit.

    a. Choose a Categorized renderer

    b. Column = speed_limit

    c. Color ramp = Greys

    d. Click Classify

   e. Select the NULL class and click the Delete ⊟ button.

   f. Click the Advanced drop down menu and choose the Symbol Levels option.

   g. In the Symbol Levels panel check Enable symbol levels. This options renders the features on the map canvas in sequence by class. This puts the roads with the highest speed limits above the other classes.

   h. Click the Go Back ◁ button. See figure 6.1.

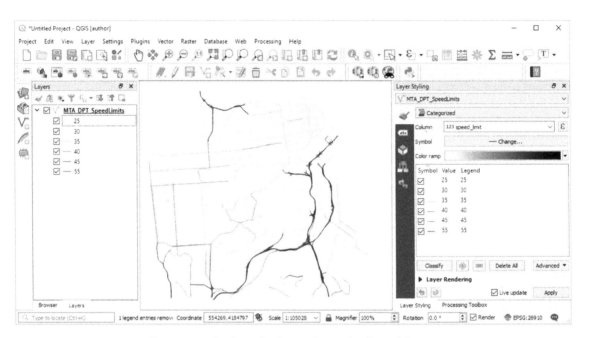

Figure 6.1: Styling the Street Layer by Speed Limit

5. Save your map as exercise6.qgz.

6. You will use a processing algorithm to find the shortest distance between two points on the network.

7. Add the Start_Points layer from the SanFrancisco GeoPackage to QGIS. Give the points a bright red fill color.

8. Open the Processing Toolbox and expand the Network Analysis tool category.

9. Locate and open the Shortest Path (Layer to Point) tool. See figure 6.2, on the next page.

   a. Set the Vector layer representing network to MTA_DPT_SpeedLimits

   b. Set the Path type to calculate to Shortest

   c. Set the Vector layer with start points to Start_Points.

   d. For End point (x,y) click the ellipsis End Point [...] button. Then pick a location in the northeastern corner of the street network, and click on it. The End point (x,y) box will become populated with the coordinates for the location you clicked.

   e. Leave the Shortest path output as a temporary layer.

   f. Click the Run button and then Close when it finishes.

   g. A new layer named Shortest path will be added to the Layers panel.

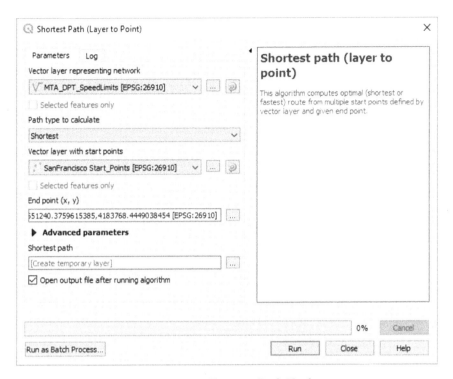

Figure 6.2: Shortest Path Tool

10. Its status as a temporary scratch layer will be indicated by the Temporary Scratch Layer ⬚ icon in the indicator space of the Layers Panel. Click on that icon to open the Save Scratch Layer window. Save it as ShortestPath into the SanFrancisco GeoPackage. The layer will be saved, and the Temporary Scratch Layer icon will disappear.

11. Give the layer a bright red line color and a width of 0.46. See figure 6.3.

Figure 6.3: Shortest Path From Start Points to the End Point

12. Now you will determine the shortest drive time from the Start Points and the destination. In the Processing Toolbox and expand the Recently Used category and open the Shortest Path (Layer to Point) tool.

a. Set the Vector layer representing network to `MTA_DPT_SpeedLimits`

b. Set the Path type to calculate to Fastest

c. Set the Vector layer with start points to `Start_Points`.

d. For End point (x,y) click the ellipsis End Point [...] button and try to click on the same destination locale.

e. Expand the Advanced parameters section and set the Speed field to `speed_limit`.

f. Again leave the Shortest path output as a temporary layer.

g. Click the Run button and then Close when it finishes.

h. A new layer named `Shortest path` will be added to the Layers Panel below.

13. With this criterion, you may get a very different solution, depending on the points you chose. See figure 6.4.

Figure 6.4: Fastest(purple) and Shortest(red) Paths From Start Points to the End Point

14. Again click on the Temporary Scratch Layer 🗒 icon to open the Save Scratch Layer window. Save it as `FastestPath` into the `SanFrancisco` GeoPackage.

15. Save your map file and close QGIS.

> For doing more complicated network analyses on larger datasets pgRouting (https://pgrouting.org/) is a fantastic tool. pgRouting is an extension to PostgreSQL and uses PostGIS. It has an ever growing suite of SQL based tools for running network analyses.

6.4   Task 2 - Allocating Service Areas

Now you will use some GRASS tools to allocate portions of the road network served by each San Francisco Police Station. GRASS (Geographic Resources Analysis Support System - `https://grass.osgeo.org/`) is a mature and powerful free and open source (FOSS) GIS software package. It has a unique data structure that can be initially intimidating. Fortunately, most of the GRASS processing tools are available via the QGIS Processing Toolbox. This makes them available to the wide array of file formats read by QGIS.

1. Open QGIS and open `exercise6.qgz` if it is not already.

2. Turn off visibility for the FastestPath, Shortest path and Start_Points layers.

3. Add the SF_Police and SF_FireStations layers from the SanFrancisco GeoPackage to QGIS.

4. Change the color of the SF_Police points to have a blue fill and the SF_FireStations points to have a red fill (figure 6.5).

Figure 6.5: Fire and Police Stations Added

5. The first step in doing a network analysis using GRASS tools is to build a network dataset. In the Processing Toolbox expand GRASS | Vector. There are a lot of tools! Type *net* into the Processing Toolbox Search box to filter the visible tools. Find and open the v.net tool.

This tool will create a linear network of San Francisco streets and attach nodes representing the Police stations.

6. Enter the parameters described below and shown in the figure 6.6, on the next page:

    a. Set the Input vector line layer (arcs) [optional] to MTA_DPT_SpeedLimits
    b. Set the Input vector point layer (nodes) [optional] to SF_Police
    c. Set the Operation to be performed to connect.
    d. Set the Threshold for connecting centers to the network (in map unit) to 300.
    e. Leave the Network output as a temporary layer.
    f. Click the Run button and then Close when it finishes.
    g. A new layer named output will be added to the Layers Panel.

7. Open the attribute table for the output layer. It has one new column named cat. Close the table.

8. Now you will save this layer into the SanFrancisco GeoPackage. At this time, GRASS tool output cannot be saved to an existing GeoPackage. That is why you saved it as a temporary layer. You will now take the additional step to export it. Right-click on the layer and choose Export | Save Features As and save it into the existing GeoPackage. Name the new layer road_network.

Now that the network dataset is constructed, you will identify the road territory that each police station should serve.

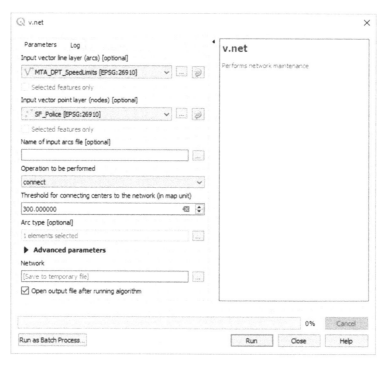

Figure 6.6: v.net Tool

9. Find and open the v.net.alloc tool. Fill out the tool form as described below and as seen in the figure 6.7, on the facing page.

    a. Set the Input vector line layer (arcs) [optional] to SanFrancisco road_network

    b. Set the Center points layer (nodes) [optional] to SF_Police

    c. Set the Threshold for connecting centers to the network (in map unit) to 300.

    d. Leave the Network Allocation output as a temporary layer.

    e. Click the Run button and then Close when it finishes.

    f. A new layer named output will be added to the Layers Panel.

10. Again export the resulting temporary layer into the SanFrancisco GeoPackage naming it policestation_allocation.

11. Set up your Layers Panel so that only the SF_Police layer and the policestation_allocation layer are visible. Position the SF_Police layer as the top most layer in the Layers Panel with policestation_allocation just below. See figure 6.8, on the next page.

12. Now you will symbolize the policestation_allocation layer. Open the Layer Styling Panel and switch to a Categorized renderer and set the Column to cat. Click Classify. The road network will now be colored by the Police Station serving each road segment.

13. Next you will label the Police stations with their name. Set SF_Police as the target layer in the Layer Styling Panel. Select the Labels abc tab.

    a. Change the label setting to Single labels

    b. Set Label with to FACILITY_N.

    c. One the Text abc tab set the Font to *Calibri*.

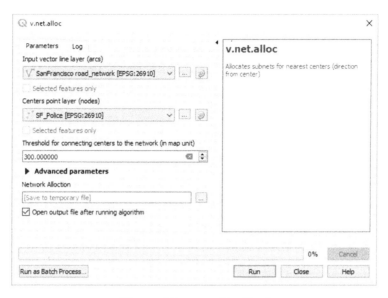

Figure 6.7: v.net.alloc Tool

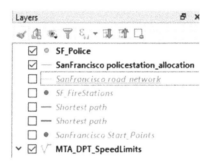

Figure 6.8: Layers Panel

    d. Set the Size to 8

    e. Set the Style to **Bold**.

    f. Click the Formatting ⁺ᵃᵇ tab and set the Wrap on character to a space and Alignment to Center.

    g. Select the Buffer abc tab and enable Draw text buffer.

    h. Switch to the Placement tab and set the Placement method to Cartographic with a Distance of 1.5

14. Your map should resemble the figure 6.9, on the following page.

6.5 Conclusion

In this exercise, you were exposed to basic network routing and allocation analysis. You calculated the shortest distance between two points via both time and distance. You then determined which portions of the network that should be allocated to each police station. There are many applications for this type of analysis including emergency management, parcel delivery, and general navigation.

6.6 Discussion Questions

1. What is a real world application of network analysis? Explain.

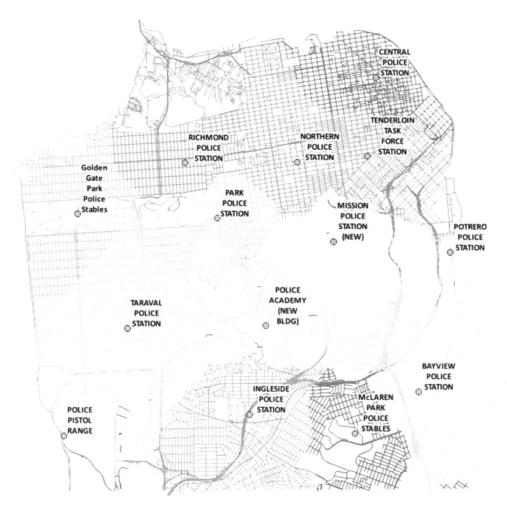

Figure 6.9: Road Allocation by Police Station

2. How can a network analysis benefit the logistics industry?

3. What other linear networks could this apply to other than roads?

6.7 Challenge Assignment

The San Francisco Police Department has shown your analysis to their colleagues at the Fire Department and they were impressed. Now the Fire Department would like the same analysis done for their stations. Repeat the steps in the second task to create the same allocation analysis for the Fire Department. Compose a map of the results of the Fire Department analysis.

Exercise 7

Raster Data Analysis - Working with Topographic Data

Objective – Learn the Basics of Terrain Analysis

7.1   Introduction

In this exercise, you will learn about topographic data and how to use it for analysis. You will learn how to create datasets such as slope, aspect, and hillshades using QGIS. You will then learn how to combine them using raster algebra.

This exercise includes the following tasks:

- Task 1 Terrain Analysis

- Task 2 Reclassification

- Task 3 Using the Raster Calculator

7.2   Objective: Learn the Basics of Terrain Analysis

The objective of this exercise is to learn the basics of terrain analysis using QGIS. This will include created hillshade images, generating slope and aspect datasets and using the Raster Calculator to perform raster algebra.

7.3   Task 1 - Terrain Analysis

7.4   Task 1.1 - Creating a Color Hillshade Image

In this task, you will use a digital elevation model to create several terrain related datasets: slope, aspect, and hillshade. These elevation derived datasets can be important in site selection and other terrain based spatial analyses.

1. Open QGIS.

2. Starting with a new project add the 35106-B4.dem raster from the exercise directory to QGIS.

This raster layer has elevation values for each cell. This type of data is referred to as a digital elevation model, or DEM, for short. This particular dataset covers the Sandia Mountains on the east side of Albuquerque, New Mexico (shown in figure 7.1, on the next page). The light areas have the highest elevation and the dark areas the lowest elevation.

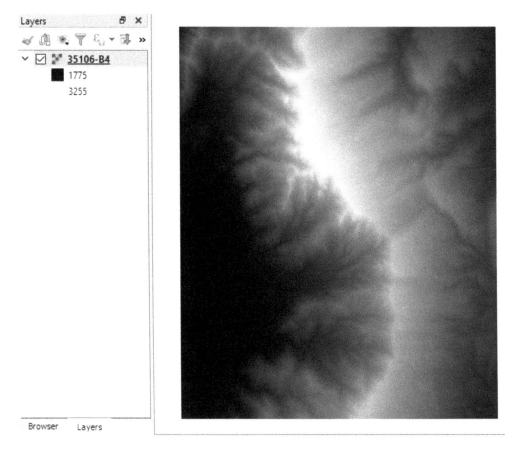

Figure 7.1: Digital Elevation Model (DEM) in QGIS

3. Let's explore the properties of the raster dataset.

4. Open the Layer Properties for the DEM and choose the Information tab. Notice that the raster is in the UTM coordinate system. UTM has X/Y coordinate values in meters.

5. Also notice that the Pixel size is 10 x 10. This means each cell represents a 10 by 10 meter area. There is other useful information here such as the Data type, Dimensions and Statistics for the values in the raster.

6. Now switch to the Symbology tab. Find the Min/max Values Settings section and expand it. The elevation values (Z) of a DEM are typically either feet or meters. The min value probably reads 1775 and the max value 3255. However, your values may differ slightly depending on your Min/max Values Settings. The default setting is Min/max. However, there are other options such as Cumulative count cut which removes data outliers and Mean +/- standard deviation.

> You can set the default behavior for Min/Max values. Click on Settings | Options and choose the Rendering tab. In the Raster section you can set default settings for raster contrast enhancement. See figure below.

7. You can also set how thoroughly QGIS scans the raster dataset for min/max values. By default the Statistics extent is set to Whole raster. Click this drop down and note that you can also set this to Current canvas and Updated canvas. The last setting will update the statistics and data rendering to just those in the visible extent and will update that as you pan/zoom the map canvas.

8. The default Accuracy setting is Estimate (faster). Click the drop down for this and note that you can also choose Actual (slower).These settings can be very useful when working with a very large raster dataset, or when you want

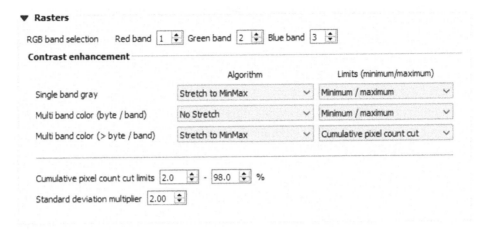

Figure 7.2: Raster Rendering Settings

statistics on just the visible extent.

9. Set the Min/max Values Settings to Min/Max, the Statistics extent to Whole raster and the Accuracy to Actual (slower) and click the Apply button. The values should now read 1775 to 3255 which are the actual min and max values of the DEM.

10. The Sandia Mountain range reaches 10,678 feet above sea level. Therefore, you can deduce that these elevation units (Z values) are in meters. Before working with DEMs, it is important to understand what unit the X, Y, and Z values are in. In this case, all three are in meters.

11. Close the Layer Properties window.

12. Save your project as Terrain.qgz in the exercise directory.

13. You will use the Raster Terrain Analysis toolset to create the several elevation related datasets. Open the Processing Toolbox.

14. Find the native QGIS Raster terrain analysis section and expand it to see the available tools.

15. First you will create a hillshade image which will allow you to get a better feel for the terrain in this area. Double click the Hillshade tool.

16. Use the following parameters (shown in figure 7.3, on the following page).

    a. Elevation layer = 35106-B4

    b. Z factor – 1.0 (this is a conversion factor between the X/Y and Z units. Since all three are meters you can leave this at 1.0)

    c. The QGIS defaults for Azimuth and Vertical angle (sun position) are 300 and 40 respectively. The Esri defaults are 315 and 45. You can experiment with those values.

    d. Save the output Hillshade layer ti the exercise_7_Data/MyData folder and name it Hillshade.tif

    e. To set the Hillshade output format, click the ellipsis button and choose Save to file.... Set the Save as type to TIF files (*.tif)

    f. Click Run and then Close.

The resulting hillshade should resemble the figure 7.4, on the next page.

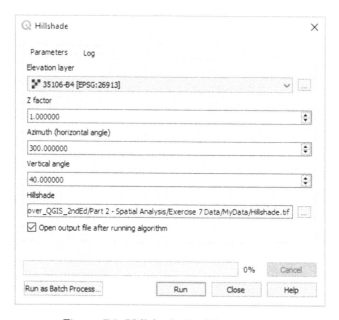

Figure 7.3: Hillshade Tool Parameters

There is also a *Hillshade* renderer available. Another suitable approach is to simply *Duplicate* the DEM layer and render the copy as a Hillshade image. When using this renderer it is best to visit the *Resampling* section and set the *Zoomed in* resampling to *Bilinear* and the *Zoomed out* to *Cubic* for better rendering. You now know how to generate a hillshade dataset. However, this approach would achieve the same end without needing to create a separate layer!

Figure 7.4: Hillshade Layer

This is a grayscale hillshade rendering. Now you will use both the original DEM and the hillshade to create a color hillshade image.

17. Make sure the Hillshade layer is above the DEM layer in the Layers Panel.

18. Select the DEM layer (35106-B4)and open the Layer Styling Panel.

19. Switch to a Singleband pseudocolor renderer.

20. Click the Color ramp drop down and choose Create New Color Ramp. Shown in figure 7.5.

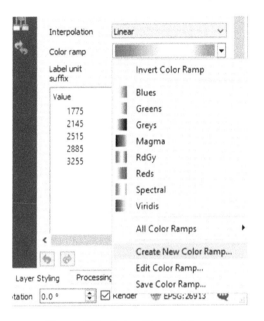

Figure 7.5: Color Ramp Menu

21. In the Color ramp type window choose Catalog: cpt-city and click OK. Shown in figure 7.6.

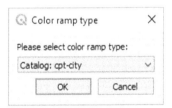

Figure 7.6: Color Ramp Type

22. In the Cpt-city Color Ramp window select the Topography category.

23. Select cd-a or sd-a and click OK.

> To save this color ramp click the drop down Color Ramp menu and choose Save Color Ramp. Name the ramp, tag as you wish and click OK. It will now appear in your list of color ramps!

24. Expand the Min/max Values Settings and ensure it is set to Min/max values and that the Accuracy is set to Actual (slower).

25. Now change the target layer in the Layer Styling Panel to the Hillshade layer.

26. Scroll down to the Layer Rendering section set the Blending mode to Multiply.

27. Your map should now resemble the figure 7.7.

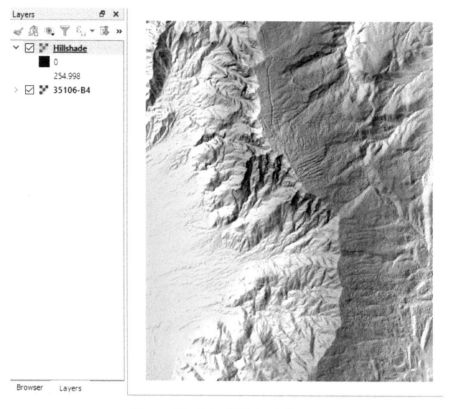

Figure 7.7: Color Hillshade Image

7.5   Task 1.2 - Calculating Slope and Aspect

1. Now you will create a Slope dataset. From the Processing Toolbox return to the Raster terrain analysis section and open the Slope tool.

2. Complete the Slope tool as shown in the figure 7.8 below then click click Run and Close when it is complete.

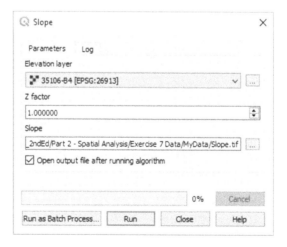

Figure 7.8: Slope Tool

The slope raster shows the steepest areas in white and the flattest terrain in black. The tool determines the steepness of each pixel by comparing the elevation value of each pixel to that of the eight surrounding pixels. The slope values are degrees of slope (shown in figure 7.10, on the following page).

> Because the QGIS Processing Toolbox contains tools from multiple providers there are often multiple tools that do roughly the same thing. If you need slope in percentages you can use the GDAL | Raster Analysis | Slope tool.

Now you will create an Aspect raster. Aspect measures which cardinal direction the terrain in each pixel is facing (north facing vs. south facing etc.)

3. From the Processing Toolbox double click on the Aspect tool. Fill out the Aspect tool as shown in the figure 7.9 below then click Run and Close when it is complete.

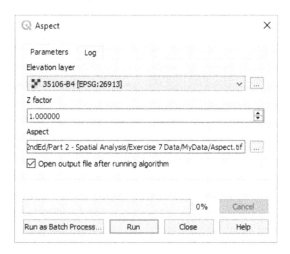

Figure 7.9: Aspect Tool

The output should resemble the figure 7.10, on the following page with values ranging from 0-360 representing degrees (0=north, 90= east, 180 = south and 270 = west).

4. Save your project.

7.6   Task 2 - Reclassification

Now that you have created the slope and aspect data you will reclassify them into meaningful categories. Raster reclassification is a method for aggregating data values into categories. In this case, you will be reclassifying them into categories important to identifying habitat suitability for a particular plant species. Once the slope and aspect data have been reclassified you will combine them in Task 3 to identify suitable habitat areas.

This plant requires steep slopes. You will classify slope raster into three categories: 0-45, 45-55, and > 55.

1. Open QGIS and open exercise7.qgz if it is not already.

2. Search in the Processing Toolbox for *Reclass* and find the Raster analysis | Reclassify by table tool.

    a. The Raster layer will be Slope.

    b. Next you will set up the Reclassification table. Click the ellipsis button to open the Fixed table window.

    c. For row # 1 set the Minimum to 0 and the Maximum to 45. Set the Value to 1.

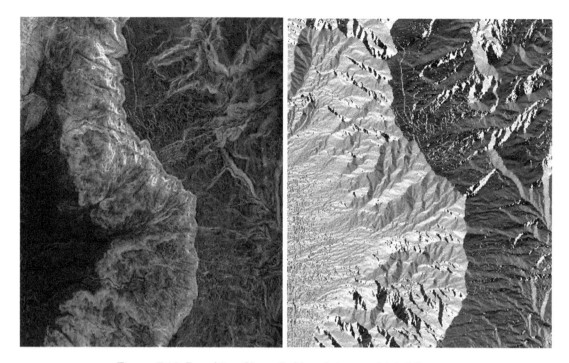

Figure 7.10: Resulting Slope (left) and Aspect (right) Layers

d. Add two more rows and set them up as shown in figure 7.11. Note the maximum cell value (75.480842590332) for row 3 was obtained from the Layer Properties | Information tab.

e. Click OK to close the Fixed table window.

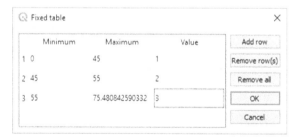

Figure 7.11: Reclassification Table Set Up In the Fixed Table Window

3. Open the Layer Styling Panel ✍ with the target being the Reclassified slope raster.

4. Set the render type to Paletted/Unique values and click Classify.

5. Make the pixels with a value of 3 dark green, those with a value of 2 a light green and those with a value of 1 white.

6. Give the layer a Blending Mode of Multiply.

7. Turn off all the layers other than the Reclassified slope raster and the Hillshade. See figure 7.13, on page 186.

Now you will recode the Aspect data in the same fashion. This plant prefers west facing slopes. Hence the west facing slopes will be set to 3, the north and south are the next best location so set them to 2, and the eastern slopes can be set 1. Remember that the values of the aspect raster are compass bearings or azimuths (270 is due west, 0 is north, 180 is south and 90 is east). You will classify the aspect data into eight cardinal directions.

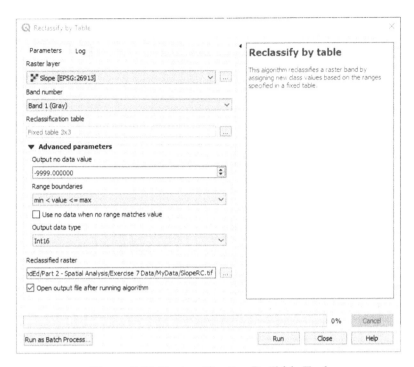

Figure 7.12: Reclassification By Table Tool

8. From the Processing Toolbox open the Raster analysis | Reclassify by table tool. Remember that it will now also appear in the Recently used category.

    a. The Raster layer will be Aspect.

    b. Next you will set up the Reclassification table. Click the ellipsis button to open the Fixed table window.

    c. Set up the table as shown in figure 7.14, on the next page.

    d. When done OK to close the Fixed table window.

9. Right-click on the Reclassified Slope layer and choose Styles | Copy Style.

10. Right-click on the Reclassified Aspect layer and choose Styles | Paste styles.

11. Rename the layers to *Reclassified Slope* and *Reclassified Aspect* respectively.

12. Save your QGIS project.

7.7 Task 3 - Using the Raster Calculator

Now you will use the Raster Calculator to combine the reclassified slope and aspect data. The Raster Calculator allows you to combine raster datasets mathematically to produce new outputs. For example, raster datasets can be added, subtracted, multiplied, and divided against one another. This procedure is also known as raster algebra. In this task you will add the two reclassified rasters together. Since each raster has ideal conditions coded with the value '3', an area that ends up with a pixel value of 6 would be ideal.

1. Open QGIS and open `exercise7.qgz` if it is not already.

2. From the menu bar choose `Raster | Raster Calculator`. The loaded raster datasets are listed in the upper right window. Below it is a panel of operators and an expression window (see figure 7.15, on page 187).

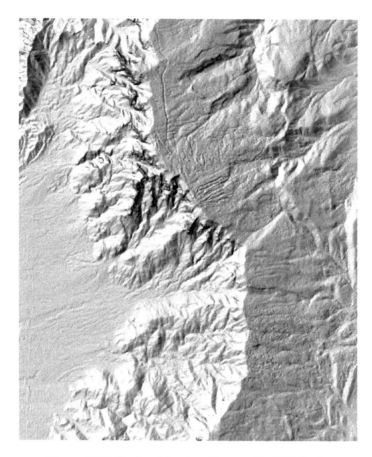

Figure 7.13: Reclassification Slope with Hillshade

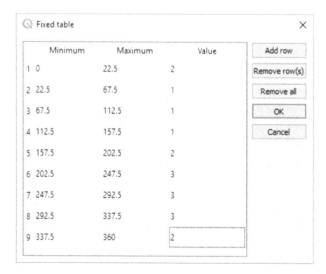

Figure 7.14: Aspect Reclassification Table Set Up In the Fixed Table Window

3. Do the following to add the two reclassified rasters:

    a. Double-click on `Reclassified Slope@1` to place it in the Raster Calculator expression.

    b. In the Operators section, click the addition sign.

c. Then double-click on the `Reclassified Aspect@1` raster.

d. In the Result Layer section name the Output layer `Exercise_7_Data/MyData/PlantHabitat.tif`.

e. Choose an Output format of GeoTIFF.

f. Click OK.

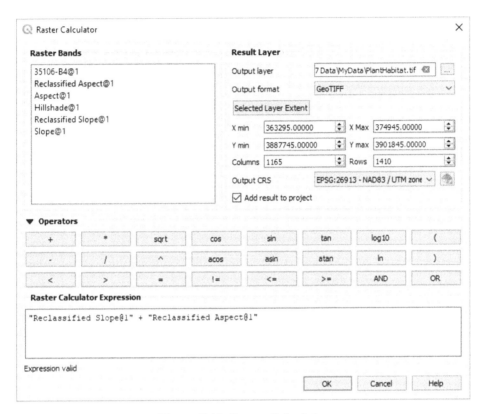

Figure 7.15: Raster Calculator

4. Using what you know apply the Paletted/Unique Values renderer to the Plant Habitat layer.

5. Select values 2-6 and select the Greens Color ramp.

6. Apply a Blending Mode of Multiply to the layer.

7. The final raster will resemble the figure 7.16, on the next page.

8. Save your QGIS project.

7.8   Conclusion

In this exercise, you were exposed to terrain analysis, creating derived datasets from elevation data (DEMs). You then went on to reclassify two terrain related datasets (aspect and slope), and combine them to produce a suitable habitat layer for a plant species. This is another method of doing site selection analysis. Raster data are well suited for these types of analyses.

7.9   Discussion Questions

1. What other real world applications of terrain analysis can you think of?

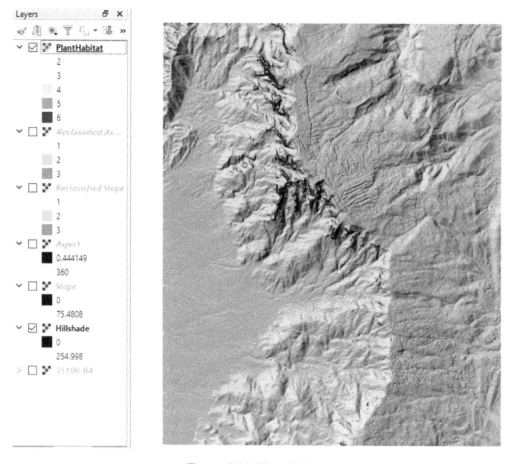

Figure 7.16: Plant Habitat

2. How does this suitability analysis compare to the site selection analysis done with the vector data model in Exercise 5?

7.10 Challenge Assignment

Another scientist is interested in developing a map of potential habitat for another species that prefers rugged, steep west facing slopes. Use the same Raster Terrain Analysis tools to develop a Ruggedness Index. Recode the Ruggedness Index into three categories:

- Min: 0 Max: 20 Value: 1

- Min: 20 Max: 40 Value: 2

- Min: 40 Max:(lookup) Value: 3

Combine the resulting reclassified ruggedness index with the reclassified slope and aspect from the exercise to create the final result. Compose a map showing the results.

Exercise 8

Raster Data Analysis - Density Surfaces

Objective – Learn Density Analysis Methods

8.1 Introduction

In this exercise you'll learn about performing point density analysis. Density analysis can be used to show areas where there is a high occurrence of data. The exercise will also cover converting between vector and raster data.

This exercise includes the following tasks:

- Task 1 Rendering Points as Heatmaps

- Task 2 Creating Point Density Rasters

- Task 3 Raster to Vector Conversion

- Task 4 Vector to Raster Conversion

8.2 Objective: Learn Density Analysis Methods

The objective of this exercise is to learn about density analysis methods and look at the conversion between the raster and vector data models.

8.3 Task 1 - Rendering Points as Heatmaps

Point density analysis can be used to show where there is a concentration of data points. In this task, you will first use one of the many unique renderers available in QGIS to render points as a heatmap. A heatmap is a point density surface. You will then learn how to create an actual heatmap raster dataset.

Radius (aka neighborhood) – When generating a heatmap you can define the search radius. The software will use this distance when searching for neighboring points. A given pixel will receive higher values when more points are found within the search radius, and lower values when fewer points are found. Therefore, you can get very different results by changing the radius value.

1. Open QGIS.

2. Using your method of choice, add both the layers found in the `texas.gpkg` in the `Exercise_8_Data` folder to QGIS. You should then have both `TexasBoundary` and `place_names` layers loaded.

3. Save your project as `Exercise8.qgz` in the exercise directory.

4. Open the Layer Styling Panel and make place_names the target layer.

5. Change the renderer from Single symbol to Heatmap.

      a. Use the default Greys Color ramp.

      b. Set the Radius to 80000 Map Units. This value was determined by experimenting with different values. See figure 8.1.

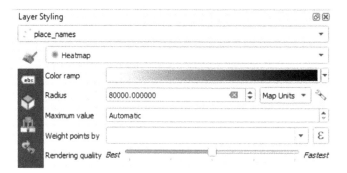

Figure 8.1: Setting up the Heatmap Renderer

You now have rendered the points as a heatmap in just a couple simple steps! Notice that you also have the options of weighting the heatmap by an attribute column. You will not use that option here but it is worth remembering. Now you will do a little work to more appropriately style the Texas boundary layer.

6. Make TexasBoundary the top most layer in the Layers Panel.

7. Set TexasBoundary as the target layer in the Layer Styling Panel

8. Select Simple fill. Change the Fill style to No brush.

One of the major goals of any cartographic endeavor is to put the focus of the map on the data you want the map reader to see first. In the next steps you will use a couple data rendering tricks to create a mask around the Texas place names heatmap.

9. Right-click on the TexasBoundary layer and choose Duplicate from the context menu.

10. Set TexasBoundary copy as the target layer in the Layer Styling Panel. Change the renderer to Inverted Polygon. This renderer styles the layer outside its boundaries. Styling a copy of the Texas layer with this renderer creates a mask layer around Texas.

11. Select Simple fill. Change the Fill style to Solid. Then change the Fill color to white. This completes the mask effect around the heatmap. See figure 8.2, on the next page.

12. Save your project.

8.4   Task 2 - Creating Point Density Rasters

Next you will learn how to create a heatmap layer versus rendering points as a heatmap. To do this you will be using the Heatmap (Kernel Density Estimation) tool. This is a preferable workflow if you need information from the point density surface versus just a rendering of it.

1. Open QGIS and open exercise8.qgz if it is not already.

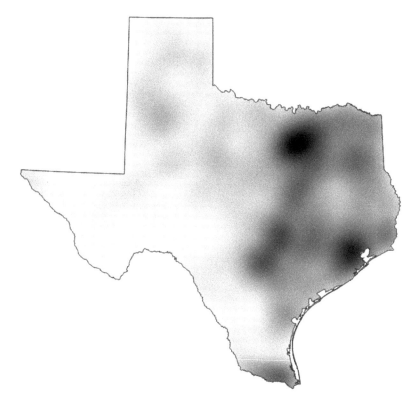

Figure 8.2: Points Rendered as Heatmap

2. Here you will learn a new method of finding tools in QGIS. In the lower left corner there is a Locator Bar (Ctrl + K). This lets you search QGIS for processing tools, layers, features, settings etc. It even acts as a quick calculator! You can precede a search with the keywords shown in the figure 8.3.

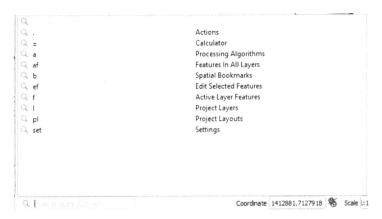

Figure 8.3: QGIS Locator Bar

3. Type *Heat* into the Locator Bar to find the Heatmap (Kernel Density Estimation) tool. See figure 8.3. Double-click on the tool in the Locator Bar to open it.

4. You will use the same radius, but notice the tool has more options than the Heatmap point renderer. Enter the following options in the tool:

  a. Point layer = place_names

Figure 8.4: Finding the Heatmap Tool via the QGIS Locator Bar

b. Radius = 80000 meters

c. Pixel size X and Pixel size Y = 2000 each

d. Expand the Advanced parameters section and set the Kernel shape to Epanechnikov. Kernel shape controls the rate at which the influence of a point decreases as the distance from the point increases. Different kernels decay at different rates. Epanechnikov gives features less weight for distances closer to the point than Triweight. Epanechnikov therefore produces smoother hotspots. You can find documentation on the different Kernel shapes here: https://en.wikipedia.org/wiki/Kernel_(statistics).

e. Heatmap output = Exercise 8 Data/MyData/TownDensity.tif

f. Click Run and Close to dismiss.

5. You will have a permanent point density heatmap loaded into your Layers Panel rendered with the default black to white color ramp. It will look similar to the rendering in Task 1 but the color ramp by default is reversed.

6. You will run the tool a second time but this time you will weight the town points by their population. Run the Heatmap (Kernel Density Estimation) tool again. This time use all the same parameters as before but also set the Weight from field parameter to POPULATION. Name the Heatmap output as TownPopDensity.tif.

Weighting the heatmap by a field provides a much more accurate picture of where the population centers are, rather than just town density (figure 8.5, on the facing page).

7. Save your project.

8.5   Task 3 - Raster to Vector Conversion

Sometimes it is necessary to convert data between the two main data models: vector and raster. Here you will convert the population-based heat map to a vector dataset. Having the data in the vector data model allows for easier area calculations and different cartographic options (border and fill).

1. Open QGIS and open exercise8.qgz if it is not already.

2. Symbolize the TownPopDensity raster with the following settings:

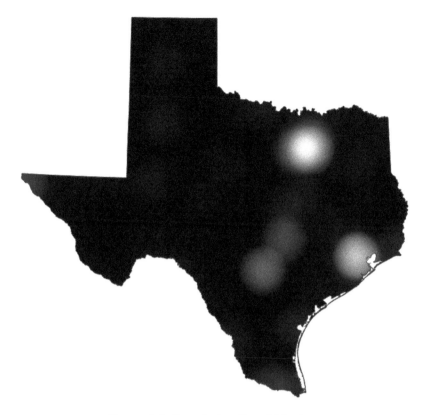

Figure 8.5: Population Based Heatmap

a. Renderer = Singleband pseudocolor

b. Color ramp = YlOrRd

c. Mode = Continuous

d. Min / Max Value Settings = Cumulative count cut

e. Min / Max Value Settings | Accuracy = Actual (slower)

The map will now resemble the figure 8.6, on the next page.

This is a more pleasing rendering and is very useful for a visual interpretation of population centers. However, if you wanted to have an actual layer of these population centers, the heat map needs to be processed further. You will now identify the highest population centers.

3. First, you need to decide on a threshold value that will constitute the population centers. There are a couple ways to do this: you can look at the values from the layer classification or look at the Layer Properties | Histogram. Here you will use values greater than 800,000 as the threshold for population centers.

4. From the menu bar choose Raster | Raster Calculator.

a. Double-click on TownPopDensity@1

b. Click on the > Operator

c. Type 800000 in as the value

d. Output layer = Exercise 8 Data\MyData\PopulationCenter.tif

e. Click Run (figure 8.7, on the following page).

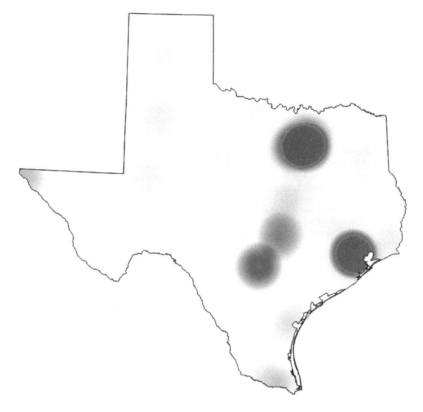

Figure 8.6: Styled Population Weighted Heatmap

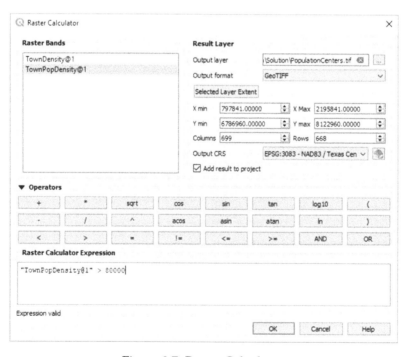

Figure 8.7: Raster Calculator

5. All the cells in the TownPopDensity raster input layer that had pixel values greater than 800,000 now have a value of 1, and the remaining pixels have a value of 0.

6. You will now convert the output to a vector layer. From the menu bar choose `Raster | Conversion | Polygonize (Raster to Vector)`.

     a. Input layer = PopulationCenters

     b. Output Vector file = `MyData/PopulationCenterPolys.shp`

     c. Click Run. (figure 8.8)

     d. Click Close when complete.

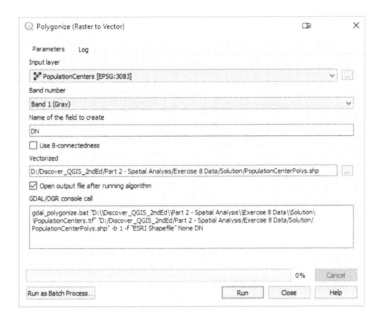

Figure 8.8: Polygonize Tool

7. When the processing is complete, make sure the new polygon layer is above the raster layer in the Layers Panel so that it is visible.

Since the output represents all the pixels in the raster you need to eliminate the non-population center polygons from this layer. To do this you will put the layer into Edit mode, select those polygons with a value of 0 and delete them.

8. Right-click on the PopulationCenterPolys polygon layer in the Layers Panel and choose Toggle editing from the context menu.

9. Open the attribute table for the layer. Click the Select features using an expression ${\cal E}$ button.

10. Expand the Field and Values section. Double-click on DN to place it in the Expression window. Click the = operator. Now click the all unique button and double-click on the 0 value to place it in the expression. (figure 8.9, on the following page)

11. Click Select Features to execute the selection then click Close.

12. Now that the records with a value of zero are selected, and the layer is in edit mode, click the Delete selected features 🗑 button.

13. Click the Toggle editing mode ✏ button and Save the changes.

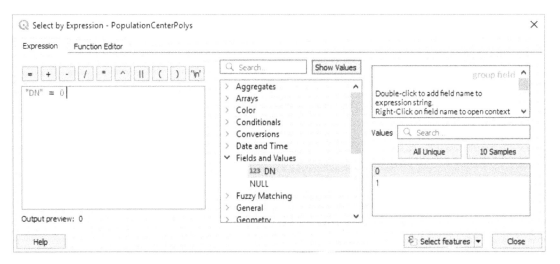

Figure 8.9: Select by Expression

Since the population centers extend beyond the state boundaries you will clip them. Here you will use a new QGIS feature named **Editing in Place** This new feature which was introduced at QGIS 3.4 allows you to run some processing tools against layers without having to produce a new output layer. You run the tool against the current layer and the changes are applied to that layer. A very novel new workflow!

14. Highlight (select) the PopulationCenterPolys layer in the Layers Panel.

15. Open the Processing Toolbox. Click the Editing in Place button.

16. Now find the Vector overlay | Clip tool and open it. Set the Overlay layer to TexasBoundary. Click Modify All Features. Now simply toggle out of editing and Save your edits. The layer will have been clipped to the state boundaries in place! (figure 8.10)

Figure 8.10: Clipping Features In Place

The population centers are now a polygon layer you can use in a final map, or perhaps to feed into another analysis (figure 8.11, on the facing page).

Now that the data are in polygon form, it is straightforward to calculate their acreage. QGIS calculates areas in the units of the coordinate reference system, therefore the layer needs to be in a Cartesian coordinate system with

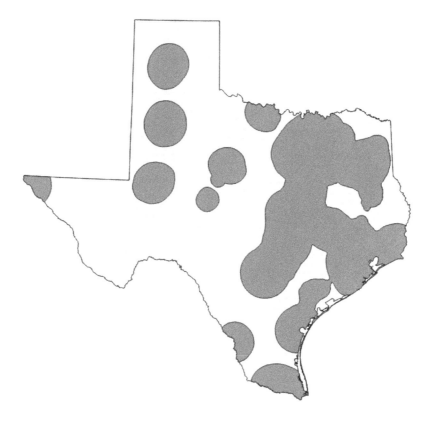

Figure 8.11: Population Centers

units of feet or meters. Currently it is in a Geographic coordinate system with values of decimal degrees. You will save the layer to a new coordinate reference system; then you can calculate the square meters of the polygons and convert those to acres or square miles, etc.

17. Open the attribute table for the PopulationCentersPoly layer.

18. Click the Toggle editing mode ✎ button.

19. Click the New column 🗒 button.

20. Name the column acres and make it a Whole number (integer) column. Assign it a Length of 7. Close the table.

21. Now you will install a plugin.

22. From the menu bar choose Plugins | Manage and Install Plugins. Switch to the All tab and search for the *Calculate Geometry* plugin and install it. Close the Plugin Manager when done.

23. Right-click on the PopulationCentersPoly layer and choose Calculate Geometry from the context menu.

24. Set the Field to acres and the Units to Acres and click OK. (figure 8.12, on the next page)

25. Toggle off editing and Save your results (figure 8.13, on the following page).

26. Now you have a layer of population centers and you have calculated their acreage!

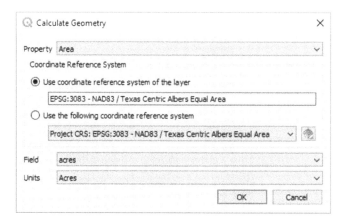

Figure 8.12: Calculate Geometry

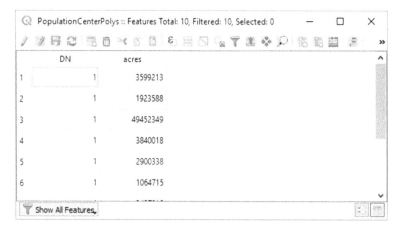

Figure 8.13: Acres Field Populated

27. Save your project.

8.6   Task 4 - Vector to Raster Conversion

It can also be very useful to have data represented in the raster data model. Rasters are very useful for analysis. In the last exercise, you saw how rasters can be combined via the Raster Calculator to conduct a site selection model. You can convert points, lines and polygons to a raster format. One must be cognizant of the effects of cell size. The data will be generalized when the conversion from precise vector locations to cells occurs. Here you will convert a vector layer to raster.

1. Open QGIS and open exercise8.qgz if it is not already.

2. Add the Nueces_Roads.shp to QGIS.

3. Right-click on the Nueces Roads layer in the Layers Panel and choose Zoom to layer (figure 8.12).

4. From the menu bar choose Raster | Conversion | Rasterize (Vector to Raster).

    a. Input layer = Nueces_Roads

    b. Field to use for a burn-in value = TLID. Note: this can be any numeric attribute. Often it will be a field that assigned some sort of weight to the output raster cells. Here we will simply use the TLID.

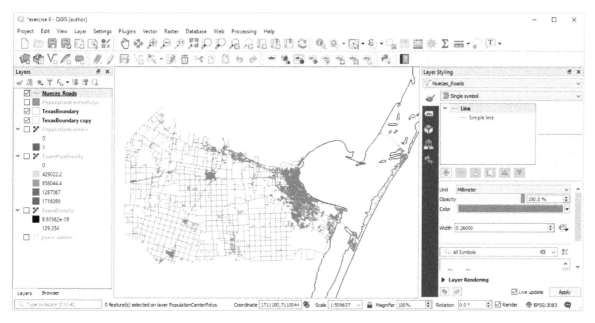

Figure 8.14: Nueces Roads in QGIS

   c. Width/Horizontal resolution and Height/Vertical resolution = 3000 each

   d. Output extent (xmin, xmax, ymin, ymax) = Click the ellipsis button to the right and choose Use Layer Extent from the context menu. When the Select Extent window appears set it to Nueces Roads and click OK.

   e. Rasterized output file = MyData\Roads_raster.tif. Note: If you get the message *The output file doesn't exist*, you must set up the output size or resolution to create it. Click OK.

   f. Take the remaining defaults.

   g. Click Run. (figure 8.15, on the following page). Click OK and Close.

5. The resulting raster has values matching the TLID values for road pixels and values of 0 for the remaining pixels

6. Symbolize the new raster with the Singleband pseudocolor render using the Greys Color ramp.

7. Zoom into the dense part of the road network to the east which is the town of Corpus Christi. (figure 8.16, on page 201).

> Another good method for raster to vector conversion is to generate contours from a raster. There are several tools in the Processing Toolbox which can be used. Searching Toolbox for the keyword *Contour* will reveal GDAL, GRASS and SAGA tools for accomplishing this. Generating contours from a DEM is a common use case.

8.7 Conclusion

In this exercise, you learned how to use the Heatmap algorithm to generate point density rasters based off of both point densities and attribute values (population). Density analyses are often used to analyze data related to crimes, or the amount of fast food stores in an area. The output provides a nice overview of how close the points are, and you can choose our own variables to weight the output. Finally, using the conversion tools we can convert between raster and vector. Having data in raster form allows you to perform raster algebra operations via the Raster Calculator. Having the data in vector form allows for geometries to be easily calculated (acreage), and for more sophisticated cartographic options (border and fill).

Figure 8.15: Rasterize Tool

8.8 Discussion Questions

1. Discuss the different uses of point density.

2. Explain how weighting a feature via an attribute changes the outcome.

3. Is there anything we can do about the degradation of data in the conversion between vector and raster?

8.9 Challenge Assignment - A

In the `Exercise_8_Data\Challenge` folder there is a shapefile containing crime data for Surrey in the United Kingdom. There is a column for crime type (`Crime_type`). Use this field to generate two heatmaps: one for 'Violent Crimes' and one for 'Drugs'. You will have to select records corresponding to each crime type, and save the selected features to a new shapefile for each. The heatmaps will be generated against the resulting shapefiles.

8.10 Challenge Assignment - B

Use the data from Task 1 to experiment with generating contours. Try some of the different tools in the Processing Toolbox to generated elevation contours from the DEM.

Figure 8.16: Rasterized Roads

Part III

Data Acquisition and Management

Exercise 1

Exploring Geospatial Data Models and File Formats

Objective – Explore and Understand Geospatial Data Models and File Formats

1.1 Introduction

There are two main data models for GIS data: vector and raster. Additionally, GIS data comes in many file formats. When gathering data for a project, it is common to acquire data from several sources. Therefore, it is also common for the data to be in several different file formats. In this exercise, you will review GIS data models and file formats.

This exercise includes the following tasks:

- Task 1 GIS Data Models
- Task 2 GIS File Formats

1.2 Objective: Explore and Understand Geospatial Data Models and File Formats

The objective of this exercise is to explore and understand geospatial data models and file formats.

1.3 Task 1 - GIS Data Models

This task will be a review of the data commonly stored in the vector and raster data models. You will explore the exercise 1 data and answer some questions.

1. Open QGIS 3.x.

2. Use the Data Source Manager to add the 35106-B4.dem file from the exercise data directory.

Question # 1 – Is this a continuous or categorical raster?

Question # 2 – In a DEM what do the pixel values represent?

3. Now use the Data Source Manager again and add the 05_35106b47.tif raster. This is a multiband raster image with red and green light combined with color infrared to create a false color image.

Question # 3 – What is the pixel resolution of this raster?

4. Now use the Browser Panel to add the LandFire_EVT.img raster.

Question # 4 – Is this a continuous or categorical raster?

5. Use the Browser Panel and add both the Roads layer found in the `Roads.gpkg` GeoPackage and the Trails layer contained in the Trails.gdb File Geodatabase to the map canvas.

Question # 5 – What is the coordinate reference system for the Roads layer?

Question # 6 – How many features are in the Trails layer?

Question # 7 – What are the two easiest methods in QGIS, for answering question number 6?

Both the File Geodatabase and GeoPackage are shown with the database ⊟ icon in QGIS Browser. The File Geodatabase (FGDB) is a proprietary format developed by Esri and the GeoPackage is an open format developed by the Open Geospatial Consortium based on SpatiaLite. Due to the fact that Esri has published an API (`https://github.com/Esri/file-geodatabase-api`) for the FGDB, QGIS can read data from one. However, the API does not support all the features of an FGDB, such as representations, topology rules and attribute domains. These data are also read only in QGIS. By using the OsGeo4W installer you can easily install the GDAL FileGDB driver (ArcGIS 10.0 and above) which allows you to both read and write data from a FGDB. Run the installer, choose Advanced install and find the driver in the Libs section. This driver allows you to both read and write data from a FGDB. Editing is still not supported so it is recomended that you convert this type of data to a GeoPackage for long-term use within QGIS. A FGDB also does not support spatial SQL which is another drawback when compared with the GeoPackage. In the next Exercise you will learn how to import File Geodatabases and other formats into a PostGIS database.

1.4   Task 2 - GIS Data File Formats

There are many different file formats commonly used in GIS. Some formats are designed to store vector data and some raster data, while others contain a myriad of other types of information. In this task, you will explore the file formats included with the exercise data.

Question # 8 – In Task 1 you added three raster datasets. What were the three file formats that those were stored in?

- `LandFire_EVT`

- `05_35106b47`

- `35106-B4`

1. Open QGIS and open the Browser Panel. Navigate to the `Exercise_1_Data` folder. The folder contains three raster datasets, three shapefiles, two XML files, and two text files.

2. There are also two folders: an `info` folder and a folder named `vegetation` (ignoring the Solutions folder present for each exercise).

3. Expand the `vegetation` folder and right-click on the `metadata.xml` file with the polygon icon next to it. Choose Layer Properties from the context menu. The Layer Properties window will open to the Metadata tab.

You can see that it is a line layer with 15,953 features and the coordinate reference system is UTM. However, you probably do not know the storage type for this layer. This is an older file format for storing vector data called a Coverage. The `info` folder holds the attributes. The `vegetation` folder is the layer name and stores the spatial features. Sometimes you will see data files ending in *.e00*. This is an exported coverage. This format is for data sharing as it is a file containing the info and layer folders, and is more easily transferred. QGIS can also natively read e00 files.

4. Close the Layer Properties window.

5. Open the Data Source Manager and select the Vector tab.

6. Switch the Source Type to Directory and the Type to Arc/Info Binary Coverage (see figure 1.1).

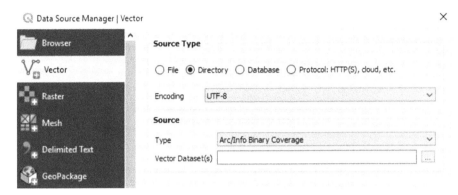

Figure 1.1: Add Vector Layer for Arc/Info Coverages

7. Click the ellipsis Browse button and navigate to the Exercise_1_Data folder.

8. Select the vegetation folder (do not enter it just select it) and click Select Folder.

9. Click the Add button.

10. The Select Vector Layers to Add... window opens. Here you are being asked to choose which components of the coverage to add to QGIS. This is because of a special property that coverages have: they can store multiple geometries. While a single shapefile stores either point, line, or polygon geometry, a single coverage can store all three geometries. This vegetation dataset has two polygon components (PAL & landfire_evt) a line component (Arc), and a point component (CNT).

11. Select the landfire_evt layer and choose OK (see figure 1.2).

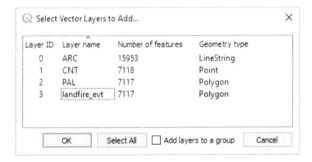

Figure 1.2: Select Coverage Component to Add

12. Click Close to dismiss the Data Source Manager.

13. The layer is added to QGIS (see figure 1.3, on the following page). This is a vector version of the LandFire_EVT raster layer.

Question # 9 – What attribute column would you use to map these vegetation types using a Categorical renderer?

Question # 10 – How would you convert the vegetation coverage to a GeoPackage?

14. Open the Browser Panel again and navigate to the exercise data folder.

15. Right-click on the Exercise_1_Data and choose Properties. This shows you the contents of the folder. Notice all the files with the *SandiaCrestSW* prefix. Compare that to the Browser Panel view. The Directory Properties

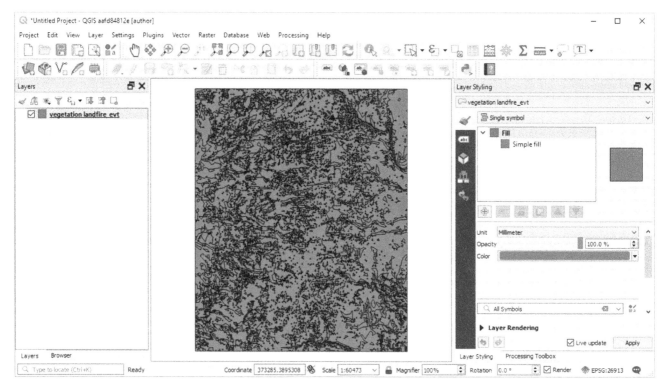

Figure 1.3: Vegetation Coverage Added to QGIS

window shows you all the components of the shapefile, whereas the Browser Panel shows just the .shp as a layer and the metadata files. Close the Directory Properties window when done.

16. Find the `Recreation_Site_pt.kmz` file in the Browser Panel that has the polygon icon. Right-click on it and choose Add Layer to Project. The Select Vector Layers to Add... window opens.

17. This KMZ file contains many layers. Select the Picnic site and Trailhead layers (hold the `CNTRL` key to select multiple entries) and click OK. (selections shown in the figure 1.4, on the next page).

1.5   Conclusion

In this exercise, you reviewed the raster and vector data models. You have explored several file formats and have been introduced to three new vector formats: the coverage, the Esri File Geodatabase and Keyhole Markup Language (KML).

1.6   Discussion Questions

1. What are the strengths of both the vector and raster data models?

2. List the vector and raster file formats you are now familiar with.

3. How does a coverage differ from a shapefile?

1.7   Challenge Assignment

Convert the KML and coverage data to a GeoPackage database.

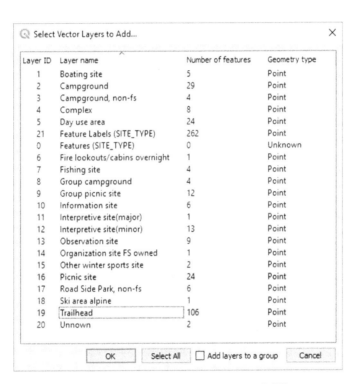

Figure 1.4: Adding KMZ Data to QGIS

Exercise 2

Setting Up a Project Database

Objective – Learn How to Normalize Data and Import It into a PostGIS Database

2.1   Introduction

There are two main data models for GIS data: vector and raster. Additionally, GIS data comes in many file formats. When gathering data for a project, it is common to acquire data from several sources. Therefore, it is also common for the data to be in several different file formats. In this exercise you will create a project geodatabase for the Gifford-Pinchot National Forest in Washington State. First, you will normalize the data. This means you'll put all datasets in the same coordinate reference system (CRS) and clip them to the study area boundary. Lastly, you'll put them all into the same file format: a PostGIS geodatabase.

This exercise includes the following tasks:

- Task 1 Investigate and Normalize Project Data

- Task 2 Create a New PostGIS Database

- Task 2 Populate the New PostGIS Database

2.2   Objective: Learn How to Normalize Data and Import it into a PostGIS Database

The objective of this exercise is to explore and understand geospatial data models and file formats.

2.3   Task 1 - Investigate and Normalize Project Data

In this task, you will familiarize yourself with the exercise data and will begin to normalize the data.

1. Open QGIS 3.x and then use the Data Source Manager open to the Browser tab. Navigate to and expand the `Exercise_2_Data` folder.

There are eight vector layers here. There are four Esri Shapefiles, two KML files, and an Esri File Geodatabase containing two Feature classes (shown in the figure 2.1, on the following page). Each of these file formats will be treated differently.

2. All the data for this project will need to be in UTM, Zone 10, NAD83. Unfortunately, not all of the data are in that coordinate system, so we will need to convert it.

3. Select the two feature classes in the `giffordPinchot.gdb` and choose Add Selected Layers to Project. (figure 2.2, on the next page) Close the Data Source Manager.

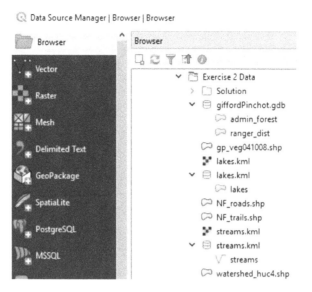

Figure 2.1: Exercise Data in the Browser Tab

Figure 2.2: Exercise Data in the Browser Tab

4. Save your project as `Exercise2.qgz`.

This layer is in a custom Albers Equal Area coordinate system. Since it is in a custom CRS, there is no EPSG code to use during import into a database. Therefore, you will first save this out to a shapefile in the desired CRS.

5. Use the Locator Bar in the lower left corner of QGIS to find and open the Reproject Layer tool. Preceding your search term with the keyword a, filters the results to show only processing algorithms. Double-click on the tool to open it. (figure 2.3, on the facing page)

> If the Locator Bar window pops up again you can press the Esc key to dismiss it.

6. With the Reproject Layer tool window open set the Input Layer to *admin_forest*. Set the Target CRS to UTM Zone 10N - EPSG: 26910. When browsing for this target CRS you can search for *Zone 10* or *26910* to locate the CRS. Save the Reprojected resulting dataset as a shapefile named `Forest_boundary.shp` to the exercise `Data` folder. Run the tool when ready. (figure 2.4, on the next page)

7. Remove the original File Geodatabase version of this dataset from the map as you no longer need it.

8. Right-click on the newly added layer and choose `Set CRS | Set Project CRS from Layer` to put the QGIS project into this same CRS.

9. Repeat the steps above to reproject the `ranger_dist` feature class to a shapefile with the same coordinate system as the `Forest_boundary` layer. Name it `Ranger_district.shp`.

The only other dataset in Albers Equal Area is the vegetation shapefile.

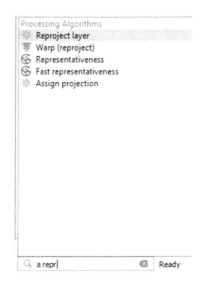

Figure 2.3: Using the Locator Bar to Find the Reproject Layer Tool

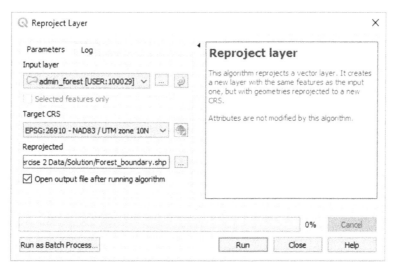

Figure 2.4: Reproject Layer Tool

10. Add the gp_veg041008.shp shapefile to QGIS and reproject this dataset as a new shapefile in UTM Zone 10 NAD83. Name it Vegetation.shp.

11. Add the NF_roads, NF_trails, and watershed_huc4 shapefiles to QGIS.

These last three layers along with the reprojected vegetation layer are all shapefiles in the correct CRS. However, they extend beyond the forest boundary. You need to clip these layers to the forest boundary.

12. Use the Vector | Geoprocessing Tools | Clip tool to clip the roads, trails, watershed and vegetation layers to the forest boundary (example clip parameters shown in the (figure 2.5, on the following page). You can give them the same output name, but end it with clip. For example, NF_roads will become NF_roads_clip.

> When running a tool repeatedly you can run it for the first layer, then switch back to the Parameters tab, set it up for the next layer, click Run and repeat until finished. Right-clicking on a tool in the Processing Toolbox also gives you the option to Execute as a Batch Process.

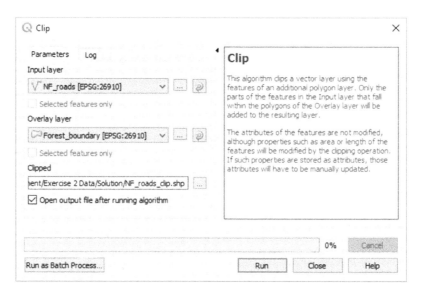

Figure 2.5: Clipping Roads to the Forest Boundary

13. Remove the original unclipped roads, trails, watershed and vegetation layers once the four clip operations are complete. Your map should now resemble the figure below (note that not all layers are visible in the figure 2.6).

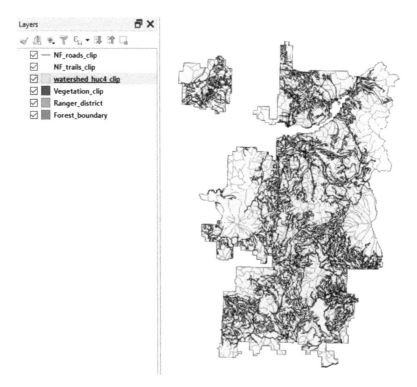

Figure 2.6: Normalized Layers

You have taken the initial steps to normalize the data. There are two more layers that you will export into the PostGIS database; rivers and lakes. However, KML files are always in a geographic CRS of WGS 1984 (EPSG:4326). These KML files can be reprojected when importing into the PostGIS database without having to be converted to another format.

14. Save your project.

2.4   Task 2 - Create a New PostGIS Database

Now that you have taken the initial steps to prepare your data, you will create a new empty PostgeSQL/PostGIS database that you will import your datasets into.

Here you will learn the basics of the FOSS enterprise database PostgeSQL and the spatial extension PostGIS. PostGIS allows you to store and manipulate spatial data layers in a PostgreSQL database. In this environment a spatial layer, for example, ranger district boundaries, is stored as a table in the database. One of the attribute columns will be the geometry of the layer.

It really has no analog in the Esri ecosystem. It is quite a bit more robust than a File Geodatabase because it is a true relational database. It is more similar to Microsoft's SQL Server or an Oracle database. However, unlike those databases PostgreSQL/PostGIS also comes with hundreds of spatial SQL functions. To be effective at using PostGIS you need to learn SQL (Structured Query Language) which is beyond the scope of this book. However, there are many resources for doing learning that language.

Completing this task also requires that you install PostgeSQL/PostGIS on your machine.

To do this visit `https://www.postgresql.org/download/` and install the PostgreSQL installer for you operating system. During this install you will be prompted to create a user and password. The default is postgres/postgres. Be sure to record this so you do not forget it. Once PostgreSQL installs you will be prompted to launch the *Application Stack Builder*. There you can choose to install the PostGIS extension.

PostgreSQL installs an interface to the database named pgAdmin 4. There are alternatives to this. The most recommended alternative is the Community version of DB Beaver (`https://dbeaver.io/download/`). For this next, task the book will use pgAdmin 4.

1. Search for pgAdmin 4 and run it. It will open in a web browser.

2. Double-click on `Servers` and you should see a server named something like PostgreSQL10

> If you do not see a server you can right-click on Servers | Create | Server. Set the host to localhost, port to 5432, and the Maintenance database to postgres. Enter your user name and password and click Save.

3. You will be prompted to enter the password you set during installation.

4. Now you can create an empty database. Right-click on Databases and choose `Create | Database`.

5. Name the Database `discover`, set the Owner to postgres, and click Save. (figure 2.7, on the following page). You have created an empty PostgreSQL database.

> Notice on the Create Database window there is a SQL tab. Everything done in PostgreSQL/PostGIS is done via a SQL command.

6. Expand the `discover` database.

7. You will see a series of objects within your new database. Expand Extensions. (figure 2.8, on the next page). You will only see plpgsql. This is the basic extension that comes with PostgreSQL and allows you to write SQL commands.

8. Expand Schemas. You will see only one, the public schema. Expand the public schema. Underneath that expand Functions. At the moment you will not have any functions. Expand Tables. Notice that you also do not have any tables.

Figure 2.7: Create PostGIS Database in pgAdmin 4

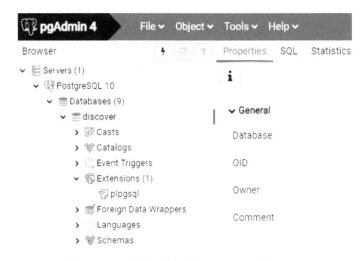

Figure 2.8: New Database in pgAdmin 4

9. Now you will create the extension PostGIS for your new database. Click on the `Tools` menu and choose `Query tool`. Enter the following SQL statement: `CREATE EXTENSION postgis` and click the Execute ⚡ button. (figure 2.9) You will recieve a message that query returned successfully.

Figure 2.9: SQL For Creating PostGIS Extension

10. Now right-click on `discover` database again and choose Refresh.

11. Revisit `Extensions` and you will see PostGIS added.

12. Revisit `Schema | Public | Functions` and then `Tables`. You will see a table plus great number of functions (over 1000!) now that you have enabled PostGIS for this database.

13. In the Query tool enter the following SQL: `SELECT * FROM spatial_ref_sys`. This is a basic SQL statement for showing all the data in a table. This table is the reference for all the CRS's that PostGIS supports.(figure 2.10, on the next page)

The SELECT portion is followed by a comma separated list of the columns you would like to return in your query. Putting an asterisk in your SELECT statement tells PostgreSQL to return all the columns. The FROM statement tells the database which table is the target of the query.

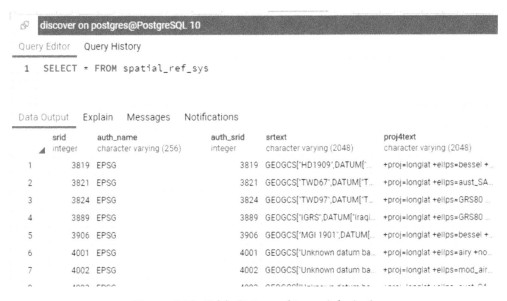

Figure 2.10: Table Returned in pgAdmin 4

It is also possible to do all of this via the command line by using the SQL Shell that is installed and configured when you install PostgreSQL.

2.5 Task 3 - Populate the New PostGIS Database

Now you will populate the PostGIS database with the eight layers.

1. Open QGIS and open Exercise2.qgz if it is not already.

2. Add the streams and lake KML layers to QGIS.

3. Now that you have created a PostGIS database you will use QGIS to upload your data into the database.

4. Open the Browser Panel and find the 🐘 PostGIS connector.

You can also use the Data Source Manager to do this.

5. Right-click on PostGIS and choose New Connection. The Create a New PostGIS Connection window will open. Set up the window as follows (figure 2.11, on the following page)

   a. Name = discoverQGIS

   b. Host = localhost

   c. Port = 5432 (this is the default port for PostgreSQL installations)

   d. Database = discover

   e. Click Test Connection. The Enter Credentials window will open. Enter your Username and Password and click OK. You should recieve a message that the connection was successful. If that's the case click OK. Back at the main connection window click OK again. If not check your settings and try again.

Figure 2.11: Creating a New PostGIS Connection

6. To upload your four shapefiles into your PostGIS database you will use the QGIS DB Manager. Click the `Database` menu and choose `DB Manager`.

7. The DB Manager (figure 2.12) lets you import/export data to and from spatial databases you are connected to and also write SQL expressions against your data. Notice that it will allow you to connect to several databases: GeoPackage, Oracle Spatial, PostGIS, SpatiaLite and something called Virtual Layers.

Figure 2.12: DB Manager

8. Expand the PostGIS section. You should see your `discoverQGIS` connection and expand it. Expand the `public`

schema. There are a few tables associated with the PostGIS extension but the database is otherwise empty.

9. To import your data click the ![Import Layer/File...] button. You will start with the stream and lake KML layers. (figure 2.13)

    a. Input = lakes
    b. Schema = public
    c. Table = lakes (it is best to use all lower case and underscores instead of spaces when working with PostGIS)
    d. Source SRID = Enable it should read EPSG: 4326
    e. Target SRID = Enable it and browse for the UTM Zone 10 (EPSG: 26910) CRS which should now be in your Recently used coordinate reference systems list
    f. Check Convert field names to lowercase
    g. Check Create spatial index
    h. Click OK.

Figure 2.13: Import Vector Layer into PostGIS

10. You should get a message that the Import was successful. Click OK.

11. Click the Refresh ![icon] button and note that you now have a polygon layer in your PostGIS db. You can click the Info, Table and Preview tabs to get information about the dataset and see previews.

12. Repeat the previous steps to import the streams KML into the database. (figure 2.14, on the next page)

Streams and Lakes were the final two layers that required a CRS reprojection. The remaining six UTM layers can now be imported. The only change is that both the input and target SRID's will be 26910 (UTM Zone NAD83).

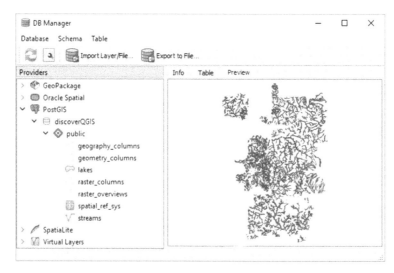

Figure 2.14: Preview of Streams in the DB Manager

13. To import your data click the Import Layer/File... button. You will start with the stream and lake KML layers. (figure 2.15, on the facing page)

    a. Input = NF_roads_clip
    b. Schema = public
    c. Table = lakes
    d. Source SRID = Enable it should read EPSG: 26910
    e. Target SRID = Enable it should read EPSG: 26910
    f. Check Convert field names to lowercase
    g. Check Create spatial index
    h. Click OK.

14. Repeat the above steps for trails, watersheds, ranger districts, vegetation, and forest boundary layers.

15. Now that all eight layers have been imported you can remove the original layers from the map.

16. The layers in the database can be added via the DB Manager, the Data Source Manager or the Browser Panel.

17. If using the DB Manager, right-click on a layer and choose Add to canvas.

18. If using the Data Source Manager or the Browser Panel, select the database and click the Connect button. Once the layers appear, you can select them and click Add, which will add them to QGIS (figure 2.16, on the next page).

19. To give you a sense of what you can do with spatial SQL open the DB Manager. Click the SQL Window button.

20. The Query (discoverQGIS) tab will open on the DB Manager. Here you can write and execute SQL against your database tables. Enter the following SQL `SELECT trl_no, ST_Buffer(geom,500) AS geom FROM trails;`. Click the Execute button.

21. To see the result on the QGIS map canvas click the Load as new layer checkbox.

Figure 2.15: Import Roads into PostGIS

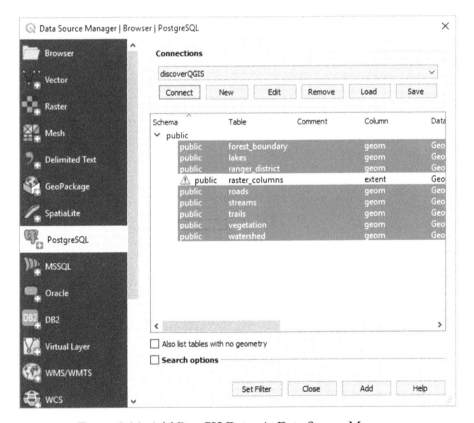

Figure 2.16: Add PostGIS Data via Data Source Manager

22. In the Load as new layer section check the Geometry column checkbox and ensure geom is listed. Enter a Layer name (prefix) as `trailbuffer`. Click Load. (figure 2.16)

You can also create what is known as a View which is simply a named SQL query.

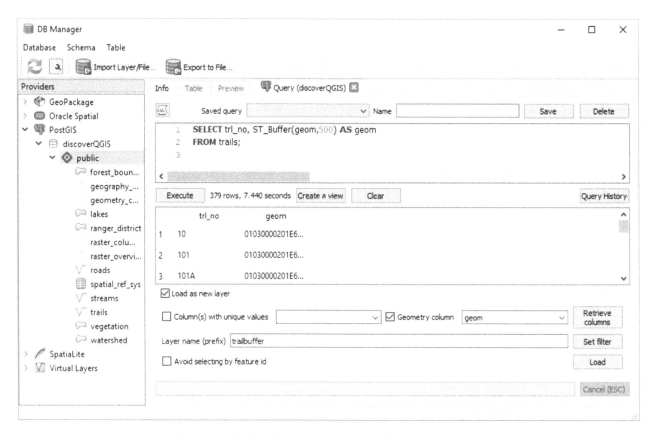

Figure 2.17: DB Manager with Spatial SQL Command

23. The layer will be added to the QGIS map canvas. Open the Layer Properties for the layer and select the Information tab. The Layer source is simply the SQL statement! Using SQL in this way allows you to conduct spatial analyses and spatial queries of your data without having to create new flat file based layers. The layer is literally just the short SQL string and therefore takes up almost no disk space.

24. Turn off all the layers except forest_boundary, trails and trail_buffer. Make sure trails is the top most of the three layers followed by the buffer and forest_boundary. Spend a few moments doing some basic styling of the data. Your map should resemble figure 2.18, on the next page.

2.6   Conclusion

In this exercise, you took data in several different file formats and CRSs and normalized them. They are all now in the same CRS, clipped to the forest boundary, and in a geodatabase. This methodology has the benefit of creating a working copy of the data—the raw data still exist. If you accidentally delete or corrupt a dataset, you still have the original files. Additionally, the data now all reside in a tidy database. Since they are all in the same CRS, you can run any geoprocessing or analysis tools against them knowing they are all in UTM Zone 10 NAD83.

2.7   Discussion Questions

1. What are the steps involved in setting up a PostGIS database?

2. What are the advantages of normalizing project data?

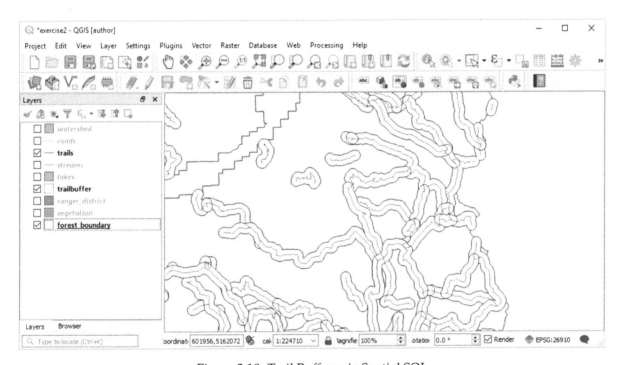

Figure 2.18: Trail Buffers via Spatial SQL

Exercise 3

Vector Data Quality

Objective – Learn to Verify the Quality of Vector Data with Topology Rules

3.1   Introduction

GIS data are referred to as models because they are simplified representations of actual real world objects. As the real world is represented, this often results in data with thousands of records and complex spatial relationships. With so many records, it can be challenging to verify the quality of such large data by visual means alone. Additionally, to verify that spatial relationships have been maintained, we can test the data using topology rules and ensure that it is well constructed.

This exercise includes the following tasks:

- Task 1 Topology Rules - Part 1

- Task 2 Topology Rules - Part 2

- Task 3 Fixing Topology Errors

3.2   Objective: Learn To Verify the Quality of Vector Data with Topology Rules

In this exercise you will be explore the spatial relationship between points, lines, and polygons. You will build topology rules and validate them to identify data errors.

3.3   Task 1 - Topology Rules - Part 1

In this task, you will use the Topology Checker plugin to investigate the quality of two datasets: bus routes and bus stops.

1. Open QGIS and add the `parcels.shp`, `Bus_stops.shp`, and `Bus_routes.shp` layers from the exercise `Data` folder to the map (shown in figure 3.1, on the following page).

2. Save your project as `exercise3.qgz` in the exercise folder.

3. From the menu bar, choose `Plugins | Manage and Install Plugins`.

4. Select the Installed tab and enable the Topology Checker plugin. Some plugins are core plugins meaning they are included with every installation of QGIS. This plugin is an example of one of those. You never need to install it. It just needs to be activated when you need it.

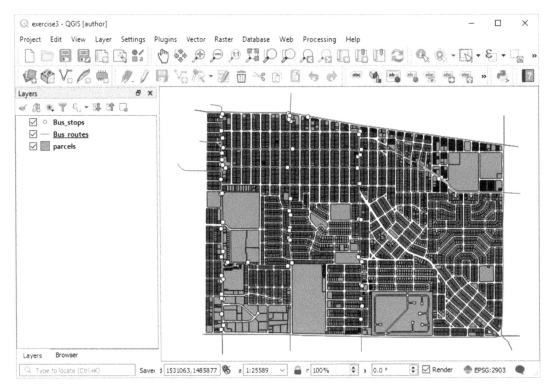

Figure 3.1: Data Layers in QGIS 3.x

5. From the menu bar choose `Vector | Topology Checker` to open the Topology Checker Panel (figure 3.2, on the next page).

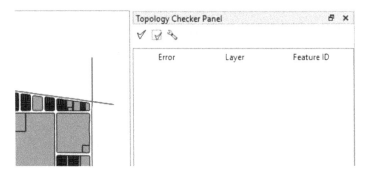

Figure 3.2: Topology Checker Panel

First, you will investigate the integrity of the Bus Stops layer.

6. Click the Configure 🔧 button in the toolbar of the Topology Checker Panel. This opens the Topology Rules Settings window. Here you can set up a variety of topology rules.

7. Select any existing rules and click the the | ▭ Delete Rule | button to remove them.

8. Under Current Rules choose Bus_stops as the layer. Click the second drop down to see what topology rules are available for point layers. Choose *must not have duplicates*. This rule will check to make sure there are no stacked points, in other words, a bus stop situated directly over another. This type of error is difficult to identify without a topology rule.

9. Click the  button to have the rule established (shown in figure 3.3, on the facing page).

Figure 3.3: Setting Topology Rules

10. Click OK to close the Topology Rule Settings.

11. In the Topology Checker Panel, click the Validate All ✓ button.

Note: You can also choose to zoom into a particular area and just validate the topology rule within the current extent by clicking the Validate Extent button.

12. The topology checker finds three duplicate geometries which are listed in the Topology Checker Panel with their Feature IDs and the rule they are violating. (shown in figure 3.3).

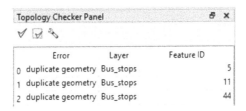

Figure 3.4: Topology Errors Found

Additionally, the duplicated points are highlighted in red on the map. Again, these errors would be difficult to find any other way. However, once identified they are easy to fix. Simply toggle on editing, select the duplicates and delete them.

Now you will examine the topology of the Bus_routes layer.

13. In the Topology Checker Panel, click the Configure button again.

14. Select and use the ⊟ Delete Rule button to remove the Topology rule for the Bus Stops.

15. Create a new rule for the Bus_routes, using must not have dangles. This means the endpoint of a dangling line will be identified. You might expect that since these data are only a portion of an urban area, and there are bus routes heading off the map that those dangling endpoints will be identified. However, there should not be any in the middle of the network (figure 3.5, on the following page).

16. Click the ⊕ Add Rule button and click OK (topology rule shown in figure 3.6, on the next page).

17. Validate the topology. The Topology Checker finds 25 errors of this type. Many are the expected ones, for example lines heading off the map edge. However, there are several in the middle of the network. Zoom in to

Figure 3.5: Bus Route Dangle Error

Figure 3.6: Bus Route Topology Rule

some of these errors and investigate.

18. Save your project.

3.4 Task 2 - Topology Rules - Part 2

Now you will implement topology rules to check the integrity of the parcels layer.

1. Open QGIS and open Exercise3.qgz if it is not already.

2. Open the Topology Checker Panel.

3. Click the Configure 🔧 button.

4. Select any existing rules and click the the ⊟ Delete Rule button to remove them.

5. Configure three rules for the parcels layer: must not have gaps, must not overlap, and must not have duplicates (rules shown in figure 3.7, on the facing page).

6. Click OK to accept the topology rules.

7. In the Topology Checker Panel, click the Validate All ✔ button.

8. The Topology Checker will report violations for each rule, sixteen errors in all.

9. Save your project.

3.5 Task 3 - Fixing Topology Errors

Now you will edit the parcel layer to eliminate the seventeen topology errors.

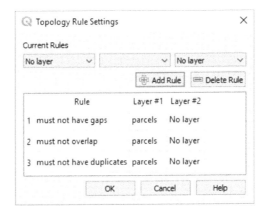

Figure 3.7: Bus Route Topology Rule

1. Open QGIS and open `Exercise3.qgz` if it is not already.

2. Re-validate the topology rules if they are not appearing.

3. First, you will work on the duplicate geometries. Right-click on the parcels layer in the Layers Panel and choose Toggle Editing.

4. Double-click on the first **duplicate geometry** error in the Topology Checker panel and it will zoom to that location.

5. Use the Select Feature by Rectangle ⬚ tool and drag a small rectangle to select the duplicate parcels on the map.

6. Open the parcels layer attribute table.

7. Change the display filter in the lower left corner to Show Selected Features.

8. Notice that for the two selected features, all of the attributes are identical.

9. Select the feature with the higher row number by clicking on the row number. This leaves just one selected record.

10. Click the Delete selected features 🗑 button to remove the duplicate parcel.

11. Repeat these steps to delete the remaining duplicate geometry topology errors. The attribute table should now show a total of 6,968 records.

Now that the duplicate geometry errors are fixed, you will turn your attention to fixing the overlaps and gaps errors. To fix these errors, we will first set our snapping tolerances to make editing significantly easier and more precise.

1. From the menu bar choose `Project | Snapping Options`.

2. Click the Enable Snapping 🧲 button.

3. Ensure the Snapping Mode is set to Active Layer.

4. Set the Mode to Vertex and the Tolerance to 10 pixels.

5. Click on the ⟨ Topological Editing ⟩ to activate it.

6. Click on ⟨ Snapping on Intersection ⟩ to activate that setting.

Topological editing maintains common boundaries in polygon mosaics. With this option checked, QGIS detects a shared boundary in a polygon mosaic and you only have to move the vertex once—QGIS will take care of updating the other boundary.

The selected snapping options are shown in the figure 3.8.

Figure 3.8: Snapping Settings

7. Close the Snapping options window. Remember that you can also use the Snapping Toolbar to make changes to the snapping environment. You can enable this from View | Toolbars.

8. From the menu bar choose Settings | Options and click on the Digitizing tab. There are many digitizing settings available here.

9. Make sure the Search radius for vertex edits is set to 10 pixels (shown in figure 3.9). Setting this to something other than zero ensures that QGIS finds the correct vertex when editing.

Figure 3.9: Project Digitizing Settings

10. Click OK to set the Options window.

11. Open the Layer Styling Panel ✎ with the target being the Parcels layer. Expand Layer Rendering and set the Opacity to 50%.

12. On the Topology Checker Panel, uncheck Show errors.

13. Double-click on the error for Feature ID 624. The map will zoom to the location of the error. With errors turned off and the transparency set, you can see the overlap issue (shown in figure 3.10, on the next page).

There are two parcels involved in the overlap. Here, the western (left) overlapping parcel boundary needs to be moved west (left) so that it does not overlap with the eastern parcel (parcel on the right).

14. Use the Select Feature by Rectangle ⬚ tool to select the western (left) overlapping parcel. Each vertex of the

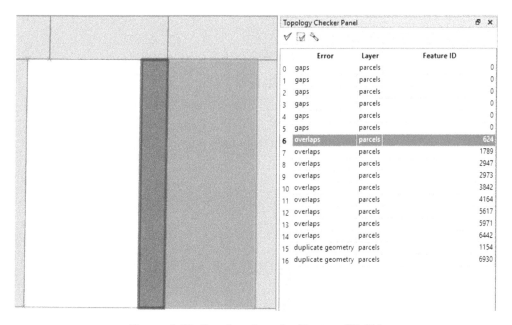

Figure 3.10: Overlap Area for Feature ID 624

selected feature will appear as a red X.

15. If it is not already, enable the Digitizing toolbar by clicking `View | Toolbars | Digitizing`.

16. On the Digitizing toolbar click on the Vertex Tool. This tool allows you to move individual feature vertices. Hovering over a vertex causes it to be highlighted as a red circle. To move a vertex requires only two single clicks. Once on the vertex to be moved and once where you want it to be repositioned.

17. Click once on the upper right vertex and click again on the at the proper location for that parcel corner (to the left - west). Two clicks and the vertex is repositioned properly.(shown in figure 3.11)

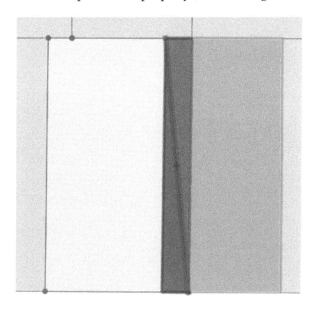

Figure 3.11: Overlap Half Resolved

18. Repeat for the lower right vertex.

19. In the Topology Checker Panel, click the Validate Extent button and the overlap topology error will no longer be listed and the overlap will be resolved

20. The remaining overlaps can be fixed in the same fashion. Each time one is resolved you can zoom to the parcel layer extent and re-validate all.

21. Zoom out From the Topology Checker Panel click on the third Gap error in the list. Again you will be zoomed in to the location of the error (shown in figure 3.12).

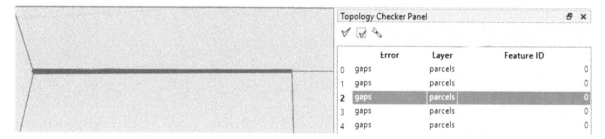

Figure 3.12: Gap Error

22. In the Topology Checker Panel, uncheck Show errors.

23. There is a small sliver between the parcels. Select the parcel to the north and then click on the Vertex Tool.

24. Using the Vertex Tool move the vertex in the southwestern corner of the northern selected parcel, so that it snaps with the vertex of the parcel to the south, closing the gap.(shown in figure 3.13)

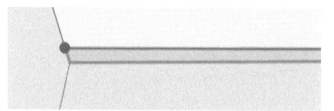

Figure 3.13: Fixing the Gap Error

25. Click Validate Extent button to ensure that the issue has been resolved.

26. You can repair other gap errors the same way.

27. When you are done repairing the topology errors, save your edits.

28. Save your project.

3.6 Conclusion

In this exercise, you learned how to test the integrity of your vector data with topology rules. These rules can involve features in two different layers or can be set to test the features in a single layer. There are different rules for points, lines and polygon features. You also learned how to use Topological editing to resolve the issues found.

3.7 Discussion Questions

1. What are the steps involved creating and testing a topology rule?

2. How would topology be useful for property data?

3.8 Challenge Assignment

See if you can think of other topology rules that could be implemented against these data sets. Use topological editing to fix all the errors found.

Exercise 4

Spatial Data Quality

Objective – Learn to Assess Data Quality, Work with Metadata and Aggregate Data

4.1 Introduction

Spatial data is becoming more common and readily available via the Internet. However, the accuracy of the data is always a concern. As we are experiencing a growth in data availability, we should choose our sources wisely. When it comes to data accuracy, not only do we look at the spatial component, but the attribute component as well. Metadata is becoming a large component to data and it is a key factor in determining the completeness of data.

This exercise includes the following tasks:

- Task 1 Exploring Data Accuracy by Mapping Delimited Text Coordinates

- Task 2 Metadata

- Task 3 Data Aggregation - Dissolving Features

4.2 Objective: Learn to Assess Data Quality, Work with Metadata and Aggregate Data

This exercise focuses on data and its accuracy. You'll be looking at the metadata and the standards of the metadata that some datasets require. You'll also look at assessing the accuracy of the data and if it is usable or not.

4.3 Task 1 - Exploring Data Accuracy by Mapping Delimited Text Coordinates

Data accuracy is an important concept and this goes for the spatial data as well as the attribute data. The spatial and attribute data can be edited and changed, but what if it is a noted problem in the data? Can we overlook certain points in the data that we know have been captured erroneously? We must be aware of the errors that are inherent in the data and the fixes that are provided. In this first task, you will create a point layer of shipwrecks from a text file containing the X and Y coordinates. You will then assess its accuracy.

1. To begin you will add a basemap to QGIS. To do this you will install and configure a plugin named QuickMapServices.

2. From the menu bar choose Plugins | Manage and Install Plugins. In the Plugin Manager search for and install QuickMapServices. Close the Plugin Manager when done.

3. The QuickMapServices will appear under the Web menu. First you will configure the plugin. From the menu bar choose Web | QuickMapServices | Settings. In the QuickMapServices Settings window switch to the More

Services tab. Click the Get contributed pack button. You should get a pop up reading *Last version of contrib pack was downloaded!* Click OK and Save.

4. Revisit Web | QuickMapServices and you will see a very large list of available basemaps, well over 100. These will now appear each time you use the plugin. Choose Google | Google Terrain. There is also a panel with this plugin that can be used to search for additional basemaps.

5. Next you will learn how to create a point layer from coordinates stored in a comma delimited text file.

6. Open the Data Source Manager and switch to the Delimited Text tab. Fill out the window as in the figure 4.1.

    a. File name = Browse to the exercise data folder and select shipwrecks.csv.

    b. Layer name = Shipwrecks

    c. File format = CSV (comma separated values)

    d. Expand the Geometry Definition section

    e. Geometry definition = Point coordinates

    f. X field = X_COORD,N,15,6

    g. Y field = Y_COORD,N,16,6

    h. Geometry CRS = EPSG:4326. It is crucial to know the correct CRS of the coordinates otherwise they will likely not fall in the correct location.

    i. Click Add and then Close the Data Source Manager

Figure 4.1: Create Point Layer from Delimited Text File

7. Right-click on the Shipwrecks layer in the Layers Panel and choose Zoom to layer.

8. Notice that one point is well away from the others.

9. Open the attribute table for shipwrecks. Notice the coordinate values for the AC Adams. The X and Y values are in the wrong columns. This was a data entry error. Close the attribute table and remove the shipwrecks layer.

When creating a point layer from a delimited text file, the coordinates are being rendered as points just within the current QGIS project. The shipwrecks layer is simply a rendering of the coordinates in the CSV file. The layer will behave like any other in QGIS, but is not a layer you could share with a colleague. This is because the data are still not stored in a true in a GIS format, such as a GeoPackage, GeoJSON or Esri Shapefile. To create a permanent GIS layer, you would right-click on the layer and save it as a file in the format of your choice.

10. Using a text editor such as Notepad or a spreadsheet program such as Open Office Calc or Microsoft Excel, open the `shipwrecks.csv` file and correct the incorrect coordinates, then save your edits.

11. Recreate the layer from the corrected delimited text file.

12. When mapped correctly all the data points should all fall near the western end of Lake Superior. Next you will symbolize and label them.

13. Set the shipwrecks as the target layer in the Layer Styling Panel. Select Simple marker. Switch to a Symbol layer type of SVG Marker. Scroll down to the SVG Groups section and find the `transport` folder. You will see a collection of SVG icons. Choose the one that looks like a ship anchor (`transport_marina.svg`).

> While there is a decent set of SVG icons that ship with QGIS, it is possible to both design your own in a program like Inkscape, or download open libraries of existing icons. For example, a very large set of MapBox Maki icons can be downloaded here: https://labs.mapbox.com/maki-icons/. You can set paths to different SVG folders on your system from Settings | Options | SVG Paths.

14. Give the icon a Width and Height of 10. Make the Fill color bright red, and the Stroke color to black. Set the Stroke width to 0.2.

15. Switch to the Labels ![abc] tab the Layer Styling Panel. Change from No labels to Single labels. Set the Label with column to `Shipwreck,C,18`. Switch to the Placement ![icon] tab and set the Distance to 4. Shown in figure 4.2, on the following page).

16. One must always be careful about data and not take their accuracy for granted. It is your responsibility to discover and fix errors. You cannot rely on the software to understand such mistakes.

> Another common issue that occurs with coordinate data are rounding errors or truncated coordinates. For example, people may round UTM coordinates to the nearest thousand when working off of USGS topographic maps. This may be due to the fact that these maps list the UTM coordinate values every thousand meters.

4.4   Task 2 - Metadata

In this task, you will be looking at the metadata section of spatial data. When data is purchased, or published online by an agency or organization, we expect to have a complete dataset. This includes the spatial data, the attribute data, and the metadata. Metadata is often described as data about data, and is the one sure way we can understand the source, how it was created, what scale it was created at, what the spatial reference is, what kinds of accuracy can we expect, etc. All datasets have some error associated with them. After all, they are simplified models of the real world.

1. Open QGIS 3.x and start a new project.

2. Add the `NM_GMU.shp` shapefile to QGIS. This is the Game Management Units (GMUs) of New Mexico.

3. Open the Layer Properties and click on the Switch to the ![icon] Metadata tab. Here you are seeing a fairly new implementation of layer level metadata in QGIS. This is new to QGIS 3.x. Shown in figure 4.3, on page 239. This

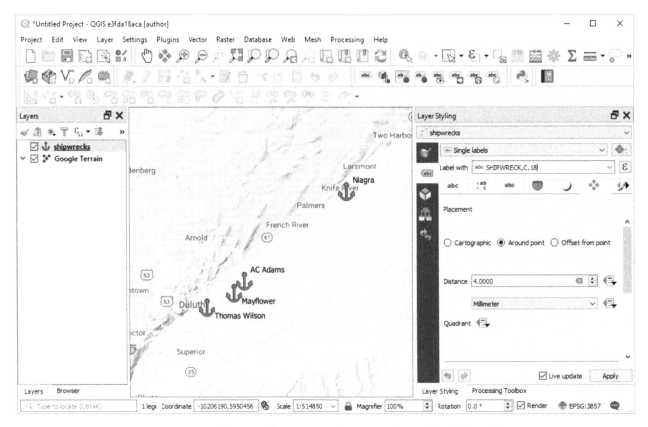

Figure 4.2: Shipwrecks Accurately Mapped and Symbolized

metadata tab is based on the Dublin Core Metadata Initiative (`http://dublincore.org`). Dublin Core is an open ISO (19115) metadata standard. Metadata standards are important, as they provide a framework organizations can use to develop consistent high quality metadata. There are several metadata standards. One of the earliest standards developed was the Federal Geographic Data Committee (FGDC) standard (`https://www.fgdc.gov/metadata/geospatial-metadata-standards`). It is still widely used within the U.S. However, the the FGDC now endorses the migration to ISO metadata standards such as Dublin Core. Tools for doing this migration from one format to another are still being developed.

One of the files that composes a shapefile is a metadata file. It can take several forms: text, HTML or XML. The Dublin Core metadata currently read by QGIS is stored as a QMD file. All of these can be opened in a text editor or a web browser.

The Dublin Core Metadata Standard contains fifteen metadata elements: Title, Creator, Subject, Description, Publisher, Contributor, Date, Type, Format, Identifier, Source, Language, Relation, Coverage and Rights.

4. Click on Identification tab. This provides a title and abstract for the data.

5. Switch to the Extent tab. Here you are presented with the CRS and spatial extent of the dataset.

6. Switch to the Contact tab. Here you are presented with contact information for the publisher of the dataset.

7. Below is a Metadata dropdown menu. This allows you to Load and Save Metadata to/from a QMD file.

8. Close Layer Properties when you have finished reviewing the metadata.

9. From the menu bar choose `Project | Properties`. Switch to the   Metadata tab. Shown in figure 4.4,

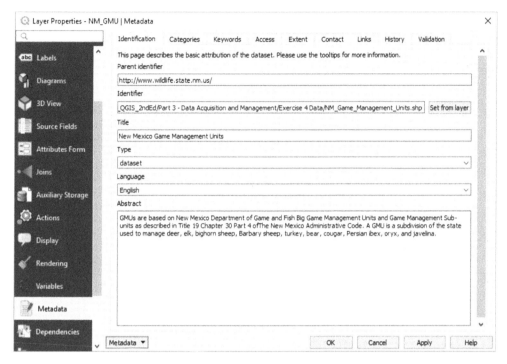

Figure 4.3: Layer Properties - Metadata Tab

on the facing page. Since this is a new project it is empty. However, this is a place for you to document a QGIS project. This can be very helpful if it is a project that will be distributed or widely used.

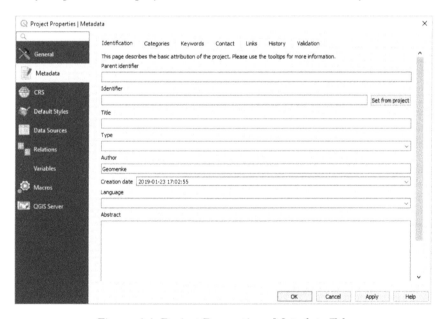

Figure 4.4: Project Properties - Metadata Tab

4.5 Task 3 - Data Aggregation - Dissolving Features

Data aggregation is the process where data is joined, merged, or generalized to suit a need. This may be done in such a way to protect the information at a lower level.

1. Open QGIS 3.x and start a new project.

2. Add the `countries.shp` shapefile to QGIS.

3. From the menu bar choose `Vector | Geoprocessing Tools | Dissolve`.

4. Set up the Dissolve tool to dissolve based on the `SubRegion` attribute field. You will do this in the Dissolve field(s) [optional] section. Click the Dissolve fields ellipsis button. The Multiple selection window will open displaying a list of attributes. Check the box next to `SubRegion` and click OK.

5. Name the Dissolved output `Sub_Regions.shp` (shown in figure 4.5). Click Run when ready.

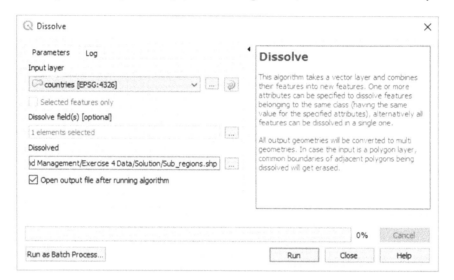

Figure 4.5: Dissolving Based on Attributes

The result is an example of data aggregation. All the data in the map will be mapped using those regions. In this scenario, all data by country will be aggregated to the sub region level.

6. Using what you know symbolize this new layer by the `SubRegion` using the Categorized renderer. Note that if using the default Random colors Color ramp, you can click on the drop down menu for that and choose Shuffle Random Colors until you get a set you are happy with.

7. Next you will learn how to use a new renderer named Shapeburst fills. Click the large Change button above the Random colors Color ramp. This opens symbol properties for all the classes.

    a. Select Simple fill.

    b. Find Symbol layer type which is set to the default setting of Simple fill. Change the Symbol layer type to Shapeburst fill.

    c. Scroll down and select Set distance and set the value to 1.

    d. Check Ignore rings in polygons while shading

    e. Click the Go Back ◀ button to return to the main layer symbology settings.

    f. Expand the Layer Rendering section and set the Opacity to 80%.

    g. Now make the countries layer the target layer and set the and set the Color to HTML notation #beb297. To do this click on the Color bar and scroll down to find the HTML notation which accepts hexadecimal colors!

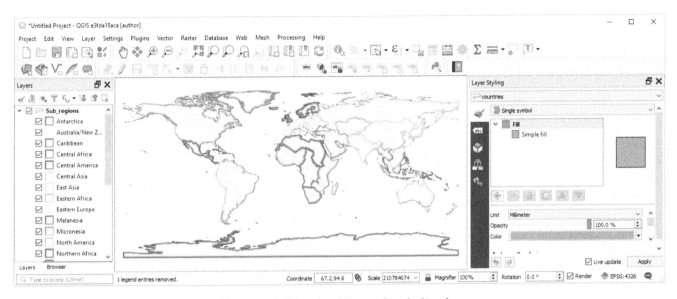

Figure 4.6: Dissolved Layer Symbolized

4.6 Conclusion

Spatial and attribute data accuracy is important. Having a complete data set and keeping track of all the edits and errors is also important. Metadata provides background on the data provided to us. It supplies us with vital information regarding the use and resolution of the data. If you read the metadata, you may be able to determine that the data is not a good fit for your project before trying to edit and manipulate it. Data aggregation is a way to abstract the data and to remove data levels from the data. In Task 3, you changed the lowest level in the data from countries to sub regions. This is important, but we need to be aware of the consequences of our actions when mapping data and how the accuracy is changed when we manipulate it. Along the way you also expanded your ever growing cartography toolkit with two new methods of symbolizing data: SVG icons and Shapeburst fills.

4.7 Discussion Questions

1. What issues do you need to be aware of when mapping data by X/Y coordinates?

2. Does metadata need to be written for all datasets? Explain.

3. Why do we need a metadata standard?

4. How can data aggregation be problematic in a real world mapping scenario?

4.8 Challenge Assignment

- Add the NM_GMU shapefile to QGIS.

- Aggregate the Game Management Units into Cougar Zones as you did with Countries into Sub-regions in Task 3.

- Add a Delimited Text layer of from the NM_GMU`cougar_sample_points. You will need to set the Geometry CRS. Hint: These coordinates are in the same CRS as the NM_GMU shapefile.

- Do all the cougar sample points fall correctly in New Mexico?

- If not can you identify the issue with any points that are not falling in the correct location, fix it and re-map them?

Exercise 5

Raster Data Structure

Objective – Work with the Raster Data Model

5.1 Introduction

Raster data is a data model in which the data is presented in a grid. Each grid cell contains one data value or attribute. For example, a digital elevation model (DEM) has cell values that represent the elevation. One important characteristic of raster data is the resolution. Raster resolution is a measure of the cell dimensions, which means the area that each cell covers in the real world. For example, a satellite image may have a resolution of 30 meters, which means that each cell covers 30 square meters in the real world. You can use raster data simply as cartographic backdrops, as datasets for digitizing, or for analysis.

This exercise includes the following tasks:

- Task 1 Merging and Clipping Raster Data
- Task 2 Raster Pyramids

5.2 Objective: Work with the Raster Data Model

This exercise focuses on working with raster data within QGIS.

5.3 Task 1 - Merging and Clipping Raster Data

Raster data are often provided in tiles, such as USGS Topographic Map Quadrangles. In such cases, it is necessary to merge the raster tiles together to form a seamless raster covering the study area.

1. Open QGIS and add the four DEM raster datasets (35106-A4.dem, 35106-A5.dem, 35106-B4.dem and 35106-B5.dem) (shown in figure 5.1, on the following page).

Each of these has cell values representing the elevation above sea level and is styled with the values stretched across a black to white color ramp. Since each dataset has different minimum and maximum cell values, the boundaries between datasets is obvious.

2. Save your project as exercise5.qgz.

3. Double-click on the 35106-B5.dem layer to open the Layer Properties.

4. Click on the Information tab.

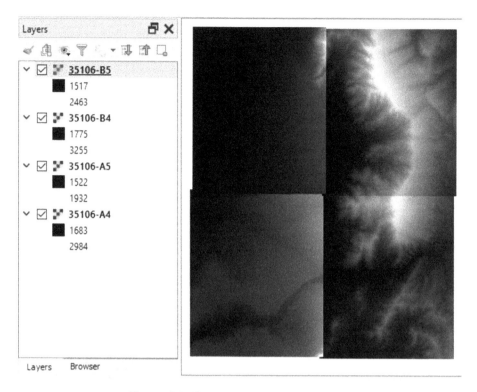

Figure 5.1: Four DEMs Added to QGIS

In the topmost Information from provider section you will find information about the file format (GDAL Driver Description), cell statistics (Band 1), Dimensions, Origin, Pixel Size (10 meters) and the Data Type.

Raster datasets are always rectangular. If the data content does not fill the rectangular area, the extra cells will be assigned a value that signifies that there is no data there.

5. Scroll down to the Bands section and you will see that the No Data value is -32767.

6. Close the Layer Properties.

7. Enable the Processing toolbox.

8. From the Toolbox choose GDAL | Raster miscellaneous | Build Virtual Raster.

9. Fill out the Build Virtual Raster tool with the following parameters: (shown in figure 5.2, on the next page)

   a. Input Layers = Click the ellipsis button to open the Multiple Selection window. Click Select All to select all four DEMs. Click OK.
   b. Resolution = average
   c. Uncheck Place each input file into a separate band
   d. Resampling algorithm = Bilinear
   e. Virtual output = Save to temporary file
   f. When parameters match the figure below, click Run.

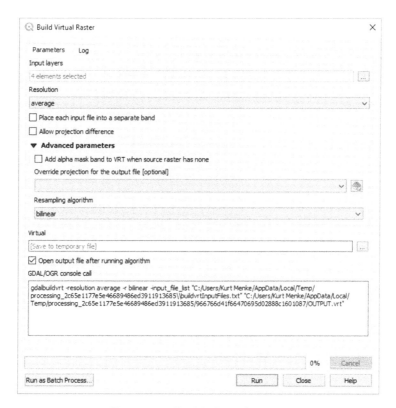

Figure 5.2: Build Virtual Raster

Notice the GDAL/OGR console output section of the Build Virtual Raster tool. This is the syntax for the equivalent operation run from a command prompt. GDAL and OGR come with a series of command utilities (https://www.gdal.org/gdal_utilities.html) (https://www.gdal.org/ogr_utilities.html). This tool is simply a GUI for the command line utility. These utilities are powerful and fast and this is a great way to begin to learn how to use them.

10. Turn off the input DEMs in the Layer Panel. You now have a seamless raster (shown in figure 5.3, on the following page).

11. Now you will clip the virtual raster to the project study area.

12. Add the StudyArea.shp shapefile to QGIS.

13. From the Toolbox choose GDAL | Raster extraction | Clip raster by mask layer.

14. Set the following parameters for the Clip raster by mask layer (shown in figure 5.4, on the next page):

    a. Input layer = OUTPUT

    b. Mask layer = StudyArea

    c. Clipped (mask) = StudyAreaDEM.tif

    d. Click Run

    e. Click Close when done.

15. Turn off the visibility for the StudyArea and OUTPUT virtual raster layers to see the clipped raster. (shown in figure 5.5, on page 247)

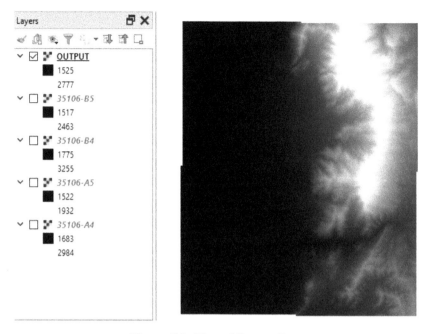

Figure 5.3: Virtual Raster Output

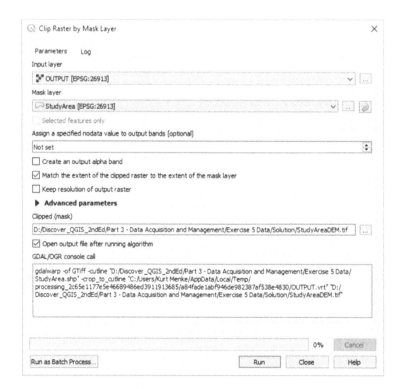

Figure 5.4: Clipping a Raster with a Mask Layer

16. Save your project.

This is a common workflow to get raster data set up for analysis.

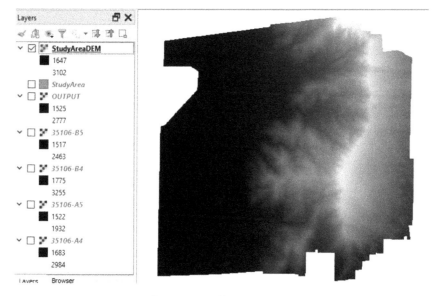

Figure 5.5: Clipped DEM

5.4   Task 2 - Raster Pyramids

Pyramids are lower resolution versions of a raster dataset that are more suitable for display on a monitor. Without pyramids, the computer will attempt to render each and every pixel in a raster dataset, whether the computer monitor can display all the detail or not. Having pyramids greatly decreases the time it takes to render a raster on screen.

1. Open QGIS and open exercise5.qgz if it is not already.

2. Open the Layer Properties for the StudyAreaDEM raster layer.

3. Click on the   Pyramids   tab. Currently this raster has no pyramids. The available resolutions are listed on the right side (shown in figure 5.6).

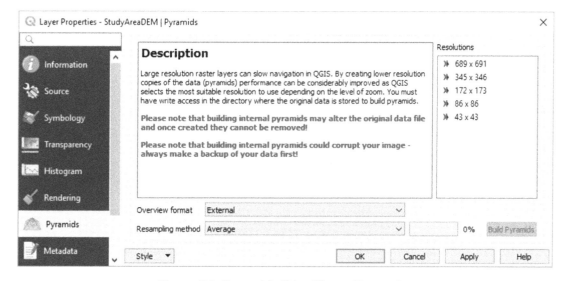

Figure 5.6: Pyramids Tab of Layer Properties

Pyramids can be embedded within the raster file, or built externally. It is safer to build them externally as this does not alter the original dataset. The external pyramid file can always be deleted if it does not have the desired results.

4. Select all resolutions: 689 x 691 to 43 x 43.

5. For the Overview format, select External.

6. Set Resampling method to Cubic.

Generally nearest neighbor technique is most suitable for discrete rasters since it will not change the values of the cells. The average, gauss, and cubic techniques are more suitable for continuous rasters such as this DEM. They will cause some smoothing of the data and may result in some values that are beyond the original range.

7. Click the Build Pyramids button.

8. Click OK to close the Layer Properties.

9. Zoom in and out on the raster to see how quickly the raster renders on the screen.

> This dataset is small enough that you may not notice an improvement in drawing speed. However, it can be quite dramatic for larger rasters over 1 GB in size.

10. Re-open the Layer Properties for the StudyAreaDEM raster layer.

11. Switch to the Information tab.

12. In the Information from provider section look for More information. You will see multiple dimension entries indicating that the pyramid resolutions were built.

13. Open a file browser (for example: Windows explorer or Finder) and navigate to the Exercise_5_Data folder. You will see a StudyAreaDEM.tif.ovr file. This is the file containing the pyramids.

5.5   Conclusion

In this exercise you focused on preparing raster data so that it seamlessly covers a study area. You also learned how to build pyramid files for a raster dataset.

5.6   Discussion Questions

1. What is a raster dataset?

2. Compare and contrast raster and vector data models.

3. Why might you use raster data? Give two examples.

5.7   Challenge Assignment

Install the SRTM Downloader plugin shown in figure 5.7, on the facing page. This allows you to download SRTM DEMs for the current canvas extent. Using the QuickMapServices plugin turn on the OpenStreetMap basemap (Web | QuickMapServices | OSM | OSM Standard). Zoom in to an area of interest and download the DEMs covering that area shown in figure 5.8, on the next page. Keep the area to the size of a large municipality so avoid too large a download. Build a virtual raster from the set of DEMs and build pyramids for the merged DEM. Create a color hillshade effect as you did in Part 2 Exercise 7.

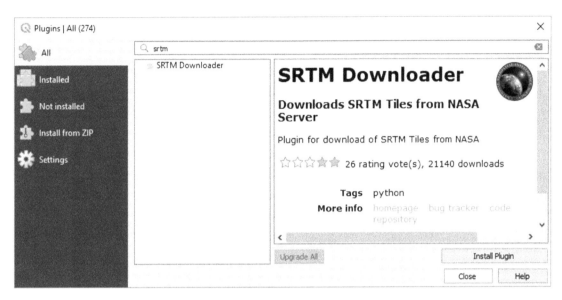

Figure 5.7: SRTM Downloader Plugin

Figure 5.8: SRTM Download

Exercise 6

Geocoding Address Data

Objective – Learn to Map Address Data via Geocoding

6.1 Introduction

Data collection is an important task in the creation of a GIS. Data can come from several sources such as GPS receivers, text files, or from the Internet as shapefiles—you may even receive a coverage. The GIS can manage all of this data. We may receive data with an address that we want to display on a map. We can geolocate items using an address via a process known as geocoding. This tool helps us take point features from a text file and tie it to an address.

This exercise includes the following tasks:

- Task 1 Geocoding
- Task 2 Building a Map

6.2 Objective: Learn to Map Address Data via Geocoding

The objective of this exercise is to learn how to geocode address-based data provided in a text file and create a map from various data sources.

6.3 Task 1 - Geocoding

In a geocoding operation, address data contained in a table or text file are mapped against a street network dataset. The street network dataset needs to have attribute fields holding the address ranges on the left and right side of each road segment. The software then extrapolates the position along the street arc. This is done based on where the numeric street address falls in relation to the address range for that segment. See figure 6.2, on page 253 below. If the address being mapped is 150 Central Ave., and the address range on the even side of the street is 102 to 200, the software will compute the position as being halfway down the block on the right side. Mapping addresses has many applications including mapping the customer base for a store, members of an organization, public health records, and crime locations. Once mapped, the points can be used to generate density surfaces and can be tied to parcels of land. This can be important in cadastral information systems.

1. Open QGIS and add the Streets layer from the DukeCity geopackage.

2. Open the Attribute table for Streets and examine the available fields of data. Notice that in addition to the STREETNAME and STREETDESI columns, the data include fields called LEFTLOW, LEFTHIGH, RIGHTLOW, and RIGHTHIGH. These fields hold the address range for each road segment. These are necessary in a geocoding operation.

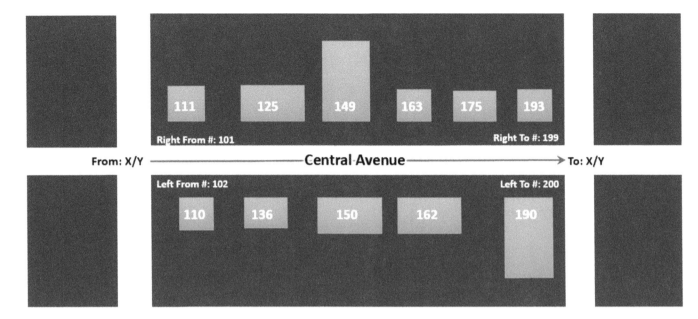

Figure 6.1: How Geocoding Works

3. Close the attribute table.

4. Now add the `Addresses.csv` table to QGIS.

5. Open the attribute table for the Addresses layer.

6. This file has an `ADDRESS` column that combines the street number, street, street type (ex: BLVD, AVE, ST), and city quadrant. There are additional fields with that address parsed out into `STREET`, `NUMBER` and `QUAD`. The tool you will be using requires separate fields in the address data for street and street number.

7. Now that you are familiar with the data, close the Addresses attribute table.

8. Search for and install the MMQGIS plugin.

MMQGIS appears as a menu in QGIS. This is a plugin developed by Michael Mann and it has a lot of useful tools in addition to the geocoding tools.

9. From the menu bar choose `MMQGIS | Geocode | Geocode from Street Layer`.

10. For the Input CSV File (UTF-8) click the [Browse...] button, navigate to the `Exercise_6_Data` folder and choose the `Addresses.csv` table. Fill in the remaining choices as (shown in figure 6.2, on the next page).

    a. First set the fields that hold street name and number in the `Addresses.csv` file.

    b. Then assign the field in the Streets shapefile that contains the street name.

    c. The Bldg. Setback (map units) field allows you to specify how far from the street arc to place the points. Street GIS data are known as street centerlines. The line falls where the median is on a large boulevard. Using this setting allows you to place the points more closely to the building's actual location. Set this to 20. The map units of this dataset are in feet. This distance roughly corresponds to the width of two road lanes.

    d. Set the Left From Number, Left To Number, Right From Number and Right From Number to `LEFTLOW`, `LEFTHIGH`, `RIGHTLOW`, and `RIGHTHIGH`.

e. The result will be a point shapefile. Name the Output Shapefile StreetGeocode.shp and save it to the Exercise_6_Data folder.

f. Geocoding operations rarely have 100% success. Street names in the street shapefile must match the street names in the CSV file exactly. The tool will save out a list of the unmatched records. Set the Not Found Output List to StreetNotFound.csv in the Exercise 6 Data folder.

g. Click OK to run. This process may take several minutes. The status of the geocoding will display in the bottom left corner of QGIS.

Figure 6.2: MMQGIS Geocode From Street Layer Tool

11. When complete the new layer is added to QGIS. The process should successfully geocode 199 of the 203 addresses

12. Open the attribute table for StreetGeocode. All of the attributes from the CSV file are brought in as attributes to the output shapefile.

13. Right click on the StreetGeocode layer and choose Zoom to Layer. All of the points look to be well mapped. (shown in figure 6.3, on the following page).

14. Zoom into a concentration of points and then zoom in farther to some within the city. Use the Identify Features tool to inspect the mapped points and the roads to ensure that the operation was successful. Here you are looking to ensure that the address from the point layer is falling on the correct block on the correct street. Never take a GIS operation for granted. Check your results with a critical eye.

15. You can also add the StreetNotFound.csv file to QGIS and study it to try and determine why the four records did not find a match.

Figure 6.3: Geocoding by Street Layer Result

16. These are good geocoding results. Now you will try the other method available: geocode using the Open-StreetMap/Nominatim geocoding service. You will not be asked to use the Google web service because it requires an API key and the terms of service change frequently.

17. From the menu bar choose MMQGIS | Geocode | Geocode CSV with Google/OpenStreetMap. This tool requires an internet connection.

18. Fill out the Web Service Geocode parameters so they match the figure 6.4, on the next page):

    a. Input CSV File (UTF-8) = Addresses.csv

    b. Address Field = STREET

    c. City Field = CITY

    d. State Field = STATE

    e. Country Field = COUNTRY

    f. Web Service = OpenStreetMap/Nominatim

    g. Output Shapefile = OSMAddresses.shp

    h. Not Found Output List = OSMNotFound.csv

    i. Click OK to run. Again, this may take a while and progress is displayed in the lower-left corner of QGIS.

19. This may take several minutes to run and in part depends on the speed of your internet connection.

20. This technique matches all 167 records. The figure 6.5, on the facing page) shows the OpenStreetMap/Nominatim addresses in yellow and the street layer geocoded addresses in red. Note how much they differ!

21. Right-click on OSMAddresses.shp and choose Zoom to Layer. These, too, seem to be well mapped. Although there is a discernible difference between the address point locations identified by the two tools. Both results cannot be correct. Add the OSMNotFound.csv file to QGIS. Study it to try and determine why the 36 records did not find a match.

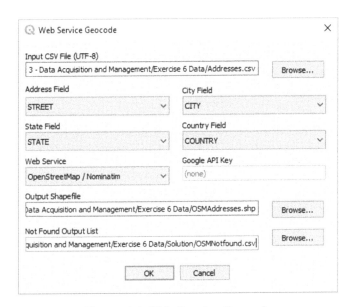

Figure 6.4: Web Service Geocode

Figure 6.5: Comparing Two Geocoding Methods

22. Again, zoom in to some sample address points and spot check the results to determine if the points are on the street they should be. Can you determine which output is more accurate?

23. Congratulations! You have created points from a table of addresses! The real challenge is determining which is most correct. Geocoding is often an iterative process. Carefully inspecting the results is necessary.

24. Save your map as `exercise6.qgz`.

6.4   Task 2 - Building a Map

At the end of your data development, a product is usually required. In this case, a map is necessary to complete the exercise. Data from several sources have been downloaded and included in your exercise data folder.

1. Open QGIS and open `exercise6.qgz` if it is not already.

2. Add the jurisdiction, biketrails, and council layers from the `DukeCity` geopackage. Jurisdiction is the municipal boundaries for Albuquerque, New Mexico. Council is the City Council Districts. Bike trails are municipal bike trails.

3. Using QGIS symbolize the layers and use the Layout Composer to compose a letter sized color map highlighting the different Facilities (StreetGeocode) by City Council District.

4. You will have to style the StreetGeocode addresses and City Council Districts using Categories.

5. Symbolize Bike Trails, Streets, and Jurisdiction as you see fit.

6. If you need a refresher on how to compose a map you can refer to Part 1 - Introduction to Geospatial Technology, Exercise 2 - Displaying Geospatial Data

7. Submit a jpg of your final map.

6.5   Conclusion

In this exercise you learned how to geocode address data using the MMQGIS plugin. Geocoding is an important vector data creation process. There are many data organized by address. Mapping such data allows you to generate density maps, measure proximity of points, and perhaps even characterize the neighborhoods the points fall in with socioeconomic data from the Census. Maps are often part of a final product of a GIS project or analysis. Data can come from various sources and be manipulated to fit the project. The data should be normalized in respect to the file format, spatial extent and coordinate reference system. Remember GIS data are often free, and there is a wealth of it on the Internet. Just use it with caution and check the accuracy of the data if at all possible. One should explore the data as much as possible before using and endorsing it.

6.6   Discussion Questions

1. Which tool created better output, the Geocoding by Street Layer or the OpenStreetMap/Nominatim web service?

2. What are some applications of geocoding? Describe.

6.7   Challenge Assignment

Use the data in the `Exercise_6_DataChallenge` folder to compose a map to do with pollutants in Nueces County, Texas. The data include:

- Airports
- Cities
- Roads
- Water_features
- Places
- Counties

Use the MMQGIS Geocode CSV with Google/OpenStreetMap tool to geocode the address data in the NuecesCounty.csv file. These addresses are Toxic Release Inventory sites from the EPA. As such, they are potential source points for pollutants.

In order to compose the map you will have to utilize Feature subsets (Layer Properties | Source tab) to limit some of the data to Nueces County.

You will have to check the coordinate systems to ensure that all data are in the same coordinate reference system.

Style data layers such as airports and rivers.

Submit a jpg of your final map.

Part IV

Cartographic Design

Exercise 1

Map Composition

Objective – Learn about inverted polygon shapeburst fills and map composition

1.1   Introduction

This map contains data pertaining to diabetes in Baltimore City, Maryland, USA. There is data on diabetes totals by neighborhood (this data is fictional and therefore is not in violation of HIPAA), food deserts and dialysis clinics. You will complete the map with some styling tricks and compose a final map.

This exercise includes the following tasks:

- Task 1 – Inverted Polygon Shapeburst Fills
- Task 2 – Composing a Map and Configuring Map Elements
- Task 3 – Creating Inset Maps

1.2   Objective: Learn about inverted polygon shapeburst fills and map composition

To achieve a properly designed map, the features on the map must be easily distinguishable, attractive to the map reader, and stand out from the grounds (supporting background information/data). In this exercise, you'll learn how to utilize some symbology tricks to focus the map readers attention on the main topic of the map. Additionally, you'll learn how to add more map elements to a print layout such as a scale bar, graticule and locator map.

1.3   Task 1 - Inverted Polygon Shapeburst Fills

In this task, you will combine Inverted Polygon styling (remember this is a way to style data outside the boundaries of a layer) , with Shapeburst fills to create Inverted Polygon Shapeburst Fills. You will learn two common use cases for this technique. The first will be to create a coastal vignette. The second will be to create a study area mask. The latter can really help focus the map readers attention on the topic at hand.

1. Open QGIS 3.x. and then open `BaltimoreDiabetes.qgz`.

2. This map has several layers related to diabetes: the prevalence by neighborhood (Neighborhood_diabetes), Food Deserts (FACCESS_BaltCity_FoodDesert) and Dialysis_Centers. Then there are a layers for the city boundary and counties.

3. These layers are already nicely symbolized, but you have no data representing the Chesapeake Bay, which is a large body of water next to Baltimore. It is simply a white hole in the MD_County_boundaries data layer. To represent this you could click on Project | Project Properties and change the background color of the map

261

to some nice shade of blue. However, you will learn how to generate a coastal vignette instead. Right-click on the MD_County_boundaries layer and choose Duplicate. A second copy of it will appear in the Layers Panel.

4. Drag the new copy so that it is between the Neighborhood_diabetes and Baltimore City Boundary layers in the Layers Panel. Turn on the visibility for the layer.

5. Open the Layer Styling Panel 🖌 with the target layer being the duplicated layer.

    a. From the renderer dropdown choose Inverted Polygons.

    b. Select the Simple fill component.

    c. Select a Symbol layer type of Shapeburst fill.

    d. Under Gradient colors you will check the Two color method.

       i. Color number one will have an RGB value of: 225/255/255 which is a light blue.

       ii. Color number two will have an RGB value of: 166/206/227 a darker blue (figure 1.1).

Figure 1.1: Setting up the Inverted Polygon Shapeburst Fill

Now area beyond the extent of the county boundaries (which is the equivalent of the Chesapeake Bay and Baltimore Harbor) is styled with a light blue to darker blue color ramp. It is also using the shapeburst fill style, which fills the area with a gradient based on the distance from the polygon edge.

6. You can also control where the gradation occurs. Under Shading style select Set distance and set the distance to 9. This controls the distance that the first color blends into the second. This setting gives you the control to visually represent the center of the channel.

7. There is also a Blur strength setting which controls how smoothly the two color blend. Set Blur strength to 10.

8. To complete the effect you will create a shoreline. Click the Add symbol layer 🞤 button to add a new symbology component.

9. Use the Move Up and Move Down △ ▽ buttons to move it above the Shapeburst fill if it isn't already.

10. It will be the default Simple fill symbol. Change from a Symbol layer type of Simple fill to Outline: Simple line.

11. Give the line an RGB color of 31 | 120 | 180 which is a dark blue. You can create great effects by using composite renderers like this.

You have symbolized the Chesapeake Bay without having a layer for it by using an Inverted Polygon Shapeburst Fill! (figure 1.2)

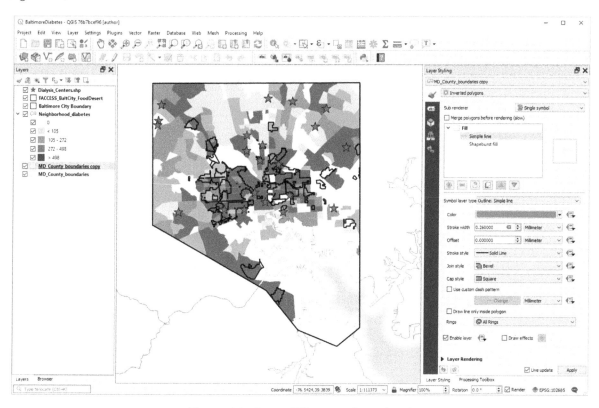

Figure 1.2: Coastal Vignette Completed

12. Save your project.

13. Next you will create a study area mask to give more visual weight to Baltimore City. You will again employ Inverted Polygon Shapeburst Fills.

14. Duplicate the Baltimore_City_Boundary layer and turn on the new copied layer.

15. Open the Layer Styling Panel targeting the new copied layer. Again change from the Single Symbol to an Inverted polygons renderer.

    a. Select Simple fill and choose the Symbol layer type of Shapeburst fill.

    b. Under Gradient colors you will again be using the Two color method.

    c. Color number one will have an RGB value of: 135 | 135 | 135 which is gray. Color number two will be white.

    d. Notice that the color for color one has a checkered pattern [▼]. This indicates it is completely transparent. When selecting the color, slide the Opacity slider to 100% making it completely opaque.

    e. Under Shading style select Set distance and set the distance to 4.

    f. Expand Layer rendering and use the Opacity slider so that Opacity is 45%.

You have now styled the area beyond the city limits. You used a gray to white color ramp with a set distance of 4 which created a mask around the city boundary. The layer is also semi-transparent so that you can still see the underlying data. It creates an effect where the area of interest pops off the map and receives more visual weight. The area beyond Baltimore City is underneath the white mask created by this styling so that visually it falls into the background (figure 1.3).

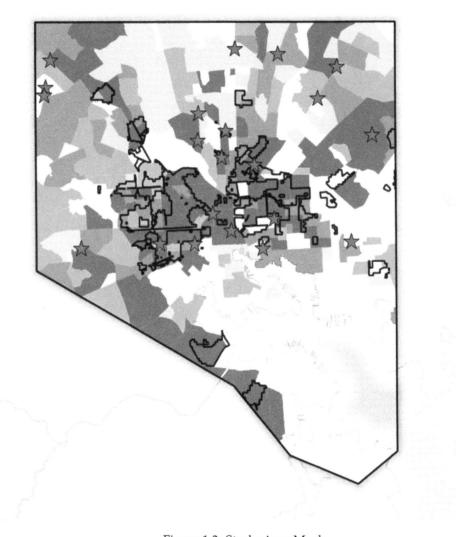

Figure 1.3: Study Area Mask

16. Save your project.

1.4   Task 2 - Composing a Map and Configuring Map Elements

In this task, you will start with a basic print layout and enhance it with variables and a coordinate grid among other map elements.

You will start by creating a new Print Layout and setting up the page.

1. From the Project toolbar choose New Print Layout ![button] button or `Ctrl + P`.

2. Name the Layout *Baltimore Diabetes*. Click OK and the new Print Layout will open.

Setting Up the Page

1. To set the sheet size right click on the blank page and choose Page Properties. Here you can specify details about the overall composition. QGIS defaults to an A4 sheet size. In the Page Size section click the Size dropdown and set it to Letter.

2. Set the Orientation to Portrait.

3. Click on the Add new map ![button] button and drag a box on the sheet of paper where the map will go. Cover the entire sheet with the map leaving a small margin. The map object can be resized after it is added by selecting it and using the handles around the perimeter to resize.

4. Here you want a regular set of margins of 0.25 of an inch. Click on the Layout tab and find the Resize Layout to Content section. Set the Margin units to in. Set the Top margin, Bottom Margin, Left Margin and Right Margin to 0.25 each. Then click the Resize Layout button (figure 1.4).

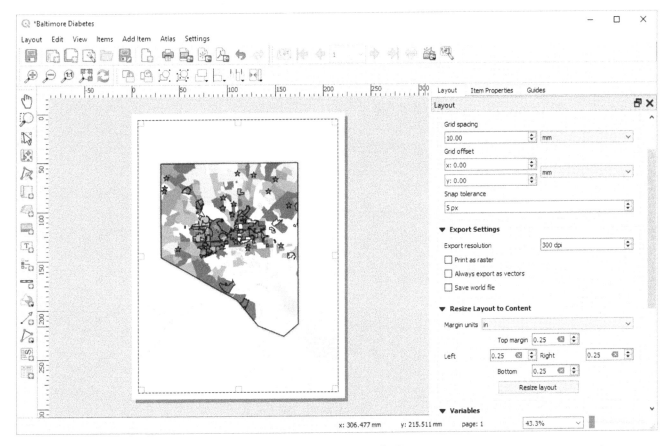

Figure 1.4: Setting up the Page

5. Now click on the Item Properties tab. With the map element selected, Item Properties will have properties of the map. In the Main Properties section set the Scale to 100000.

6. Use the Move Item Content ![button] button to pan the map so that it is centered.

7. As mentioned in Part 1 - Exercise 2 there are a series of buttons above Main Properties which were introduced at QGIS 3.6 Noosa.

From left to right these are:

- Update Map Preview
- Set Map Extent to Match Main Canvas Extent
- View Current Map Extent in Main Canvas
- Set Map Scale to Match Main Canvas Scale
- Set Main Canvas to Match Current Map Scale
- Interactively Edit Map Extent
- Labeling Settings

Note that these tools replace the *Set to map canvas extent* **and** *View extent in map canvas* **buttons, found in all QGIS versions back to QGIS version 2.0 and earlier!**

8. Click the Set Main Canvas to Match Current Map Scale button. Notice the scale changing in the main map canvas.

9. Now you will add a frame around your map object. Scroll down in Item Properties and check the Frame option. Increase the Thickness to 0.50 mm.

1.5   Task 2.1 - Setting Up the Map Title

The purpose of a map title is to quickly convey the content and focus of the map to the map reader. It should be concise and prominent.

1. Use the Add new label button and drag a box across the top of the composition. On the Item Properties tab replace *Lorem ipsum* with the following title: *Food Deserts and Diabetes in Baltimore City*.

2. Click the Font button to open the Text Format window. Set the Font to Times New Roman, Size 36 with a Font style of Bold. Click OK to accept the font settings. You may need to resize the text box after these font settings have been made so that the entire title can be seen.

3. Note that you can also click the drop-down menu for Font and access a handy context menu (figure 1.5). From there you can interactively set the font size, pick from Recent Fonts, and modify and copy the format.

Figure 1.5: Layout Font Widget

4. Under Appearance, set both Horizontal Alignment and to Center and the Vertical Alignment to Middle.

1.6 Task 2.2 - Setting Up the Legend

The purpose for the legend is to identify what symbols and colors on the map represent. Legends are used for data layers that are non-intuitive or require more explanation. For example, a blue line labeled *Amazon River* does not need to be included in a legend, it is obvious what it is. However, the range of diabetic patients per class does. Otherwise the map reader will have no way of knowing what they are looking at.

1. Add a legend using the Add new legend button. Drag a box in the empty area south of the western portion of the city to add it to the composition.

2. There are several layers that are only being used for cartographic purposes and do not need to be in the legend. You will remove these unnecessary legend entries. On the Item properties tab uncheck Auto update. Now the buttons below the Legend Item portion of the Item properties tab are active.

3. You do not need Baltimore City Boundary copy layer in the legend. Select it and click the Remove button to remove it from the legend.

4. Also remove the MD_County_boundaries copy and MD_County_boundaries layers.

5. The Legend still needs some editing. Layers come into QGIS with the file name as the layer name. As you learned, you can rename these in QGIS by going to the Layer Properties | General tab. However, you can also edit these names directly in the Legend. Select the Dialysis_Centers.shp legend entry and click the Edit button.

6. Take out the underscore and the .shp to make it an English readable layer name and click OK.

7. Rename the FACCESS_BaltCity_FoodDesert legend entry to *Food Deserts*.

8. Rename the Neighborhood_diabetes legend entry to *Diabetes Morbidity by Neighborhood* (figure 1.6).

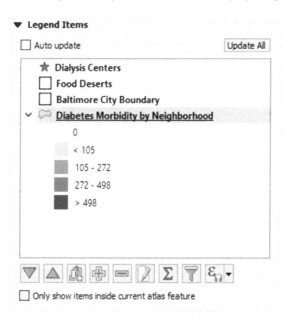

Figure 1.6: Editing the Legend

1.7 Task 2.3 - Descriptive Text

It good practice to include credits for both data sources and cartography on the map. It can also be helpful to include things like the date.

1. Next you will enter some descriptive text that tells the map reader where the data was obtained, who the cartographer was and the date created. This will be done using the Add new label tool, the same tool you used to add the title. Add the label below the legend. Add the following text in the Main properties window of the Item Properties tab.

Data Sources: Maryland Food System Map, Baltimore City View and Open Baltimore Cartographer: <your name> Created on: <todays date>

2. For the date use an expression as you did in Part 1 - Exercise 2. `concat('Created on:  ', to_date($now))`. If you need a refresher on how to do that revisit that exercise.

3. Set the Font Size to 8.

4. Drag the text element so that it lines up with the left side of the legend. With an element selected, you can also use the arrow keys on your keyboard to nudge (figure 1.6, on the previous page).

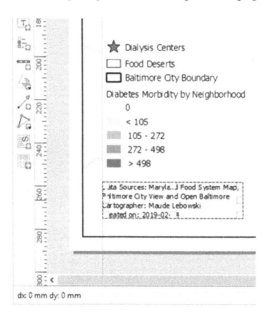

Figure 1.7: Lining Up the Text Box with the Legend

Did you know there is a recent enhancement to QGIS 3.6 that allows for custom layout checks? An example would be checks to warn a cartographer if desired map elements have been added or properly configured. These checks can help ensure maps meet a set of minimum organizational design criteria. Read more here: http://bit.ly/2G852H8

1.8 Task 2.4 - Using Variables for Adding Your Name as Author

QGIS allows you to store variables. This means any type of constant such as a unit conversion factor or your name. Variables can be set at several levels: Global, Project and Layer. Here you will create a new Global variable with your name as cartographer.

1. Bring up the main QGIS desktop application.

2. From the menu bar choose Settings | Options.

3. Click on the ℰ Variables section.

4. These are where Global variables are found.

5. Click the Add variable ⊞ button.

6. Replace new_variable with *cartographer*.

7. Click in the Value cell to the right and type your name (figure 1.8). Click OK.

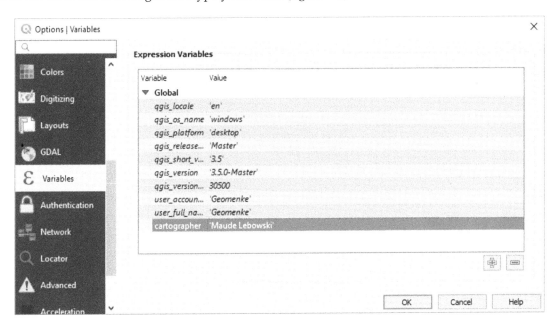

Figure 1.8: Setting Up a New Global Variable

8. Bring up the Print Layout window again.

9. Select the text you were most recently working with.

10. Highlight the name you entered and click the Insert an Expression button.

11. Scroll down in the list of functions to the Variables section and expand it. Find the variable you just created named cartographer. Double-click on it to add it to your expression. When you select it also notice that the value of that variable is displayed in the right hand pane of the expression window (figure 1.9, on the next page).

12. While you have the Expression window open, notice that there is a Recent section. Expand it and you will find the date expression you created. You can use this Recent section to bring up recently used expressions and use them without having to recreate them!

13. Click OK.

14. The text in the Items Properties panel now reads: (figure 1.10, on the following page).

15. You have used two expressions to automate your text. The @cartographer variable will always be available until you delete it. Variables and other expressions can be used throughout the QGIS interface to make your job easier! The date expression will update automatically each time the map is modified.

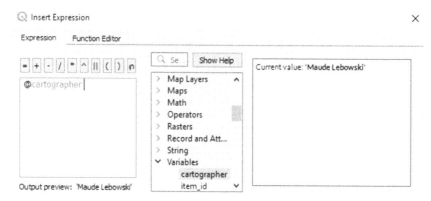

Figure 1.9: Inserting Your Cartographer Variable

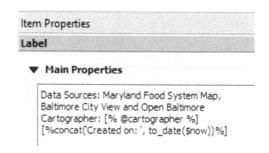

Figure 1.10: Text with both Expression and Variable

1.9   Task 2.5 - Adding a North Arrow

Often it is nice to add a north arrow to a map composition to help orient the map reader. One should especially be added if north is not up on the map. Here you will learn how to add this to your map. QGIS does not have a dedicated north arrow tool, rather you add an image. That means you use the same tool to both add a logo and a north arrow.

1. Click on the Add image ![icon] button.

2. Drag a small box into the empty space in the lower right corner of the legend.

3. On the Item Properties tab expand the Search Directories section. A series of SVG graphics included with QGIS will appear.

4. Scroll down until you see a series of north arrow graphics. Select a suitable graphic (figure 1.11). It will appear in your image box on the composition.

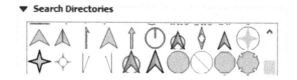

Figure 1.11: Search Directories for North Arrow Graphic

5. Scroll down to the Image Rotation section of Item Properties. Check Sync with map and set the map to Map 1 (figure 1.12, on the facing page).

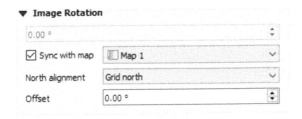

Figure 1.12: Aligning the North Arrow to Grid North

6. Scroll up to the Main Properties section and change the Resize mode to Zoom and resize frame.

7. Resize the north arrow graphic and move as needed so that it is well placed (figure 1.13).

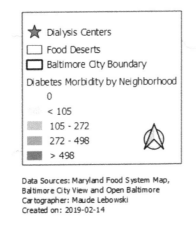

Figure 1.13: North Arrow on Map

1.10 Task 2.6 - Inserting a Scale Bar

Scale bars give the map reader a way to approximate distances on the map. There are three types: graphic scale bar, scale text and a verbal description, i.e., *One cm equals 2 kilometers.* Here you will learn how to add a graphic scale bar.

1. Click on the Add new scalebar ⬚ button.

2. Click to the right of the descriptive text to add the scalebar to the map.

3. On the Item Properties tab, in the Units section change the Scalebar units to Miles. This sets the scalebar units to miles.

4. In the Segments section, set the left to 1 and the right to 2.

5. In the Main Properties section change the Style to Line Ticks Middle. Notice that one of the styles is Numeric which would add scale as scale text (*1:100,000*).

6. In the Fonts and Colors section, change the Font to size 10.

7. Use the Select/Move Item ⬚ tool to place the scalebar in a good position next to the descriptive text (figure 1.14, on the following page).

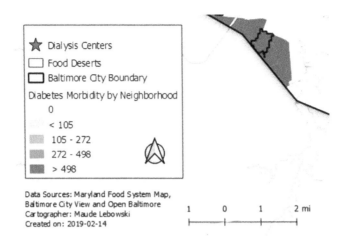

Figure 1.14: Scale Bar Added

In the northern hemisphere map readers assume that north is up. On the Item Properties tab for the map object there is a Rotation section. This allows you to rotate the map. Sometimes rotating the map frame helps fit your study area onto the sheet of paper. If you have rotated your map you should always include a north arrow.

1.11 Task 2.7 - Creating a Coordinate Grid (graticule)

Coordinate grids are a technical map elements. As such they are not always required. However, depending on the target audience for your map they can be a nice addition.

1. Select the map object on the Print layout.

2. Find the Grids section on the Items Properties tab and expand it.

3. Click the Add a new grid [⊕] button to add a grid. A grid named Grid 1 will be added.

4. Select it and click Modify grid.

5. The Map Grid Properties panel opens within Item Properties. Here you can specify several grid styles, the coordinate system, the X and Y intervals and details about the frame and labels.

     a. In the Appearance section, set the Grid type to Solid.

     b. Click the CRS Change button and search for EPSG 26918. Find the CRS and select it. Here the map is in US State Plane. However, you will put a UTM grid over the map. This is the UTM zone for this part of the world.

     c. Set the X and Y Interval units to 5000 Map units. This will result in a 5000 meter UTM grid.

     d. Click the button for Line style.

     e. Select Simple line.

     f. Click Use custom dash pattern and click Change.

     g. Set the Dash to 3 and the Space to 2 and click OK.

     h. Click on the Black color bar and open the color picker and make the color gray instead of black. Perhaps an RGB of 105 | 105 | 105.

     i. Click the Go back ◁ button twice to get back to the Grid Properties.

    j. You have given your map a frame, so you will skip the Frame section.

    k. Find the Draw Coordinates section and activate it. These are settings for the coordinate labels.

    l. For Format choose Decimal with suffix and down below set the Coordinate precision to 0.

    m. Set all four cardinal directions (Left, Right, Top and Bottom) to Inside Frame.

    n. Set Left and Right to Vertical ascending.

As you can see there are a lot of settings you can use to set up a grid exactly as you need it (figure 1.15).

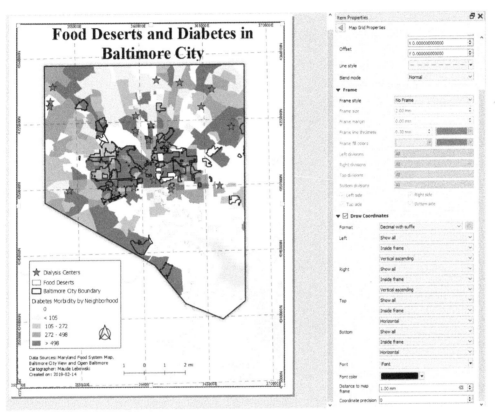

Figure 1.15: Graticule Added to Layout

> Did you know that there is also a Create Grid tool in the Processing toolbox? It can be found in the Vector creation section. This tool allows you to create a grid layer with specific spacing. It is similar to the ArcGIS Fishnet tool. Plus you can set up a visual grid as a Decoration by clicking View | Decorations | Grid. This has many of the same options as creating a layer as described above.

1.12 Task 2.8 - Finishing and Exporting the Map

1. To avoid the graticule from disrupting the title you will give the title a background the same color as the map. Select the Title object. Find the Background section on the Layer Properties panel and check it to enable a background. Click the Color drop-down menu and choose Pick Color. With the eyedropper cursor, click on the yellow county fill near the title (figure 1.16, on the following page).

2. Repeat this step for the Descriptive text box and the Scale bar box. The color should now be listed in the Recent color category making it easier to find. These are the subtle changes that can really increase the readability of a map, but that will likely go unnoticed, except to an experience cartographer or designer.

Figure 1.16: Title With Background

3. Now that you have finished the map you will export it. The buttons below the Settings menu allow you to print the composition and export it into a variety of formats. These same options are available from the Layout menu.

4. Click the Export as image ▣ button. This will allow you to save the map out to an image file.

5. The Save Layout As... window opens. Navigate to the exercise folder. By clicking on the Save as type dropdown, you will see the range of image formats you can export to. Choose JPG. Name the file and click Save.

6. The Image Export Options window will open. It gives you the export settings including the pixel dimensions and the resolution you chose on the Composition tab of the Print Layout. Here you can change these setting if need be. Click Save. Note that it also has an option to Generate a world file!

7. You will receive the message that Export layout: Successfully exported layout to...* (figure 1.17). This message includes a hyperlink to the folder where the map was exported. You can click on this to open your operating systems file browser and see the result.

Figure 1.17: Export Successful Message with Hyperlink

8. Now click the Export as PDF ▣ button. Again navigate to the exercise folder, name the file and click Save.

9. Your final map should resemble the figure 1.18, on the facing page.

10. Save you project and exit QGIS.

1.13   Task 3 - Creating Inset Maps

In this task, you will learn how to work with map themes to create inset maps. These are smaller than the main map. They provide a broader spatial context, showing where the main body of the map is located. In this context they have a smaller scale than the main map. Sometimes a detail map at a larger scale is needed. Either case can be handled by the following technique.

1. Open QGIS 3.6 and open ACoruna.qgz

2. This is a map of the town of A Coruña, Spain. In March of 2019 the 22nd QGIS Developer Meeting (Hackfest) was held there. The map has layers for Roads, Land, Water (using an inverted polygon shapeburst fill) and the Hackfest which employs a Raster Image Marker. You will work more with this renderer in the Mapping Photopoints exercise in Part 5. There is also a Countries layer which is currently turned off.

3. A simple Print Composition has been started. Open the Map print composition. It is zoomed in to A Coruña. What will be helpful to the map reader is to add an inset map showing where A Coruña is located in Spain.

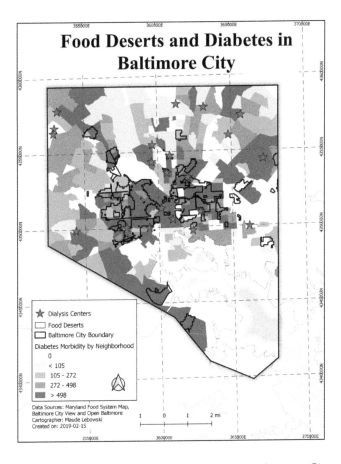

Figure 1.18: Food Deserts and Diabetes in Baltimore City

4. Return to the main QGIS Desktop window. Select all the four visible layers and choose Group Selected from the context menu. Name the group Main Map (figure 1.19).

Figure 1.19: Layers Grouped

5. Now you will set the current view as a map theme. Locate the Manage Map Themes ⚭ drop down menu at the top of the Layers Panel and click on it. Choose Add Theme and the Map Themes window will open. Name the new theme Main Map and click OK.

6. Return to the Map print composition. Select the map object with the Select/Move Items ▸ tool. On the Item Properties tab find the Layers section. Click the box for Follow map theme and change it from none to Main Map

(figure 1.20).

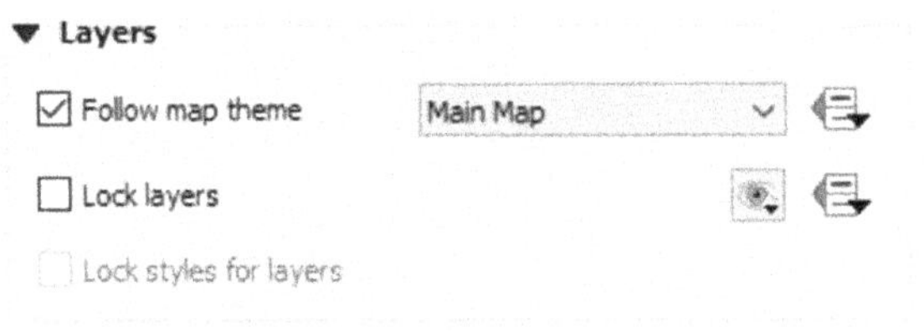

Figure 1.20: Setting the Map Object to Follow a Map Theme

7. Return to the main QGIS Desktop window. Click `Ctrl + Shift + H` to Hide All Layers. This is a keyboard shortcut that allows you to quickly turn off all the layers in a project. Turn on the Countries layer and zoom out until you can see all of Spain.

8. Click the Manage Map Themes drop down menu and once again choose Add Theme. This time name the theme Inset map.

9. Return to the Map print composition. Click the Add a new map to the layout button and drag a box in the lower left corner to add the inset map there. On the Item Properties tab again find the Layers section. Click the box for Follow map theme and change it from none to Inset Map

10. Next you will create an overview so that the position of the Main Map on the Inset Map is visible. Scroll down to find the Overviews section and expand it. Click the green Add a new overview button. Select the newly created Overview 1 and set the Map frame to Map 1.

11. To make the overview show well at this scale you need to adjust the symbology for the Frame style. Click the Frame Style button. Select Simple fill and change the Symbol layer type to Centroid fill. Select the Simple marker component and increase the Size to 4.

12. Click the button to return to the main Item Properties panel. Your final map should resemble the figure 1.21, on the next page.

1.14   Conclusion

In this exercise, you have learned how to use inverted polygon shapeburst fills to both create a coastal vignette and a study area mask. You then designed a print composition. Along the way you learned how to add and configure all the common map elements.

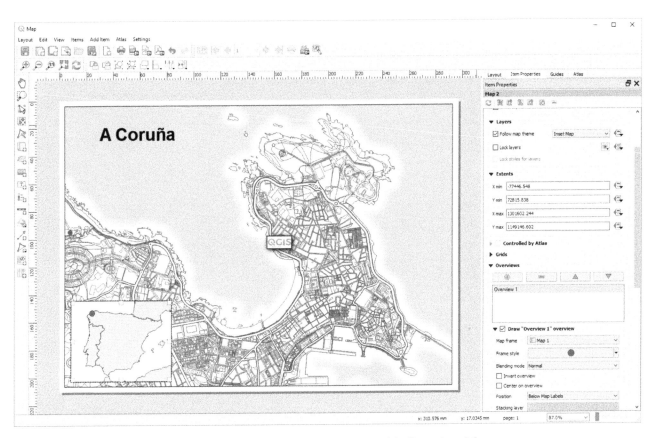

Figure 1.21: Final Print Composition with Overview Map

Exercise 2

Creating an Atlas

Objective - Create a Map Atlas

2.1 Introduction

This exercise will focus on building an Atlas. This is a handy feature found in a Print Layout that allows you to generate a series of maps. In this exercise, you will work with the same Baltimore Diabetes data from the previous exercise. You will set up an atlas to create a map of each of the 271 neighborhoods in Baltimore in one step.

This exercise includes the following tasks:

- Task 1 – Setting Up an Atlas
- Task 2 – Creating Dynamic Map Elements
- Task 3 – Highlighting the Coverage Feature
- Task 4 – Previewing and Exporting the Atlas

2.2 Objective: Create a Map Atlas

Create a map atlas.

2.3 Task 1 - Setting Up an Atlas

In this first task, you will learn the basic Atlas settings.

1. Open QGIS 3.x. and then open `Baltimore_Atlas.qgz`.

2. This is a very similar map to the one you worked with in the previous exercise. Here there is a Google Road basemap in place of the county boundary layer. The Neighborhoods layer has been given a Multiply Blending Mode so that the basemap is visible. Plus the Food Deserts and Diabetes Clinics have been given Live Layer Effects. You will learn more about those in Part 5 - Exercise 1.

3. Open the existing Print Layout by clicking the Show Layout Manager ⬜ button on the Project Toolbar. Select the Atlas layout and click Show (figure 2.1, on the following page).

4. Click on the Atlas tab. If it is not there, you can enable it from the menu bar by choosing `Atlas | Atlas Settings` or from `View | Panels`. You can also use the Atlas Settings ⬜ button to open this panel.

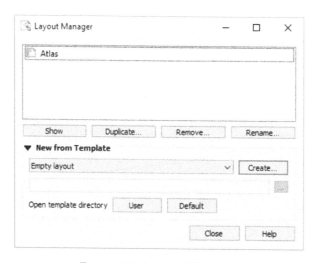

Figure 2.1: Layout Manager

5. Click Generate an Atlas.

6. Set the Coverage Layer to Neighborhoods. This is the layer that the Atlas will be based on.

7. Set the Page name to the NAME field. This is the field that will be used to create each page in the Atlas.

8. Turn your attention to the Output section. This is where you can form an Output filename expression to name the output files. Uncheck Single file export when possible. Then replace 'output_' with 'Diabetes_in_'. The expression 'Diabetes_in_'||@atlas_featurenumber uses the concatenation || operator to merge two pieces of text: Diabetes_in_ and the variable @atlas_featurenumber. This variable will be equal to the Page name as the atlas iterates through the neighborhood features. Notice that you can also set the Image export format here (figure 2.2).

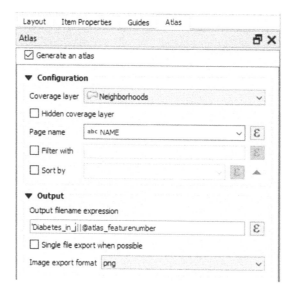

Figure 2.2: Atlas Panel

9. Use the Select/Move Graphic ![cursor] tool to select the map object.

10. Switch to the Item Properties tab

11. Click the Controlled by Atlas box. This is the final step in setting up a basic atlas.

12. Select Margin around feature and increase to 20% (figure 2.3).

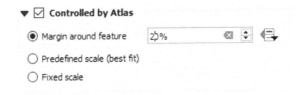

Figure 2.3: Map Properties

13. Click the Save ![save icon] button to save your project. Clicking Save in a Print Layout saves the entire project. Notice that when you have unsaved changes to your QGIS project the project name will be preceded by an asterisk. This will also appear in your Print Layout name.

2.4   Task 2 - Creating Dynamic Map Elements

You have set up a basic atlas, but in order for it to be really useful, each map needs a custom title. Plus you don't want anything appearing in the legend that is not visible on the map. This would confuse your map readers. In this next task, you will learn how to create dynamic titles and legends.

1. Open QGIS and open Baltimore_Atlas.qgz if it is not already.

2. First you will work on the title. Use the Select/Move Graphic ![tool icon] tool to select the Title text.

3. Turn your attention to the Item Properties tab. Highlight the *Baltimore City* text and click the Insert an expression button to open the Insert Expression window.

4. In the center functions section, scroll down and find the Variables section. Expand it and look for @atlas_pagename. You can also use the Search box at the top to find this. Double-click on the @atlas_pagename variable to add it. Notice the suite of variables related to Atlas! These may come in handy later. Click OK. Your title text should now look like (figure 2.4).

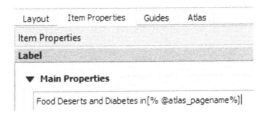

Figure 2.4: Atlas pagename Variable Added to Title Text

5. Next use the Select/Move Graphic ![tool icon] tool to select the Legend object.

6. On the Item Properties tab and find the Legend Items section. Check Only show items inside current atlas feature (figure 2.5, on the following page).

7. Save your project.

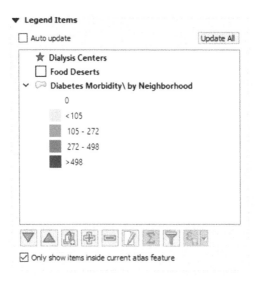

Figure 2.5: Legend Atlas Settings

2.5   Task 3 - Highlighting the Coverage Feature

In this task, you will learn how to use variables and Rule-based Symbology to highlight the current coverage feature (neighborhood).

1. Open QGIS and open `Baltimore_Atlas.qgz` if it is not already.

2. Bring up the main QGIS desktop window.

3. Duplicate the Neighborhoods layer and move the duplicated version to the top of the Layers Panel.

4. Open the Layer Styling Panel ✎ with the target layer being the duplicated layer.

   a. Change the renderer to a Single symbol
   b. In the Layer Rendering section find the Layer Blending Mode setting. Set the mode to Normal and the Opacity to 100%.
   c. Select the Simple Fill component and set the Fill style to No brush.
   d. Set the Stroke Color to a bright yellow (255 | 255 | 0) with a Width of 0.86. Set the Stroke Style to Solid Line.

Next you will set this layer up with a Rule-based renderer based on another Atlas Variable. This will make this layer equal to only the current atlas feature. The Rule-based renderer lets you set rules for what is rendered. When doing this you can leverage the expression engine to generate the rules. This means you can use any Variables or Functions included with QGIS.

5. Switch from a Single Symbol to a Rule-based ⊟Rule-based renderer.

6. Expand the Layer Rendering section and activate Draw Effects. Click on the Customize effects 🖫 button. This opens the Effects Properties panel within the Layer Styling panel.

7. Add a default Drop Shadow to the layer (figure 2.6, on the next page).

8. Click the Go back ◁ button to return to the main symbology panel.

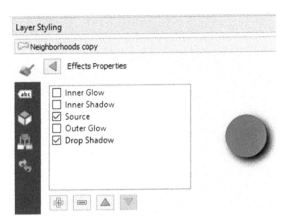

Figure 2.6: Adding A Drop Shadow

9. There is just one renderer listed. Currently it reads (no filter) in the Rule column. Double-click where it reads (no filter) to open up the Edit rule panel.

a. Enter a Label of *Coverage Feature*. This is the name of the rule.

b. Enter the following expression in the Filter box: @atlas_featureid = $id. You can also click the Expression ε button to open the Expression String Builder and create this expression there. You can find @atlas_featureid by Searching the Variables section. You can find $id in the Records and Attributes section. Highlighting these in the Expression String Builder window will tell you what each returns in the right-side help box (figure 2.7).

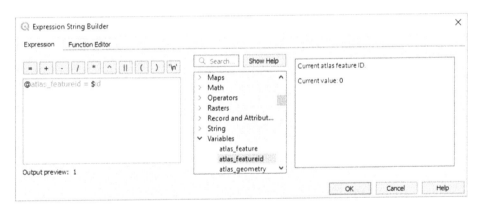

Figure 2.7: Expression for the Coverage Feature

This expression makes this layer equal to the current atlas feature. Therefore, as Atlas cycles through the maps the current neighborhood will be highlighted with a thick yellow outline and a drop shadow (figure 2.8, on the next page)!

10. Save your project.

2.6 Task 4 - Previewing and Exporting the Atlas

In this final task, you will see how to preview your atlas and export the images.

1. Open QGIS and open Baltimore_Atlas.qgz if it is not already.

Figure 2.8: Setting the Rule for the Coverage Feature

2. Open the Atlas Print Layout.

3. Click the Preview Atlas button.

4. This will activate the Atlas. The Atlas toolbar lets you cycle through each page in the Atlas to preview it. You can use the First Feature, Previous Feature, Next Feature and Last Feature buttons to preview pages. You can also use the Atlas dropdown menu to find specific pages (figure 2.9). As you preview the maps you may see changes that could be made to make the maps look betters. For example, it might provide nicer maps to reduce the segment length of the scale bar tool 200 feet. Notice that the Legend changes to match the content of each map.

Figure 2.9: Atlas Toolbar

5. You can use the Export Atlas button to export the series. Since this is a large series of maps you can decide if you want to export the entire series. A few sample maps are shown in figure 2.10.

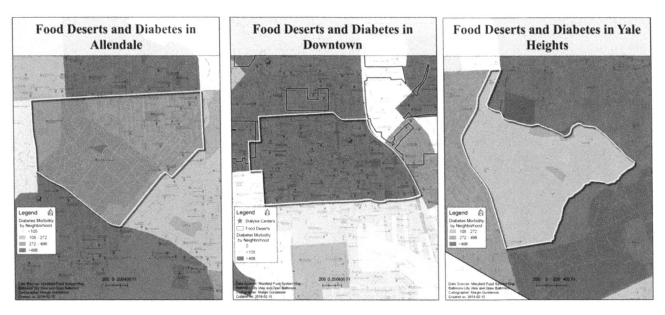

Figure 2.10: Three Sample Maps from the Atlas

2.7 Conclusion

In this exercise, you learned how to use the Atlas feature to generate large series of maps in a few minutes. This can be a huge time saver. The Atlas variables provide an efficient means to customize the various map elements.

Exercise 3

Exploring Coordinate Systems and Map Projections

Objective – Explore and Understand Coordinate Systems and Map Projections

3.1 Introduction

In this exercise, you'll explore the effects of various map projections on the characteristics of a map using QGIS.

This exercise will focus primarily on shape and area distortions and will examine projections useful for mapping on the global scale as well as on the national and state level.

This exercise includes the following tasks:

- Task 1 – Setting Map Projections and Coordinate Systems in QGIS

- Task 2 – Exploring World Map Projections

- Task 3 – Exploring National Map Projections & Defining a Custom CRS

- Task 4 – Exploring State Map Projections & Layer Reprojection

- Task 5 - Exploring the Universal Transverse Mercator (UTM) Coordinate System

3.2 Objective: Explore and Understand Map Projections and Coordinate Systems

The map projection is a fundamental part of the mapping process, and provides the backbone, or framework, for the map. It is important for the GIS Specialist to understand the qualities of the mapped region that are preserved by a given projection, and the qualities that will be distorted or skewed. Additionally, for cartographers, selection of an appropriate map projection is a crucial part of the map design process. This is because we are all used to seeing different parts of the world mapped using specific standard projections that make these areas "look right."

The transformation of the ellipsoid shape of the earth onto a two-dimensional surface cannot be accomplished without some element of distortion, through shearing, tearing, or compression. For mapping small Earth areas (large-scale mapping), projection is not a major issue, but as the scale becomes smaller, as in the mapping of continents or subcontinents, distortion becomes a significant factor.

Projections have two main characteristics: the developable surface and the properties it maintains. There are three main developable surfaces: Cones (conic projections), Cylinders (cylindrical projections), and Planes (azimuthal projections). You can see examples of these here: https://en.wikipedia.org/wiki/Map_projection. Properties maintained can include: Equal Area, Conformal (maintains shapes), Equidistant (maintains correct scale along one or two lines), and Azimuthal (maintains directions/azimuths). The names of many projections include these characteristics. Albers Equal Area Conic maintains areas and is based on a conic developable surface.

Distortion of area, shape, distance, and direction are important properties to consider. For example when making a map that displays density you should use a projection that is equal area. This is because density is a value per area (people per square kilometer) and to accurately portray the data an equal area projection should be used. There is no perfect projection. It is impossible for one projection to maintain all of these properties simultaneously.

Equal-area (or equivalent) maps, for example, preserve area relationships, but tend to lose conformality (preservation of shape). Conformal projections, on the other hand, maintain shape over small areas but produce areal distortion. In thematic mapping, it is important to maintain correct area properties. Therefore, shape is at times compromised through the choice of an equivalent projection. For small-scale maps, in fact, conformality cannot be maintained over the entire area; rather, the projection may preserve shape best along a standard line, with shape distortion increasing with distance from the line. Another property to consider is distance preservation (equidistance), which preserves distance measurements along great circle arcs. Finally, direction preservation (azimuthality) maintains correct direction from one central point to all other points.

There are hundreds of possible projections from which to choose. Some distort less in certain ways than others. It is up to the map designer to select the projection that produces the least amount of unwanted distortion. Many software packages now allow the GIS specialist to easily switch between various projections, allowing the choice of the one most appropriate. In the selection of a projection, several key elements must be considered:

- Projection properties - Are the properties of the projection suitable to the map's purpose? Considering the properties of shape, distance, direction, and area, which ones must be preserved, and which can be sacrificed? Or is compromise of all four the best choice?

- Deformational patterns - Is the amount of deformation acceptable?

- Projection center - Can the projection be centered easily on the area being mapped?

- Familiarity - Is the appearance of the map recognizable to the map reader or will it detract from the map's purpose?

3.3 Task 1 - Setting Map Projections and Coordinate Systems in QGIS

In this task, you will explore the effects of various projections on the characteristics of a map. We will focus primarily on shape and area distortions. We will examine projections useful for mapping on the global scale.

1. Open QGIS Desktop.

2. Open QGIS 3.x. and then open World View.qgz (Figure 3.1, on the facing page).

There are are two polygon themes, Circles and Land, a point theme, Cities, and a line theme, Graticule. If these circles were displayed on a globe they would be perfect circles. Here you can begin to visualize the distortion in the projection by the distortion in the Circles theme. This map is is a geographic coordinate system and is considered unprojected. The display is essentially a Plate Carrée projection. The software is using latitude and longitude measured in geodetic decimal degrees, which displays a simple rectangular coordinate system in which the length of one degree of longitude is consistently equal to one degree of latitude. With a projection that preserves shape, the polygons on the Circles theme will appear as true circles. In In a Plate Carrée projection, linear scale, area, and shape are all distorted increasingly toward the poles as demonstrated with the Circles theme.

The circles will be used in this exercise for illustrating the area and shape distortion that occurs with various projections. While this method does not actually quantify the distortion, as does Tissot's indicatrix[1], it does visually demonstrate the skewing, tearing, and shearing that occurs with certain projections.

First we will examine the map units and distance units set for this *unprojected* map.

---

[1]https://en.wikipedia.org/wiki/Tissot%27s_indicatrix

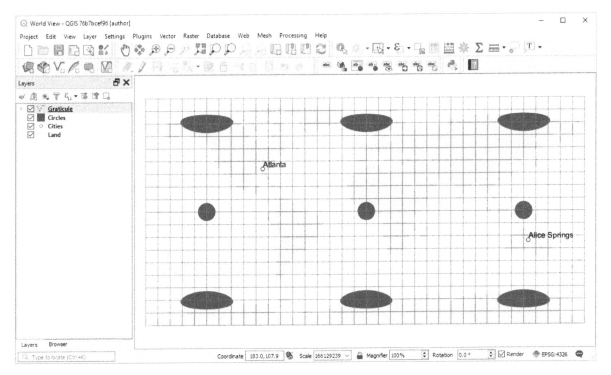

Figure 3.1: World View QGIS Project

3. Click the Current CRS 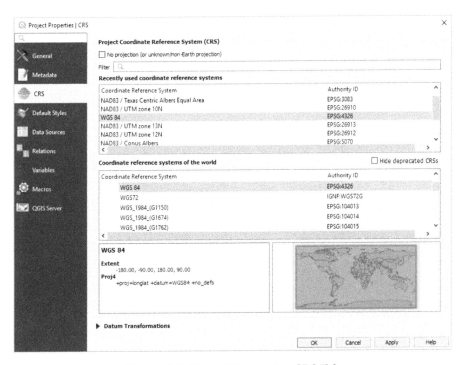 button to open the Project Properties window open to the CRS tab (Figure 3.2).

Figure 3.2: Project Properties CRS Tab

Notice that the selected coordinate system is set to WGS 84, which is an unprojected coordinate system. Also notice the valid extents preview. This is present in all CRS windows. It shows the valid spatial envelope for this CRS. Since this is a geographic coordinate system it is valid globally.

4. Click Cancel to close the Project Properties window.

Now we will do some distance measurements on this map for later comparison to maps in which a projection is set.

5. Click on the Measure Line ☷ tool on the Attributes Toolbar. The Measure box window will open (Figure 3.3).

Figure 3.3: Measure Tools

6. Set the units to kilometers. Click on the point for Atlanta, in the United States.

7. Move the cursor to the point for Alice Springs, Australia, then right-click to end the line. The distance between Atlanta and Alice Springs will be displayed in metric in the Measure box (Figure 3.4).

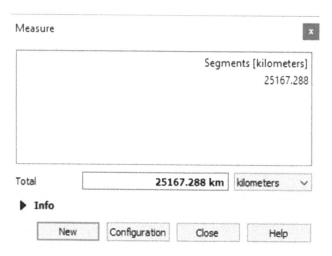

Figure 3.4: First Measurement

The measured distance is about 25,300 kilometers (your distance will vary slightly). This is not the actual distance between Atlanta and Alice Springs. With a geographic coordinate system QGIS defaults to Planimetric measurements. In other words the earth is not treated as a spheroid. QGIS measured directly between Atlanta and Alice Springs (along your measure line) heading east from Atlanta. What it should do is measure to Alice Springs by heading west from Atlanta instead of east, since heading west is a shorter distance. However, QGIS does not know that the *World is round*. This geographic CRS does not maintain spherical distance measurements, and distorts shape, direction and area.

You need to tell QGIS that you are, in fact, working with a world-based coordinate system and wish to measure on a round world.

8. From the menu bar, select Project | Project Properties. Select the General tab.

9. In the Measurements section set the Ellipsoid to WGS 84. Click OK to close Project Properties.

10. Using the Measure Line 📏 tool, again measure the distance between Atlanta and Alice Springs again (Figure 3.5).

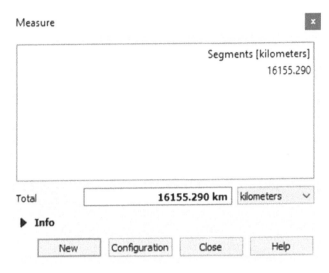

Figure 3.5: Second Measurement

The measured distance is about 16,000 kilometers (your distance will vary slightly). This is the actual distance between Atlanta and Alice Springs. This view maintains spherical distance measurements, but still distorts shape, direction, and area.

Next you will change the projection on this view to the Mercator projection.

11. Click the Current CRS 🌐 EPSG:4326 button to open the Project Properties window open to the 🌐 CRS tab.

12. In the Filter box, type in 3395, which is the EPSG code for the WGS 84 / World Mercator projected coordinate system. This filters the long list of Coordinate Reference Systems so we can easily find the one we are searching for.

EPSG Codes are unique codes for each projection/coordinate system. To learn more about EPSG codes, visit http://www.epsg.org/.

13. Select WGS 84 / World Mercator from the filtered Coordinate reference systems of the world list (Figure 3.6).

Figure 3.6: WGS84 World Mercator Selected

14. Click OK to view the map. You should see the map shown in the figure 3.7, on the following page.

The Mercator projection, a conformal projection (except at the poles), has straight meridians and parallels that intersect at right angles. Scale is truest along the equator, and becomes more distorted at higher latitudes, as evidenced by the increasing size of the circles. The Mercator projection was designed for marine navigation and gives all straight lines on the map as lines of constant compass bearing. For global scale thematic maps, however, the Mercator has too much areal distortion for accurate use.

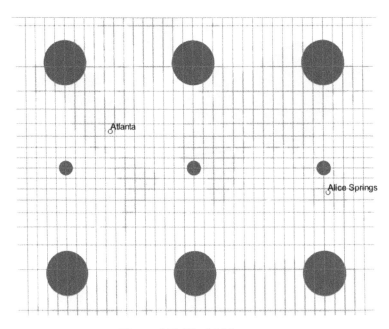

Figure 3.7: World Mercator

The Mercator is best for larger scale projections of areas at low latitude. Small-scale maps have much distortion of area and distance.

The Mercator map is much less desirable for mapping continents than other projections as it has significant distortion and can promote geographical misconceptions. In general, rectangular maps are not recommended for use in mapping the world. Equivalency (the property of equal area) and conformality are better preserved using non-rectangular maps. Task 2 will examine a map projection more suitable for mapping the world.

Keep the World View.qgz project open, it will be used in Task 2 as well.

3.4   Task 2 - Exploring World Map Projections

In this task you will examine a map projection more suitable for mapping the entire world: the Eckert IV projection. This projection is an equal-area pseudocylindrical map projection with straight parallel latitude lines and equally spaced meridians.

Here you will change the projection to Eckert IV:

1. Open Project Properties and again select the CRS tab.

2. In the Filter box, type in *Eckert*. This filters the long list of Coordinate Reference Systems so we can easily find the one we are searching for by name.

3. Select World Eckert IV (EPSG:54012) from the filtered Coordinate Reference System list. Click OK to view the map. You should see the map shown in the figure 3.8, on the next page.

The Eckert IV is useful for world maps as it is equal-area and is pleasing to the eye. Its standard parallels are at 40° 30'N and 40° 30'S. This map is only distortion free where the standard parallels intersect the central meridian.

We will see how the distance property fares.

4. Using the Measure tool, measure the distance from Atlanta to Alice Springs.

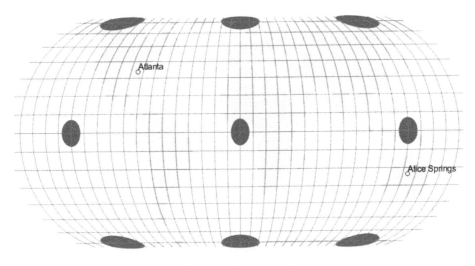

Figure 3.8: Eckert IV

The distance measures approximately 20,848 kilometers. The Eckert IV is therefore not an equidistant projection and should not be used for distance measurement.

Did you know that QGIS supports the new Equal Earth Projection? This is a special projection that is quickly becoming a standard for global maps. It is unique because it is a global projection which maintains equal areas. In the next task you will learn how to define a custom CRS. To set up QGIS with the Equal Earth projection, 1) from the menu bar choose *Settings | Custom Projections*. Create a custom definition with this string *+proj=eqearth +datum=WGS84 +wktext*, 2) Select the new CRS, which you will find under *User Defined Coordinate Systems*.

3.5   Task 3 - Exploring National Map Projections & Defining a Custom CRS

Projections suitable for mapping the world are not necessarily the best for mapping smaller areas, such as continents or countries. When mapping at such a scale in the mid-latitudes it is important to use a projection that centers on the area being mapped and has a standard line, or lines, passing through the area being mapped.

In this task, you will look at a map of the contiguous United States using a few different projections.

Exploring Different National CRS's

1. In QGIS, open the Country View.qgz project (figure 3.9, on the following page).

Country View.qgz is an unprojected map of the lower 48 states. The project has three layers: United States, LA & NYC, and Circle (centered on -97.50, 39.00). You can see it does not look quite right given the default projection. The circle shows some obvious skewing.

The distance property is more difficult to judge. The known distance between Los Angeles and New York is approximately 3,962 kilometers. We can see how the unprojected map controls distance distortion.

2. As before, use the Measure tool to measure the distance between Los Angeles and New York City in kilometers.

The measurement will should be about 3,962 kilometers. Remember, for this projection in QGIS, coordinates are treated as spherical latitude and longitude. Distance is calculated as if along a great circle arc and so the actual ground distance is preserved. Shape and areal properties, however, are distorted.

Now we will project the data using the Eckert IV projection. The Eckert IV did a nice job with the whole world, but we will see how it fares with a single mid-latitude country.

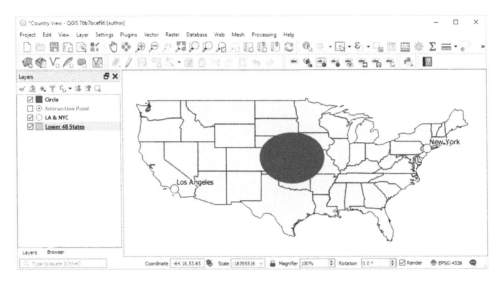

Figure 3.9: Eckert IV

3. Open the Project Properties and select the CRS tab. Choose World_Eckert_IV from the recently used coordinate reference systems box.

4. Click OK to set the CRS. You may need to click the Zoom Full 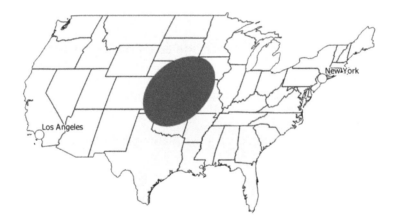 tool (Ctrl + Shift + F) to see the lower 48 states (figure 3.10).

Figure 3.10: Eckert IV Applied the USA

Defining a Custom CRS

There clearly is a great deal of distortion using this projection, most obviously the shearing. Part of the problem lies in the fact that this projection is centered at 0 degrees longitude. We can center the projection on the United States by creating a custom CRS based on the World_Eckert_IV projection.

1. From the menu bar choose Settings | Custom Projections.... This will open the Custom Coordinate Reference System Definition window.

2. Click the Copy parameters from existing CRS [icon] button to open the Coordinate Reference System Selector window.

3. Select World_Eckert_IV from the Recently used coordinate reference systems list (figure 3.11).

Figure 3.11: Eckert IV CRS in the CRS Selector

4. Click OK to return to the Custom Coordinate Reference System Definition window. The Parameters section will now be filled with the copied CRS parameters.

You need to change the central meridian so that the projection is centered at -96.000 degrees longitude instead of 0.000. This will center the projection down the middle of the country.

5. To accomplish this, replace lon_0=0 with lon_0=-96.0 (thus replacing the central meridian of 0 with -96.0). The CRS Parameters should now look like: +proj=eck4 +lon_0=-96.0 +x_0=0 +y_0=0 +datum=WGS84 +units=m +no_defs.

6. In the Name box, enter USA_Eckert_IV. This will serve as the name for your new Custom CRS (shown in figure 3.12).

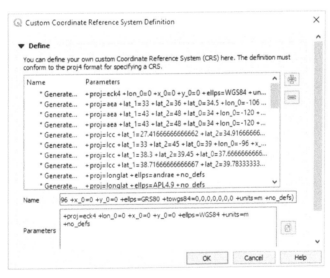

Figure 3.12: Eckert IV CRS in the CRS Selector

7. Click OK.

Your custom CRS is now added to QGIS Desktop for us to use. You can then choose your USA_Eckert_IV projection to see how it projects our map.

8. Click the Current CRS ⊕ EPSG:54012 button to open the Project Properties window open to the ⊕ CRS tab.

9. In the Coordinate reference systems of the world list, scroll all the way to the bottom until you see the User Defined Coordinate Systems section.

10. Expand the User Defined Coordinate Systems entry and choose USA_Eckert_IV. Click OK to apply the CRS.

11. You may need to click the Zoom Full ⊞ button to have the states fill the map canvas (figure 3.13).

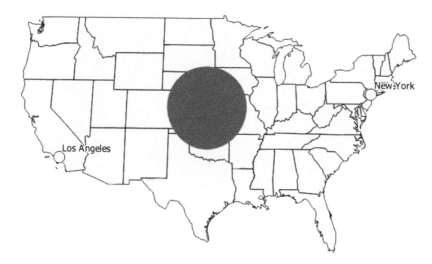

Figure 3.13: Custom Eckert IV USA CRS

This is a distinct improvement in shape, but there is still some skewing. The Eckert IV projection is primarily used for mapping the entire world. For mapping large countries, at mid-latitudes, such as the United States, other projections are more appropriate.

The Lambert azimuthal, Albers equal-area, Bonne equal-area, and Lambert conformal conic projections are examples of suitable projections for mapping east-west oriented continental areas like the continental U.S.

Because it has two standard parallels, the Albers equal-area projection is particularly good for larger countries with a significant east-west extent. We can also try Albers on our map.

12. Once again, click the Current CRS ⊕ USER:100000 button to open the Project Properties window open to the ⊕ CRS tab. Search for and select the USA_Contiguous_Albers_Equal_Area_Conic (EPSG: 102003) as the new project CRS. Click OK (figure 3.14).

Figure 3.14: Custom Eckert IV USA CRS

The Albers conic projection has low scale distortion for an area the size of the continental U.S. As the area being mapped decreases in size, distortion is less of an issue.

You will try another map projection to see what changes.

13. Open Project Properties again to the CRS tab, and choose USA_Contiguous_Lambert_Conformal_Conic (EPSG: 102004) as the CRS. Click OK to set the CRS.

14. You may need to Zoom Full to have the lower 48 states fill the map canvas.

Not too much changed between Albers and Lambert. They are both similar map projections. Lambert does have more options in its CRS parameters list, so let us examine the custom options so we can more fully understand what options can be set when creating a custom CRS.

15. From the menu bar again choose Settings | Custom Projections....

16. Click the Add new CRS button.

17. Click the Copy parameters from existing CRS button to open the Coordinate Reference System Selector window.

18. Select USA_Contiguous_Lambert_Conformal_Conic from the Recently used coordinate reference system list and click OK to copy the parameters.

19. Change the Name to Modified_USA_Contiguous_Lambert_Conformal_Conic. Your Custom CRS Parameters should look like the figure 3.15. Click OK to accept.

Figure 3.15: Modified USA Contiguous Lambert Conformal Conic

20. Open Project Properties and change the project projection to the newly created Modified_USA_Contiguous_Lambert_Confor Remember this will be found in the User Defined Coordinate Systems section.

QGIS uses Proj4 (https://proj4.org/) for CRS management.

Did you know that you can click on Help | About to open a window with detailed information about your QGIS version along with what libraries it is compiled against such as PROJ? (figure 3.16, on the next page)

CRS Parameters

A CRS has several components:

- Projection (Lambert, Albers etc.)

- Datum (NAD27, WGS84 etc.)

- Parameters (Central meridian, Standard parallels etc.)

- Units (decimal degrees, meters, feet etc.)

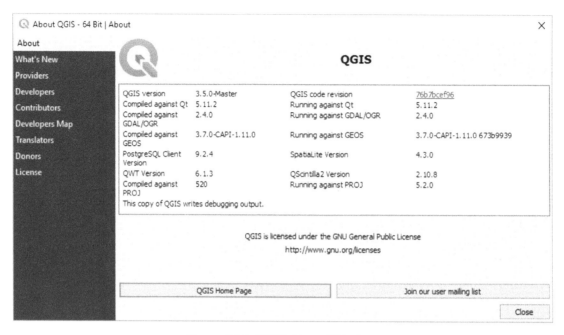

Figure 3.16: QGIS About Window

There are many ways that you can customize this CRS. This is usually done by changing the one or more of the Parameters. One common customization is centering the projection on the area of interest, for instance, a study area. In this task, the study area is the United States. To center the projection east-west you can simply redefine the central meridian. You may also want to redefine the standard parallel(s), reference latitude, or false easting and northing. The choice of parameters varies depending on which projection is being used.

In the following section these terms are defined along with where they can be modified in the CRS Parameters. Each term will be followed by the parameter in the CRS Parameters inside of parentheses.

- False easting (x_0) – the x-coordinate value for the x-origin. For example, if the central meridian for your projected map is -96.00, and the false easting is set to 0.00, then all locations along that meridian are assigned a value of 0.00. All locations to the west of the central meridian (x-origin) are assigned a negative value, and all locations to the east of the central meridian are assigned a positive value, as in a typical Cartesian plane.

- False northing (y_0) – the y-coordinate value for the y-origin. For example, if the reference latitude for a conic projection is 37.00, then all locations along that parallel are assigned a value of 0.00. All locations to the south of the reference latitude (y-origin) are assigned a negative value, and all locations to the north of the reference latitude are assigned a positive value, as in a typical Cartesian plane.

- Central meridian (lon_0) – the longitude on which a map is centered (x-origin).

- Standard parallel(s) (lat_1, lat_2) – the latitude on which a map is centered (sometimes the y-origin), or for conic projections, the parallels along which the cone touches the earth.

- Latitude of Origin (lat_0) – the latitude on which a map is centered (y-origin).

In setting map projections, the choice of spheroid, or reference ellipsoid, is also an important consideration. In this example, the spheroid is currently set to GRS_1980.

- Spheroid (ellps) – a model of the earth's shape used in transforming a projection. The reference spheroid, or ellipsoid, is generated by choosing the lengths of the major and minor axes that best fit those of the real earth. Many such models are appropriate for different locations on the earth.

Closely related to the concept of the spheroid is the concept of the datum. The North American Datum of 1927 (NAD27) uses the Clarke 1866 reference ellipsoid, whereas the North American Datum of 1983 (NAD83) uses the Geodetic Reference System (GRS) 1980 reference ellipsoid.

- Datum (datum) – selecting and orienting a specific spheroid to use for a location.

- Coordinate Units (units) – Coordinate Units are used to define distances when setting x and y coordinates.

1. In the Layers Panel, turn off the Circle layer to see southeastern Kansas, the location where the x and y origins intersect.

2. Turn on the Intersection Point layer to see where the x and y origins intersect.

3. Open Project Properties and switch to the General tab. In the Coordinate Display section change the Display coordinates using setting to Map units (meters) (figure 3.17).

Figure 3.17: Coordinate Display Settings

The Intersection Point layer represents the intersection of the x and y origins. At this point the x and y coordinates are 0.00, 0.00 (figure 3.18).

Figure 3.18: Intersection Point For X and Y CRS Origin

4. You can view the coordinates of your mouse cursor in the coordinate display box below the map canvas. Move your cursor from the point to the northeast. Both the x and y coordinates are positive. The figure 3.19) shows an example.

Figure 3.19: Coordinate Display

The values of the x and y coordinates are expressed in meters from the origin. As you move to the southwest of the intersection, the x and y coordinates are both negative. Experiment with the changing coordinate values and other projections on your own.

The conic projections function quite well for mapping the larger states in the U.S. In terms of thematic mapping, it is important that maps at this scale are equal-area. Any other properties important to the particular map should also be considered when selecting a proper projection. We will now examine projections and grid systems for large-scale maps, such as for small states, counties, or local regions.

3.6 Task 4 - Exploring State Map Projections & Layer Reprojection

The State Plane Coordinate System (SPCS) (figure 3.20) was developed to provide a simple rectangular coordinate system for large scale mapping use (i.e. small areas of the earth) within the U.S. It is largely used in surveying and engineering projects. It is also used by U.S. County governments and municipalities. Some boundaries are based on county boundaries so that each county falls entirely into a single zone. There are other countries which have developed national coordinate systems.

Figure 3.20: State Plane Coordinate System

The SPCS is a series of separate coordinate systems, each covering either an entire state, or a portion of a state. The SPCS is only used in the United States of America and, therefore, it is not appropriate to use SPCS for other countries or regions of the World. SPCS is popular due to its high accuracy in large-scale mapping because of the relatively small size of each SPCS zone. The SPCS is composed of 120 zones which follow county boundaries (except in Alaska) and often divides a state into multiple zones. There are two main projections used with the SPCS. States with a north-south axis are mapped using the Transverse Mercator projection, and designate zones between a range of 'North' and 'South' (e.g. Minnesota North). States with an east-west axis are mapped with the Lambert Conformal projection and designate zones between a range of 'East' and 'West' (e.g. New Mexico Central).

The original state plane system, developed in the 1930s, was based on the North American Datum of 1927, with coordinates measured in feet. Today the state plane system is based on the North American Datum of 1983, and coordinates are in meters.

The coordinate grids cover small areas with minimal areal or distance distortion. For small states, one grid is sufficient, while for larger states, more are required to cover the entire area. Alaska, for example, needs ten grids.

The state plane system, therefore, is only appropriate for mapping small Earth areas, such as the smallest states, city grids, or local regions. Your study area will need to fit within a State Plane Zone for this to be an appropriate choice of coordinate system. The smallest states, which only have one state plane zone, can be represented in their entirety using the SPCS.

You you will create a map display of Vermont, using the State Plane Coordinate System. Vermont is one of the smaller states and only has one state plane zone.

1. In QGIS, open the `Vermont.qgz` project (figure 3.21).

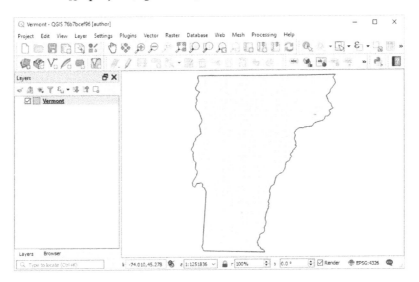

Figure 3.21: Vermont QGIS Project

2. Open Project Properties again to the CRS tab,

Note that the project projection is WGS 84 (EPSG: 4326). There is only one layer in this project and that layer also has a CRS of WGS 84 (EPSG: 4326). The QGIS project will adopt the CRS of the first layer added. That is why this project is in WGS 84 (EPSG: 4326). As you have seen you always have the option of changing the CRS of the project. If the project is in a CRS that differs from that of one or more layers, those layers will be projected on-the-fly into the CRS of the project.

To make the map of Vermont in SPCS, we have two options:

- Put the map into the NAD83 / Vermont coordinate system, EPSG: 102745.

- Project the Vermont shapefile in to NAD83 / Vermont and set the Project's coordinate system to match.

On the fly CRS transformation allows us to work with data that are in different map projections in the same QGIS Project. However, sometimes it is best to project the data in to the coordinate system we wish to map in.

Next you will project the Vermont shapefile the Vermont SPCS CRS. You will then set the Project coordinate system to match.

3. In the Layers Panel, right-click on the Vermont layer and choose Export | Save Features As... from the context menu. This opens the Save Vector Layer as... window.

4. Set the following options to project the Vermont layer, save it to a new GeoPackage, and add it to the map (figure 3.21).

a. Format = Esri Shapefile

b. Filename = Browse to the Exercise 3 folder and name the shapefile Vermont_SPCS.shp.

c. CRS = NAD_1983_StatePlane_Vermont_FIPS_4400_Feet (EPSG:102745)

d. Click OK

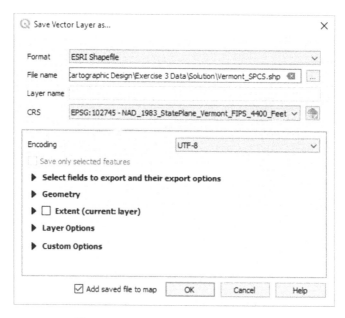

Figure 3.22: Vermont QGIS Project

5. QGIS will project the Vermont layer and add it to the map. It will look just like the existing layer, but the color of the newly-added Vermont layer may differ. Remember that styling is random on layers added to QGIS. The new layer is being reprojected on-the-fly from Vermont State Plane into WGS 84.

> Did you know QGIS 3.x allows you to run a geoprocessing algorithm such as a clip, with each layer being in a different CRS! The output CRS will match the CRS of the Input Layer.

Remember there is also a Reproject Layer geoprocessing algorithm in the Processing Toolbox in the Vector General category. In that same section of the Processing Toolbox there is a Find Projection and Assign Projection algorithms.

6. Right-click on Vermont_SPCS and choose Set CRS | Set Project CRS from Layer from the context menu.

You should now see that Vermont looks 'skinnier' as it is now being displayed in NAD1983 StatePlane Vermont FIPS 4400 Feet (EPSG:102745) and not WGS 84 (figure 3.23, on the facing page).

7. Open Project Properties and select the CRS tab.

Look at the Selected CRS Parameters at the bottom of the properties window (shown in figure 3.24, on the next page)). Note that the projection used is Transverse Mercator proj=tmerc and the scale factor is k=0.9999642857142857. The spheroid is +ellps=GRS80. The central meridian is -72.5 lon_0=-72.5 , which runs through the center of the state. The reference latitude is lat_0=42.5, which is just south of Vermont. The false easting is set to x_0=152400.3048006096, which is equivalent to 500,000 feet. The false northing is set to y_0=0. So, the false origin will be to the west (500,000 feet west of -72.5) and south (42.5) of the state of Vermont.

8. Click OK to close the Project Properties.

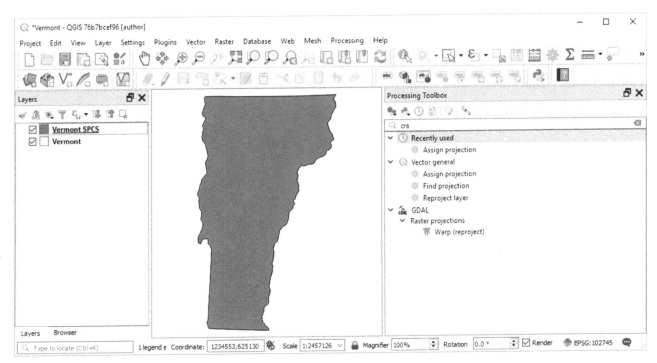

Figure 3.23: Vermont in SPCS

NAD_1983_StatePlane_Vermont_FIPS_4400_Feet

Extent
    Extent not known
Proj4
    +proj=tmerc +lat_0=42.5 +lon_0=-72.5
    +k=0.9999642857142857 +x_0=500000.0000000001 +y_0=0
    +ellps=GRS80 +units=us-ft +no_defs

Figure 3.24: Vermont SPCS Parameters

GIS layers can be removed from the Layers panel (and map window) as easily as they were added. For example, we do not need the original Vermont layer. We can just work with the version of Vermont in SPCS. To remove a layer simply right-click on it within the Layers Panel and choose Remove from the context menu. A confirmation dialog will appear. Click the OK button to confirm the removal of the layer.

9. Remove Vermont from the Layers Panel (not Vermont_SPCS!).

Scroll around the state and notice the changing coordinates. If you have a USGS topographic map of any part of Vermont, based on NAD83, the coordinates displayed here will match the UTM coordinates shown on the hardcopy map.

3.7   Task 5 - Exploring the Universal Transverse Mercator (UTM) Coordinate System

The Universal Transverse Mercator (UTM) grid (shown in the figure below) is a plane coordinate system that spans almost the entire globe. It is probably the best known plane coordinate system of international scope. For the UTM system, the globe is divided into sixty zones, each comprised of six degrees of longitude. Each zone has its own central meridian. The limits of each zone are 84 degrees north and 80 degrees south. UTM uses the Transverse Mercator projection. The zones are numbered 1 to 60, where zone 1 begins at -180° longitude and zones increase heading east back to +180° where zone 60 ends.

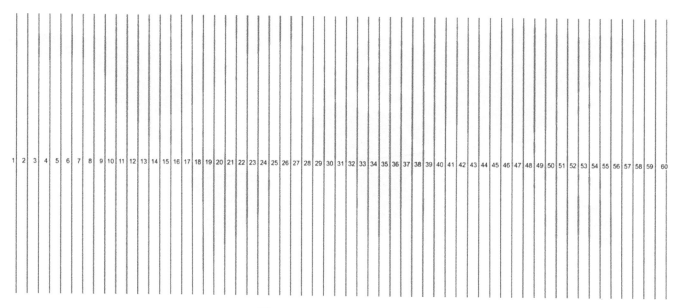

Figure 3.25: UTM Zones

1. There are separate versions of both the Country View and World View QGIS project files with a UTM Zone polygon theme. In each QGIS project document, the UTM theme is labeled with the UTM zones so you can see what zones cover your part of the country.

2. These QGIS project documents are named `World View UTM.qgz` and `Country View UTM.qgz`.

3. Using what you have learned in this exercise, experiment with the putting these UTM World and Country View maps into the UTM system.

4. Open up one of these projects.

5. Open Project Properties and open the CRS tab.

6. Via the Filter, search for *UTM*. Choose a UTM zone in your part of the country to put the map into. There are UTM definitions with different datums. Choose one from the NAD83 UTM zone projection series.

Note: Many U.S. federal agencies use this system, such as the U.S. Forest Service and the U.S. Bureau of Land Management. Like the State Plane Coordinate System, it is important that your study area fit entirely within a UTM zone.

For more information on the UTM Coordinate system, read the USGS Fact Sheet 077-01, available at `http://pubs.usgs.gov/fs/2001/0077/report.pdf`

3.8 Conclusion

In this exercise, you have explored coordinate systems and map projections. Each map projection distorts the earth differently. You are able to modify the map projections provided in QGIS to suit your mapping needs. It is important that you set the correct map projection for each data layer, and for the project.

When you import spatial data into QGIS, you must know the projection, if any, the grid system, and the datum, of your data. Mostly you will find the data in decimal degrees, that is, latitude and longitude coordinates. Base maps with underlying coordinates that are geodetic decimal degrees are the most versatile when constructing a

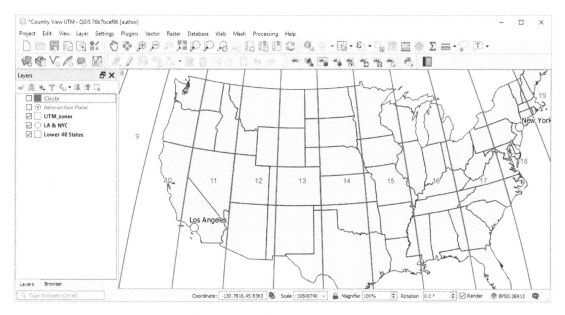

Figure 3.26: Country View UTM

map database. It is important that if you plan on doing any spatial analysis with your data, that you first project the data into the same coordinate system to get maximum accuracy.

3.9 Discussion Questions

1. Based on the world map projections covered in this exercise, which industries would best be served by each projection (provide two examples)? Does the entire industry need to agree on a single one? What problems could arise from the use of different projections?

2. Can your GIS data be in a different Coordinate Reference System than your QGIS project? Explain.

3. What UTM zone does Nevada fall into?

4. Inspect the CRS Parameters for the three Exercise 1 maps (Lower 48.qgz, Alaska.qgz, Hawaii.qgz). List the two standard parallels for each map projection. Explain why you think the standard parallels were placed where they were.

3.10 Challenge Assignment

Create a new custom CRS for the Equal Earth Projection? You will use the following projection definition: +proj=eqearth +datum=WGS84 +wktext. Using the global data in this chapter make a global map in this CRS. Turn in the final map to your instructor.

Exercise 4

Working with Labels

Objective - Learn techniques for labeling features including placement and rendering

4.1 Introduction

Labels help orient a map reader by directly tying a feature name to a feature on the map. They are very useful. When a map is well labeled you can usually minimize what is included in the legend because the map is much more intuitive to your map reading audience. There is a lot that can go into labeling features. Label placement can be complex and having labels stand out on a busy map can be tricky. In this exercise, you will learn several techniques for working with labels.

This exercise includes the following tasks:

- Task 1 - Automatic Label Placement

- Task 2 – Labeling Expressions

- Task 3 – Manually Placing Labels

- Task 4 – Working with Labels in a Print Layout

4.2 Objective: Learn techniques for labeling features including placement and rendering

4.3 Task 1 - Automatic Label Placement

In this first task, you will get familiar with label placement.

1. Open QGIS and open Iberia.qgz.

2. This is a simple map of the Iberian peninsula made with data from Natural Earth. There are layers representing the country and state boundaries, cities and rivers.

What effect was used to create the water?

3. You will begin by labeling the countries. Open the Layer Styling Panel ✍ with the target layer being Countries.

4. Switch to Labels abc tab. Click the drop-down menu which currently reads No labels and switch it to Single labels.

5. The Label with section is where you specify which attribute fields to use for labeling. Choose SOVEREIGNT. Country names will appear in a default font.

Below the Label with section is a series of tabs you can use to adjust the look and placement of your labels. The first Label text **abc** tab is where you can adjust the font settings. Change the Style to Bold.

There are a couple labels that are problematic. The label for Gibraltar which reads United Kingdom is confusing. The label for Andorra doesn't fit within the country boundaries. The label for Spain looks like it could be the label for a city.

6. Switch to the Placement ✤ tab. This allows you to adjust how the label is placed. Switch the Placement to Horizontal (slow). This setting solves the issue with the Spain label.

7. Switch to the Rendering ✐ tab. Here you will find controls for label visibility. There is a Scale dependent visibility section for setting scale thresholds for label visibility. These can be used to control where labels are visible as you zoom in and out. Find the Feature options section. Click the box for Only draw labels which fit completely within feature (figure 4.1).

Figure 4.1: Countries Labeled with Some Placement Settings

8. Another trick to assist with label readability is to use a halo around labels. The label for France is covering a river and the label for Morocco is very near a city icon. These sorts of conflicts are very distracting. Switch to the Buffer **abc** tab. Here you can create a buffer (halo) around the labels. You can control the Size, Color, Opacity and apply a Blending mode. Click the Draw text buffer box to enable buffers for these labels. You do not want the halo to have much visual weight. You want it to be unnoticeable. Instead of the default white click the color drop-down and choose Pick Color. Using the eye dropper cursor click on one of the countries to apply that color to the label buffer. Increase the Size to 2.0 (figure 4.2).

Figure 4.2: Countries Labeled with Halos

9. Next label the Rivers using the name field. Use an Arial Font and make the Style Italic. Use a dark blue Color (figure 4.3, on the facing page).

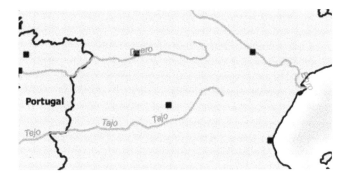

Figure 4.3: Rivers Labeled

10. One issue is that there are repeated river names (Tajo). This can often be solved by selecting the Rendering ✏ tab. Then in the Feature options section click Merge connected lines to avoid duplicate labels box. However, in this case it is due to this feature having both Rivers and Lake Centerlines represented. To deal with this situation, you will now switch this layer from Single labels to Rule-based labeling. Rule-based labeling allows you to set rules for how features are labeled. You worked with Rule-based rendering in the Atlas Generation exercise, and this is similar. Click where it reads No filter in the Rule column to open the Edit rule panel. Click the Expression button. Create this expression "featurecla" = 'River'. Give your rule the Description of *River*. Click the Go back button to return to the main labeling panel.

11. You will make one more change to how the river labels are rendered. Switch to the Placement ❖ tab and set the Placement to Curved (figure 4.4).

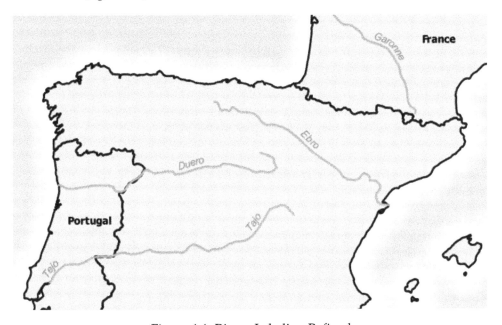

Figure 4.4: Rivers Labeling Refined

The Morocco label is still obscuring the nearby Ksar El Kebir city point. Another way to avoid label conflicts is to set another layer as a blocker. This prevents labels from being placed over those features.

12. Switch the target layer in the Layer Styling Panel to Cities.

13. On the Labeling tab switch the setting from No labels to Blocking. This will prevent the country or river labels from being rendered over City points.

14. Save your project.

4.4   Task 2 - Labeling Expressions

In this task, you will get familiar with labeling expressions. These allow you to combine multiple fields in a label. They also

1. Continue with the Iberia.qgz. QGIS project.

2. This countries dataset includes translations of the country name into different languages. Here you will label countries by their Spanish name and then the English name in parentheses.

3. Switch the target layer in the Layer Styling Panel to Countries. Click the Expression ε button the right of the Label with section to open the Expression Dialog window.

   a. Put your cursor to the left of the SOVEREIGNT field text. Expand Fields and Values and double-click on NAME_ES.

   b. To combine text elements you need to add a String Concatenation ‖ operator between them. Click on the String Concatenation ‖ operator. Now you have two fields concatenated. Look at the Output preview. They are just jammed together on the same line with no spaces.

   c. You want the English label on a second line. Click the New Line '\n' operator. Then add a second String Concatenation ‖ operator. The New Line operator is technically a piece of text and therefore also needs to be surrounded by String Concatenation operators on each side.

   d. Lastly you will place the English name (SOVEREIGNT) in parentheses. Each parenthesis is a piece of text, and therefore also needs to be surrounded by String Concatenation operators.

4. Your label expression should be: "NAME_ES" || '\n' || '(' || "SOVEREIGNT" || ')' (figure 4.5). Click OK to accept.

Figure 4.5: Labeling Expression

5. Switch to the Formatting ᵗᵃᵇ tab. Here you can control label alignment. Set the Alignment to Center. The result should be reflected on the map canvas (figure 4.6, on the next page).

There are many useful functions that can help a labeling expression. If you want to use only a portion of the text in a text field within a label you can use the substr() function to replace a word with nothing. If you are using a number in a label you can reformat it in the label expression with the format_number() function. You will use that in Part 5 - Exercise 3 - Task 3! Similarly there is an format_date() function for date fields.

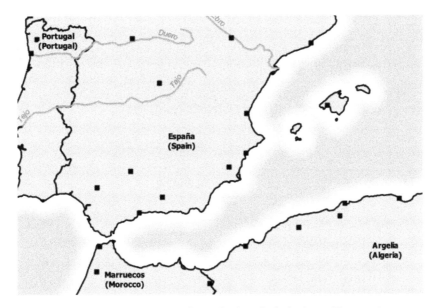

Figure 4.6: Countries with Multi-line Label via an Expression

4.5 Task 3 - Manually Placing Labels

In this first task, you will learn how to manually place labels. Sometimes no matter how many label placement options you set, you still find the need to manually place labels. Fortunately with QGIS 3.x this is very straight-forward.

1. Continue with the Iberia.qgz QGIS project.

2. Label the Cities with the NAME field (figure 4.7).

Figure 4.7: Cities Labeled

3. Another useful label placement option is wrapping labels onto a new line even if they are using just one field. Switch to the Formatting ⁺ab tab. Enter a Space for the Wrap on character. Set the Alignment to Center.

4. Switch to the Placement  tab. Change the Placement to Cartographic and the Distance to 2. This distance controls how far from the point symbol the label is placed. With larger icons, especially SVG icons, it is common to need this value increased so that there is enough separation between the label and feature.

5. These settings have helped but in this case manually placing some of these labels will be the only way to get them perfect. Make sure you have your Label toolbar enabled (figure 4.8).

Figure 4.8: Label Toolbar

6. Look for a city label you would like to move. Highlight the Cities layer in the Layers Panel. Find the Move Label and Diagram tool on the Labeling toolbar. Click on the tool and click on the label. The Auxiliary Storage: Choose Primary Key window opens. Choose the default fid field and click OK (figure 4.9). This step only needs to be done initially. Now you can click on any Cities label with the Move Label and Diagram tool and shift it's position.

Figure 4.9: Auxiliary Storage - Choose Primary Key

So how does this work? At the beginning of the workbook the QGIS project file was described. Recall that a QGIS project is saved as a *.qgs file. A new feature of QGIS 3 is that a project database (*.qgd) is also saved with the project. The *.qgd file is a spatialite database. At QGIS 3.2 projects began being saved as *.qgz files. These are zipped project files that contain both the *.qgs and *.qgd files.

These label positions are stored in the project database. They are joined to your layer without you having to manage any of it. These label positions are stored in the project.

7. Switch to the Placement tab. Notice that in the Data Defined section the Data Defined Overrides for Coordinate X and Y are active (yellow). Click the Data Defined Override to see the context menu. Notice that the option Store Data in the Project is checked.

Before this development it was still possible to create custom label positions. Prior to QGIS 3.x this was done by pointing that same Data Defined Override for Coordinate X and Y to attribute columns in the layer. That method is still possible. However, this new method is preferable because the coordinates are stored in the project versus the layer.

8. Now open Layer Properties for the Cities layer and select the Auxiliary Storage Auxiliary Storage tab. Here you can see the columns set up when you chose the primary key before moving the first label.

The map should resemble something like the figure 4.10, on the next page) below.

9. Save your project.

Figure 4.10: City Labels Moved

4.6 Task 4 - Working with Labels in a Print Layout

In this final task, you will learn about a new feature that allows you to set Print Layout objects as label blockers. This means you can control how map labels interact with a legend or title box. Note that there are features in the task that require QGIS v3.6 or later.

1. Continue with the `Iberia.qgz` QGIS project.

2. Set up a basic Print Layout like the figure 4.11).

Figure 4.11: Basic Print Layout with Title and Legend

3. Despite having set up labels carefully in QGIS Desktop, it is still common to have labels falling off the edge of a Print Layout. Fortunately, you can control that. Bring up the main QGIS Desktop window. In the Layers Styling Panel set the target layer to the Cities layer. To the right of the Label with option find and click the Automated Placement Settings 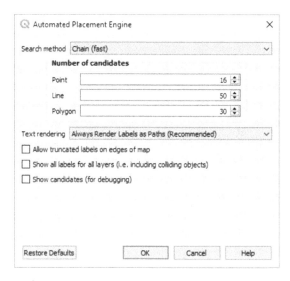 button. The Automated Placement Engine window opens. Uncheck Allow truncated labels on edges of map option (Figure 4.12). Notice that there is also a Search method option. Click OK.

Figure 4.12: Automated Placement Engine Window

4. Bring up the Print Layout again. This should have helped with any labels near the edge.

5. Now you will learn how to set individual map objects as label blockers. Select the map object. Click the Label Settings button and the Label Settings panel will open.

6. In the Label Blocking Items section, click the box for the Legend (Figure 4.13).

Figure 4.13: Label Blocking Items in the Print Layout

7. Now drag and drop the Legend over different portions of the Print Layout with labels. Notice how they moved! Below the Legend was placed where the Algeria label had been (Figure 4.14, on the next page).

4.7   Conclusion

In this exercise, you learned the many ways labels can be manipulated. Configuring and placing labels can be time consuming. However, there are some very convenient label manipulation tools available.

4.8   Discussion Questions

1. How can labeling features impact what is included in a legend?

2. Describe some of the techniques you can use to automatically place labels?

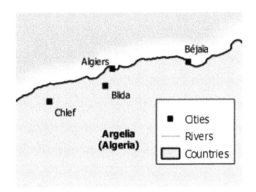

Figure 4.14: The Legend as a Label Blocker

3. How can blend modes help make halos more discreet?

Exercise 5

Creating a Colorful U.S. State Map with Expression-based Symbols

Objective - Design and construct a colorful map of the USA.

5.1   Introduction

In this exercise, you will use some styling tricks to create a modern take on this historic colorful U.S. State map downloaded from `https://wmasteros.co.` (`http://bit.ly/2EiZ8lt`)

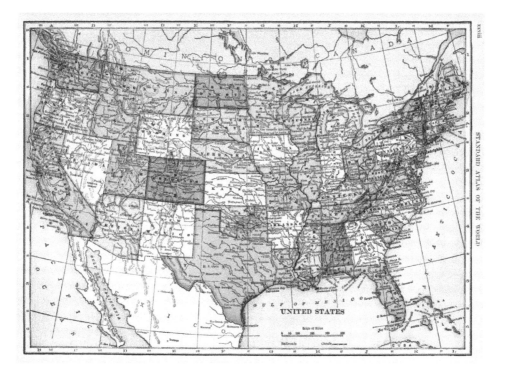

Figure 5.1: Historic USA Map

This exercise includes the following tasks:

- Task 1 – Implementing Topological Coloring
- Task 2 – Implementing Shapeburst Fills

317

- Task 3 – Creating a Random Dot Boundary Using a Marker Line and a Data Defined Override
- Task 4 – Finishing Touches
- Challenge: Repeat with World Countries or National Administration Areas

5.2   Objective: Design and construct a colorful map of the USA.

To design and construct a colorful map of the USA using some tricks. This exercise will include learning about the Topological Coloring processing algorithm, using expression based symbology, duplication of layers, and shapeburst fills.

5.3   Task 1 - Implementing Topological Coloring

In this first task, you will use the Topological Coloring tool.

1. Open QGIS 3.x and use the Browser Panel to drag and drop the USA/USA.gpkg layer onto the map canvas.

2. Now you will use a cartographic tool introduced to QGIS at version 3.0, the Topological Coloring tool. This tool computes a color index for a layer in such a way that no adjacent polygons (States) share the same color index, while minimizing the number of colors required.

3.   Find the tool in the Processing Toolbox and set it up as shown in the figure 5.2. Notice that the tool is in the Cartography section of the Processing Toolbox. Save the output to the same geopackage with the new layer named: statesColored. To do this click on the ellipsis button to the right of the Colored output and choose Save to Geopackage. Browse to the USA.gpkg and select it. Then name the layer statesColored. Run the tool.

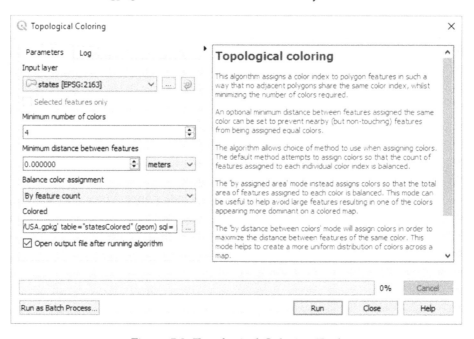

Figure 5.2: Topological Coloring Tool

4. Save your map document as ColorfulStates.qgz.

5. Open the attribute table for the new layer.

What new attribute column is added?

6. Turn the original states layer off and move the statesColored layer to the top of the Layers Panel.

7. **NOTE:** The output layer may be named `statesColored` or `Colored` depending on your Processing settings. Click `Settings | Options | Processing` and expand the General section. You can choose to Use filename as layer name or not. Here the instructions are based on using the filename as the layer name.

8. Open the Layer Styling Panel ✎ with the target layer being `statesColored`.

9. Change the symbology for the `statesColored` layer. Use a Categorized renderer against the new column, using the default random colors (figure 5.3).

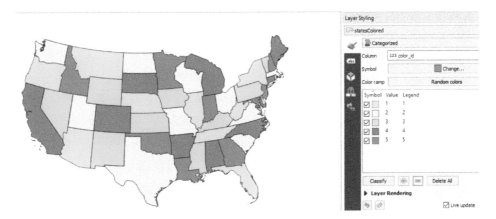

Figure 5.3: States with Topological Coloring

10. Note if you are not happy with the initial set of random colors, you can click the dropdown for the Color Ramp and choose Shuffle Random Colors from the context menu until you get a set you like (figure 5.4).

Figure 5.4: Shuffle Random Colors

11. Save your project.

5.4   Task 2 - Implementing Shapeburst Fills

In this next task, you create a second copy of the topologically colored layer and work with shapeburst fills.

1. Open QGIS and open `ColorfulStates.qgz` if it is not already.

2. Right-click on the layer named `statesColored` and choose Duplicate to make another copy of it. The new copy will be named `statesColored copy`. Turn off the layer named `statesColored` and turn on the duplicated layer so that now the only layer turned on is `statesColored copy`.

3. Now you will work with the statesColored copy layer. Make sure that the target layer in the Layer Styling Panel is statesColored copy.

    a. Click the Change button (figure 5.5). This button lets you change parameters for all the classes at once.

    b. Select Simple fill

    c. Change the Symbol layer type to Shapeburst fill.

    d. Click Set distance and set the value to 4.

    e. Click the Go back ◀ arrow to return to the main symbol window (figure 5.6).

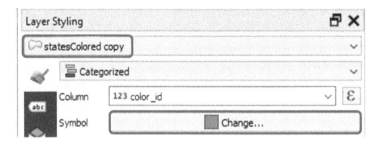

Figure 5.5: Master Change Button

4. Save your project.

Figure 5.6: States with Topological Coloring and a Shapeburst Fill

5.5 Task 3 - Creating a Random Dot Boundary Using a Marker Line and a Data Defined Override

In this next task, you will create another copy of the states layer and give it a random dot boundary symbol. For this you will use a Data Defined Override with an expression.

1. Open QGIS and open `ColorfulStates.qgz` if it is not already.

2. Duplicate the `statesColored copy` layer. The result will be named `statesColored copy copy`. Turn on this new copy and make it the top most layer in the Layers Panel.

3. Make sure the target layer in the Layer Styling Panel is `statesColored copy copy`.

    a. Change to a Single symbol renderer

    b. Select Shapeburst fill

    c. Change the Symbol layer type to Outline: Marker line (figure 5.7).

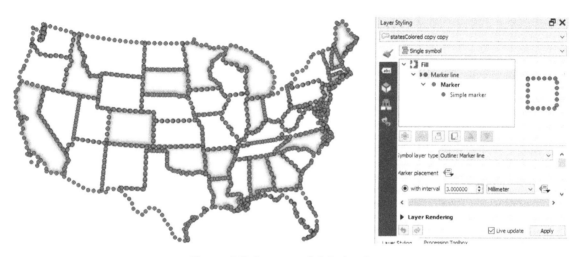

Figure 5.7: States with Marker Line

4. Now you will refine the Outline: Marker line

    a. Select the Marker line symbology component

    b. Set the with interval to 0.2. This parameter controls the spacing of the marker points. Here you are making them more dense.

    c. Next select the Simple marker component and find the Offset section. Offset controls how far a marker line point will be from the polygon boundary.

    d. Notice the series of Data Defined Override icons along the right side of the Layer Styling Panel. There is a lot of power in these Data Defined Overrides and they are available in many places. You can use them to point a symbology parameter to an attribute column containing values to be used for a particular symbol element. Or you can use them to enter an expression for a particular symbol element. Here you will do the latter for the Offset.

    e. Click on the Data Defined Override and from the context menu choose Edit. The Expression String Builder window will open.

    f. Enter the following expression `concat('0,',3 * randf(0,1) ^ 3)` and click OK.

g. About now the map is looking crazy but you are just about to finish this effect. Set the Simple marker Size to 0.2.

h. Set the Fill color to dark gray (i.e., RGB – 100 | 100 | 100)

i. Set the Stroke color to the same dark gray.

j. Click the Go back ◁ arrow to return to the main symbol window(figure 5.8).

Figure 5.8: Random Dot Boundary Complete

So what did that expression do? It feeds the Offset parameter for the Marker line a random number value with some limits. The random number is from 0 to 3 * a random floating point number between 0 and 1 to the third power. Concat() merges strings together. Randf() returns a random floating point number. This is just a taste of what can be done with Data Defined Overrides and expressions in QGIS. You learn more use cases for these in Part 5 - Exercise 4 - Mapping Photopoints.

> Note a new feature in QGIS 3.6 Noosa is a *Project Colors* section in data defined buttons which are linked to a color value. The color menu contains all colors defined as part of the current project's Project Color Scheme (which is defined through Project Properties).

5. Save your project.

5.6   Task 4 - Finishing Touches

In this final task, you will finalize your colorful map.

1. Open QGIS and open ColorfulStates.qgz if it is not already.

2. Turn on the original topologically colored `statesColored` layer. Move it so that it is above the `statesColored` `copy` layer (shapeburst fill) and below the `statesColored` `copy` `copy` layer (random dot boundary).

    a. Give it a Layer Blending mode of Multiply.

    b. Give it an Opacity of 25%

3. Turn on the `statesColored` `copy` layer (shapeburst fill).

    a. Give it a Layer Blending mode of Multiply

    b. Give it an Opacity of 80%

4. Now using QuickMapServices the Google road layer. Your map should resemble the figure 5.9.

Figure 5.9: Final Historic Colorful Map Effect

5.7 Challenge Assignment

Repeat with World Countries or National Administration Areas

Use these techniques to create a colorful map of the world, or of another countries administrative areas. If you choose the latter option, select the administration areas for that country from the `Countries_States_Provinces` layer and export the selected features to a new layer. You will find these data in the `Challenge` folder in the `WorldCountries.gpkg`.

5.8 Conclusion

In this exercise, you learned some more advanced cartographic techniques involving different Symbol layer types (Shapeburst fills and Marker lines) and Data Defined Overrides with an expression. This is a great segue to the Advanced Data Visualization section of this workbook. There you will learn more advanced cartographic techniques.

Part V

Advanced Data Visualization

Exercise 1

Using Live Layer Effects

Objective – Learn About Special Effects Available via Live Layer Effects

1.1   Introduction

Up to this point you have seen a couple examples of Live Layer Effects being used. This exercise will provide a fuller introduction to one of the unique and powerful data styling features found in QGIS: Live Layer Effects. This feature allows you to add effects such as drop shadows, inner glows and outer glows to your vector features. Each effect has parameters you can use to customize it. These will allow you to create some truly stunning cartographic visuals.

This exercise includes the following tasks:

- Task 1 – Exploring Live Layer Effects

- Task 2 – Lifting Features Off of a Busy Background

- Task 3 – Neon Cartography

- Task 4 – Bathymetry

1.2   Objective: Learn About Special Effects Available via Live Layer Effects

In this exercise, you will explore Live Layer Effects and learn some use cases for them.

1.3   Task 1 - Exploring Live Layer Effects

In this first task, you will get familiar with the different effects available and how to work with them.

1. Open QGIS 3.x and open the `LiveLayerEffects.qgz` project. The map canvas is zoomed into one food dessert in Baltimore City, Maryland, USA. You will use this as a playground for learning about Live Layer Effects.

2. Open the Layer Styling Panel 🖌 .

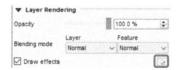

Figure 1.1: Enabling Draw Effects

3. Expand the Layer Rendering section and check the box for Draw effects. To the right a small yellow star icon 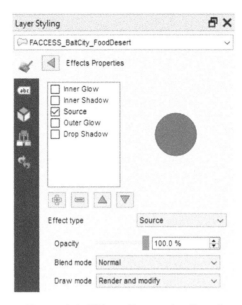 will become active. (Figure 1.1, on the preceding page)

4. Click on the Customise effects [ ] icon to open the Live Layer Effects panel (Figure 1.2).

Figure 1.2: Effects Properties Panel

5. Click on Drop Shadow (Figure 1.3). Notice that you can control the Offset, Blur radius, Opacity, Color, Blend mode and Draw mode of the drop shadow effect! Those parameters relate to whichever effect you have selected (highlighted) in the list above.

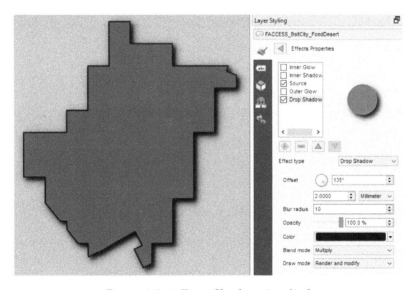

Figure 1.3: A Drop Shadow Applied

6. You can also use multiple effects simultaneously. Check Outer Glow so that you have that enabled along with Drop Shadow.

7. The Source effect is the current symbology of the feature not including effects. If you turn off Source you will be left with just the Drop Shadow and Outer Glow (Figure 1.4, on the next page).

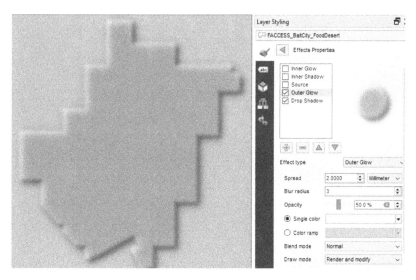

Figure 1.4: Source Turned Off

8. Notice the Effect type menu. In addition to the popular effects listed in the box above, this list includes Blur, Transform and Colorise. If you choose Blur, Transform or Colorise that effect will replace which ever effect you had selected (highlighted) in the list above (Figure 1.5).

Figure 1.5: Effect Types

9. Highlight Outer Glow in the list box and then go to the Effect type menu and choose Blur. Turn off the Drop Shadow effect so that you just have Blur and Source. Now highlight Blur so that you can see the properties of the Blur effect in the panel. Set the Blur Strength to 10 (Figure 1.6).

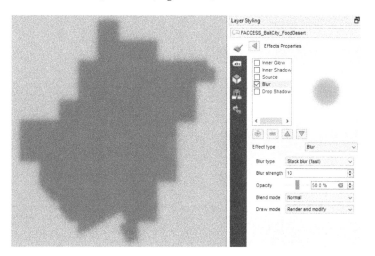

Figure 1.6: Blur Effect

10. Continue to experiment with these effects until you feel comfortable manipulating them.

11. Close QGIS.

1.4   Task 2 - Lifting Features Off of a Busy Background

In this first task, you will learn how to use Live Layer Effects to lift features off of a busy basemap. This is probably the most commonly use case. One of the most important cartographic principles is to focus the map readers attention on the topic of the map. This can be difficult when a basemap is also needed or wanted.

1. Open QGIS 3.x and open the `BaltimoreClinics.qgz` project. This is a simple map with the Baltimore City boundary and Dialysis Clinic points.

2. Use QuickMapServices to add the `Web | QuickMapServices | Google | Google Satellite` basemap to QGIS. The image provides nice context to the map but is dark and saturated making it difficult to see the features.

3. Use LiveLayerEffects to add a Outer Glow with default settings to the Baltimore City Boundary.

4. Next add a Drop Shadow with an Offset of 1mm to the Dialysis Clinics (Figure 1.7). This helps these features stand out more. Obviously there are more than one technique that can be used to make features more visible. Live Layer Effects can be a great solution in this circumstance.

Figure 1.7: Lifting Features Off a Busy Basemap

5. Save your project and close QGIS.

1.5   Task 3 - Neon Cartography

In this task, you will use Live Layer Effects to create a neon effect.

1. Open QGIS 3.x and open the Neon.qgz project. This map contains airports, flight paths and U.S. States.

2. **You will begin by working on the airport symbology.**

   a. Select the SVG marker component of the symbol. Change the Fill Color of the SVG symbol to this RGB value: 255 | 0 | 254.
   b. Change the Stroke Width to 0.2
   c. Select the Marker component of the symbol. Change the Size to 10.
   d. Apply a default Drop Shadow. (Figure 1.8)

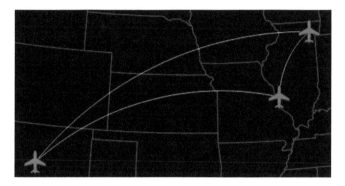

Figure 1.8: Pink Airports

3. **Next you will work on the Flight Paths.**

   a. Change the Color to the same RGB value (255 | 0 | 254) used for the airports. The easiest way to do this is to click the drop down color menu and choose this color from the Recent colors section.
   b. Change the Stroke Width to 1.26.
   c. Apply an Outer Glow.
   d. Now you will configure the Outer Glow. Increase the Spread to 6.
   e. Keep the Blur radius at 3.
   f. Choose the Color ramp option and click the drop-down color ramp menu and choose Create New Color Ramp.
   g. The Color ramp type window will open. Choose Gradient as the type and click OK.
   h. The Select Color Ramp window will open. Set Color 1 to the same hot pink you have used (RGB 255 | 0 | 254). Again you can pick this from the Recent colors section. Set Color 2 as black (RGB 0 | 0 | 0). You are setting Color 2 to match the fill color of the States layer. Set the Type as Continuous. Click OK to accept the changes and dismiss the Select Color Ramp window.

4. Finally to complete the neon effect you will add another Symbol Layer to the Flight Paths. Click the Go back ◁ button to return to the main symbology panel for the layer.

5. Click the Add Symbol Layer ⊞ button to add a second Simple Line to the layers symbol. Make sure it is above the previous symbol by using the Move Symbol Up/Down ▲ ▼ buttons. Select the new Simple Line and assign it a lighter pink color (RBG 255 | 185 | 255). Give it a Stroke Width of 0.46 (Figure 1.9, on the following page).

6. Save your project and close QGIS.

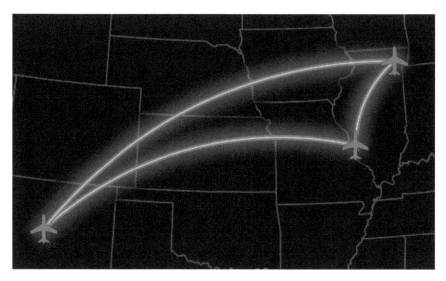

Figure 1.9: Neon Flight Paths

1.6   Task 4 - Bathymetry

In this final task, you see how to use Live Layer Effects to create a 3D looking map of bathymetry.

1. Open QGIS 3.x and open the Bathymetry.qgz project. This map contains individual bathymetry layers from the Natural Earth data. Each layer represents an ocean depth. There is also a shaded relief layer and a land layer.

2. Open the Layer Styling Panel ✎ and set the target layer to ne_10m_bathymetry_L_0.

3. Expand Layer Rendering and just activate Draw Effects. An effect has already been created, you will just enable it beginning here with the bottom most bathymetry layer. Continue doing this for each Bathymetry layer. As you do this watch the map carefully to see the effect being created as you continue enabling Draw Effects.(Figure 1.10, on the next page)

4. Open the effect properties for one of these layers to see what the effect is. It is an Inner Shadow effect.(Figure 1.11, on the facing page)

5. Finally set the target layer in the Styling Panel to the Land layer. Expand Layer Rendering and set a Layer Blending mode of Multiply. Blending modes are available in other graphic software and allow you to visually blend a layer with layers below it. Here you are applying a Blending mode to Land which allows you to see the full detail of the shaded relief below. You will explore Blending modes in more detail in the next exercise. (Figure 1.12, on page 334)

1.7   Conclusion

In this exercise, you have learned the basics of working with Live Layer Effects to achieve special cartographic looks. You have also seen some specific use cases for several effects. You have also been introduced to Blending modes which you will explore in much more detail in the next exercise.

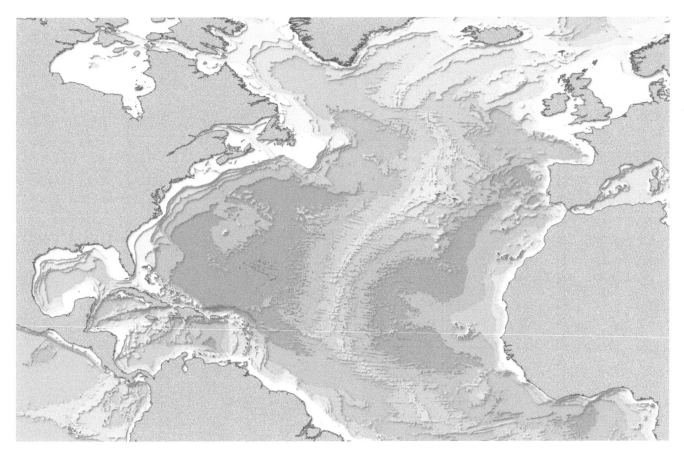

Figure 1.10: Bathymetry with Inner Shadows

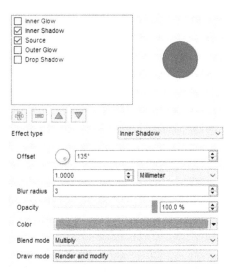

Figure 1.11: Inner Shadow Settings

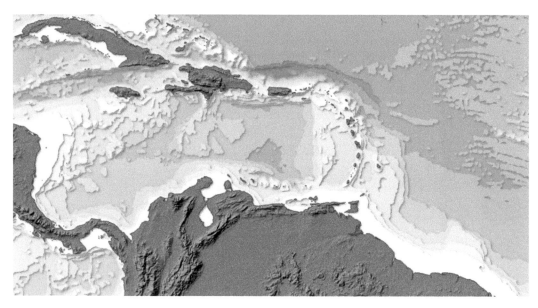

Figure 1.12: Land with a Multiply Blending Mode

Exercise 2

Creating Effects with Blending Modes

Objective – Learn Use Cases for Blending Modes

2.1 Introduction

Up to this point you have seen a couple examples of the Multiply Blending Mode being used. Blending modes determine how two layers interact visually. When a blending mode is applied to a layer it will be blending with the layer below. There are dozen different blending modes in QGIS and they can be applied at the layer level or at the feature level. There are descriptions for each in the QGIS Documentation (`https://docs.qgis.org/2.18/ en/docs/user_manual/introduction/general_tools.html?highlight=blending#blending-modes`).

This exercise includes the following tasks:

- Task 1 – Opacity Versus Blending Modes

- Task 2 – Feature Blending Mode

- Task 3 – Dodge Blending Mode

2.2 Objective: Learn Use Cases for Blending Modes

Here you will be exposed to several use cases for blending modes and will learn how to apply them at both the layer and feature level.

2.3 Task 1 - Opacity Versus Blending Modes

In this first task, you will learn a classic use case for blending modes, combining a polygon layer (land ownership) with a hillshade image below. Historically in GIS software, this would be achieved by making the land ownership data semi-transparent. This can work. However, the more transparent you make the land ownership data the more washed out the colors become. Conversely, the more opaque you make the land ownership data the less detail you see in the hillshade image. Using a blending mode you get full color saturation in the land ownership data, and all the detail in the hillshade image simultaneously!

1. Open QGIS 3.x. and then open `Jemez.qgz`.

2. This project contains one raster layer: a digital elevation model, and three vector layers: land ownership, PLSS Townships, and streams. The data covers the Jemez Mountains (`https://en.wikipedia.org/wiki/Jemez_ Mountains`) which is a massive volcanic caldera in northern New Mexico.

3. You will first render the DEM as a hillshade image. Open the Layer Styling Panel ✎ with the target being the JemezDEM raster.

4. Change the renderer from Singleband gray to Hillshade. Scroll down to find the Resampling section. Change the Zoomed in resampling method to Bilinear. Change the Zoomed out resampling method to Average. The default of Nearest neighbor is not the best choice. This is because the Nearest neighbor can produce blocky results. It is best used for categorical rasters as it will not change cell values. Bilinear, Cubic and Average resampling are best for continuous data such as a DEM. Bilinear interpolation averages the values of the four nearest cells.

5. Turn on the Land Ownership layer. Because it is a solid polygon layer it obscures the hillshade image. First you will experiment with Opacity. Switch the target of the Layer Styling Panel to the Land Ownership layer. Expand the Layer Rendering section and start dragging the Opacity slider down making the Land Ownership layer increasingly transparent. When you get to around 30% the colors are really washed out. Reset Opacity to 100%.

6. Now find the Layer Blending mode drop down menu and choose Multiply. This blending mode shows both layer at full saturation. It is probably the most commonly used one in the suite. Using Multiply for layers above a hillshade is also probably the most common use case. Very similar to what you did in Part 2 Exercise 7. Zoom in and explore the map. You will see that this is a tremendous improvement over using the Opacity slider. This blending mode is so named because it multiplies the numbers for each screen pixel of the top layer (Land Ownership), with the corresponding screen pixels for the bottom layer (JemezDEM).

7. Next set the Layer Blending Mode for the PLSS Townships to Overlay. This mode combines the multiply and screen blending modes. Light parts become lighter and dark parts become darker. The PLSS Township lines take on the a more saturated version of the landownership color they pass through (Figure 2.1).

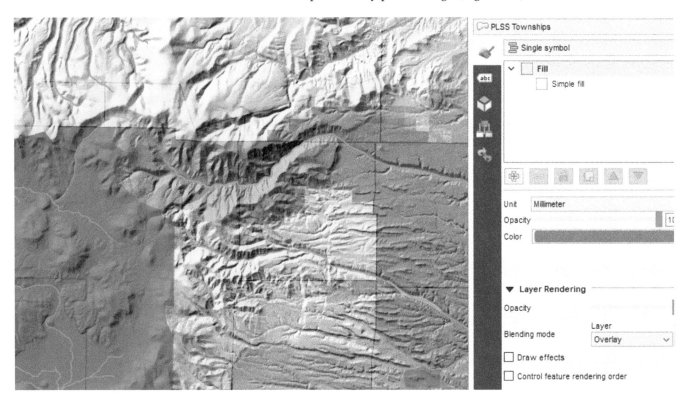

Figure 2.1: Landownership with a Multiply Blending Mode

You may also want to experiment with the Brightness setting under Layer Rendering for the elevation data. If the hillshade is too dark you can brighten it a bit.

Blending modes come in four groups: Lighten, Darken, Contrast, and Inversion/Cancellation. Multiply is in the Darken group and Overlay is in the Contrast group.

8. Blending modes are available elsewhere in QGIS. For example, you can use apply them to Label Buffers (halos), Live Layer Effects and items in a Print Layout. From the menu bar choose `Project | Layouts | Blending Modes`. This is a simple print layouts. In your data folder is a QGIS logo created by Klas Karlsson named `MadewithQGISlogo.png`. You can find the original here: `https://github.com/klakar/qgis_logo`. Use the Add New Picture ![icon] tool to add this logo to the upper right corner of the composition.

9. In the Resize Mode section of Item Properties set it to Zoom and resize frame. Make it roughly 50mm wide (Position and Size | Width |Height).

10. It is a black and white logo and looks fine. However, you will now apply a Blending mode to it to create a different look. In the Rendering section of Item Properties set a Blending mode of Multiply. This causes the white to become transparent (Figure 2.2).

Figure 2.2: A Logo with a Multiply Blending Mode Applied

These are available for all all objects in the Print Layout. There may not always be an appropriate use for them, but remember these are an option. In the previous exercise you learned about Live Layer Effects. These Blending modes are also available for each one of those effects. They can be especially effective when used in combination with Outer Glows.

2.4 Task 2 - Feature Blending Mode

In this next task, you will learn about a new blending mode and how to apply blending mode at the feature level.

1. Open QGIS 3.x. and then open `DK_roads.qgz`. This project has a Country Boundaries layer (black), a Water layer (gray), and an Denmark OSM roads (bright blue). The map is zoomed in to the island of Zealand where Copenhagen is located. The country to the east with no roads coverage is Sweden.

2. Explore the source file for the Country Boundaries layer and the Water layer by hovering over each in the Layers Panel. Are they sourced from different shapefiles?

3. The background color of the map could have been set to a dark gray via Project Properties (`Project | Properties | General`). However, here the Country Boundaries layer was Duplicated and styled with the Inverted Polygon renderer. Remember that this causes the layer to be rendered beyond it's native geometry. So Countries become Oceans. Open the Layer Styling Panel ![icon] with the target being the Water layer to see how this was done (Figure 2.3).

Figure 2.3: Inverted Polgyon Rendering

4. Change the target layer in the Layer Styling Panel to the Denmark OSM roads layer.

5. Instead of setting a Layer Blending Mode you will set a Feature Blending Mode which applies the effect to the individual features versus the layer as a whole. Set the Feature Blending Mode to Addition (Figure 2.4). At this scale the road features are stacked on top of one another. As they are rendered, their colors are being blended together additively. This increasingly brightens the screen pixels where the greatest overlap occurs, thereby visually highlighting road density.

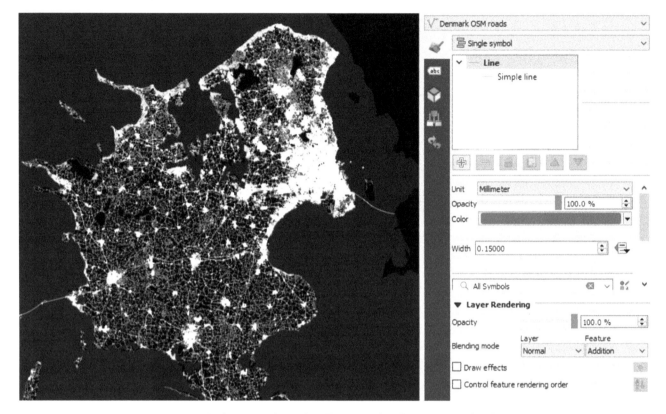

Figure 2.4: Styling Roads with a Feature Blending Mode of Addition

6. Because the effect is created due to the crowding of features, it will change as you zoom in. Experiment by zooming in and out to see how the effect changes. This particular effect works best against a dark background. Importantly this isn't producing any metrics of road density. It is simply a method of visualizing that density.

You have now seen three blending modes. Remember there are twelve in all! Many produce very similar effects so you will need to try different ones when trying to achieve a specific effect with your data. Some may be enhanced by working with layer Opacity settings or combining with Live Layer Effects and project background colors.

2.5   Task 3 - Dodge Blending Mode

In this final task, you will learn a case for the Dodge blending mode.

1. Open QGIS 3.x. and then open Dodge.qgz. This project has a country boundaries layer (white outline), a Residential Areas layer, and a Denmark OSM Roads layer. The background of the map has again been set to a black via Project Properties.

According the QGIS documentation: *"Dodge will brighten and saturate underlying pixels based on the lightness of the top pixel. So, brighter top pixels cause the saturation and brightness of the underlying pixels to increase. This works best if the top pixels aren't too bright; otherwise the effect is too extreme."*

Here you will use the Dodge blending mode to highlight roads within Residential areas.

2. **You will begin working with the Denmark OSM roads.**

    a. Turn on the layers visibility.

    b. Style them as blue lines (0 | 98 | 255).

    c. Set Line Opacity to 10%-15%.

    d. Move this layer so it is the bottom layer in the Layers Panel.

3. **Next you will work on the Residential Areas.**

    a. Move so it is below Country Boundaries in the Layers Panel.

    b. Style as teal (126 | 224 | 231) polygons with a Stroke Style of No Pen.

    c. Apply Layer Blending Mode of Dodge. (Figure 2.5)

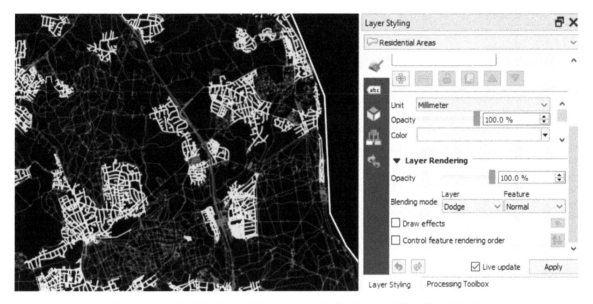

Figure 2.5: Highlighting Features with the Dodge Blending Mode

4. The roads passing through Residential Areas are now highlighted. Increasing the Opacity of the Denmark OSM roads will make the ones not passing through Residential Areas more visible but will steadily decrease the highlight effect. Experiment with different Opacity settings for Denmark OSM roads and colors for the two layers to see how the effect changes. A good way to experiment with color is to use the Color Wheel via the Layer Styling Panel ✎ (Figure 2.6, on the next page).

2.6 Conclusion

Blending modes in provide you will a powerful tool for creating nice visual effects. These have been available for quite some time in graphics software such as Adobe Photoshop and Illustrator, GIMP and Inkscape. However, having them available in a GIS is still rather novel.

Many produce very similar effects. You will need to experiment with them especially as you begin to apply them to different data and coloring schemes. Some may be enhanced by working with layer Opacity settings or combining with Live Layer Effects.

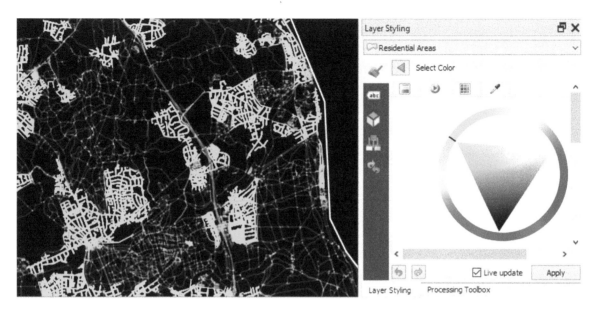

Figure 2.6: Using the Interactive Color Wheel to Experiment with Colors

2.7   Discussion Questions

1. Were you able to arrive at other more interesting color combinations and Opacity settings for the Dodge blending mode? Describe.

2. Can you think of other applications for Blending modes? Describe.

Exercise 3

The Power of Geometry Generators

Objective – Learn about working with Geometry Generators

3.1 Introduction

QGIS has a wide variety of Symbol Layer Types which act like sub-renderers (Figure 3.1). The default Symbol Layer Type for polygons is Simple fill. You have also seen use cases for Line Pattern fills (Part 1 - Exercise 2), Shapeburst fills (Part 4 - Exercise 1 and 4) and Marker Lines (Part 4 - Exercise 4). Here you will learn about a very powerful and unique renderer: Geometry generators.

Figure 3.1: Symbol Layer Types for Polygons

This exercise includes the following tasks:

- Task 1 – Rendering Polygons as Centroids

- Task 2 – Creating Interior Buffers

- Task 3 – Creating Label Callouts

3.2 Objective: Learn About Working with Geometry Generators

Geometry generators allow you to modify the geometries of features just in the way they are rendered. You do this by using the QGIS expression engine along with spatial functions like `centroid()`, `buffer()`, `make_point()`, `make_line()` and `wedge_buffer()`. The resulting geometry (point, line, polygon) does not need to match the original.

3.3   Task 1 - Rendering Polygons as Centroids

In this first task, you will learn how to render polygons as centroids (points).

1. Open QGIS 3.x. and then open `GeometryGenerators.qgz`.

2. This project contains one vector layer, the hunting units in the state of Colorado, USA (CO Big Game Hunting Units). These are how Colorado manages big game hunting.

3. Right-click on the one layer and choose Duplicate from the context menu.

4. Rename the duplicated layer *Centroids*, turn on its visibility, and move it above the original in the Layers Panel.

Open the Layer Styling Panel 🖌 and make the Centroids layer the target layer.

5. Select the Simple fill symbology component. Change the Symbol layer type from Simple fill to Geometry generator. You have two options that appear: the Geometry type and an expression window with the $geometry function (Figure 3.2).

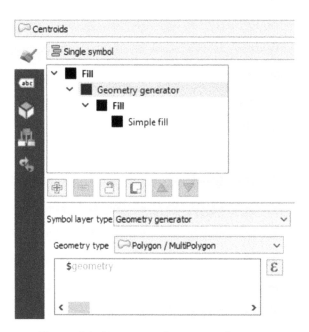

Figure 3.2: Geometry Generator Options

6. $geometry is a constant variable that returns the geometry of the current feature. You can use this with spatial functions to create new geometries. Again nothing will change on disk, you are simply changing the geometries in the way the features are being rendered.

7. Click the Expression ε button to open the Expression Dialog window. Use the central Search box to find the `centroid` function. Find the `centroid` function in the Geometry section and select it. Notice the syntax documentation to the right. This tells you that the `centroid` function takes one parameter: $geometry. Double-click the centroid function to add it to your expression. Note that QGIS inserts a red pointer where it identifies a syntax error in your expression centroid($geometry . You need a closing parenthesis to complete the expression. Enter the closing parenthesis (Figure 3.3, on the facing page). Notice that the Output Preview reads <geometry: Point>.

8. Click OK to accept. Finally change the Geometry type to Point/MultiPoint. You will instantly see the centroids represented by default red points! (Figure 3.4, on the next page).

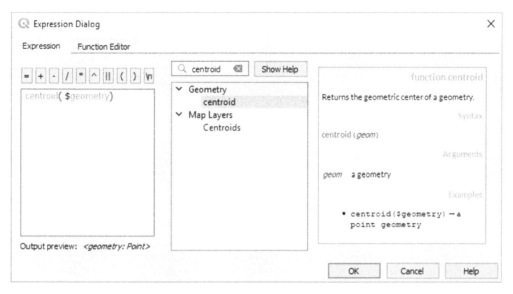

Figure 3.3: centroid($geometry) Expression

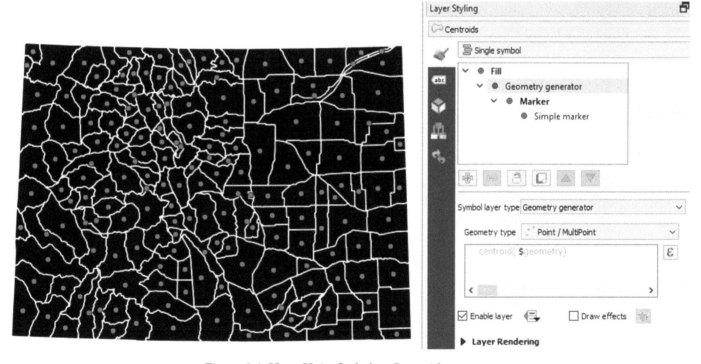

Figure 3.4: Hunt Units Styled as Centroids

Note that using the Expression window is not required. If you already know the expression, *centroid($geometry)* for example, you can just enter it into the expression box in the Layer Styling Panel.

9. Save your project.

3.4   Task 2 - Creating Interior Buffers

In this next task, you see how to create another version of the Colorado Hunt Units layer, this time as an interior buffer.

1. Open QGIS and open `GeometryGenerators.qgz` if it is not already.

2. Right-click on the original CO Big Game Hunting Units layer and choose Duplicate from the context menu.

3. Rename the duplicated layer *Interior Buffers,* turn on its visibility, and move it above the original but below Centroids in the Layers Panel.

4. Make the Interior Buffers layer the target layer in the Layer Styling Panel.

5. Again select the Simple fill symbology component and change the Symbol layer type from Simple fill to Geometry generator.

6. This time you will be using the buffer() function. Again open the Expression Dialog window. Search for the `buffer()` function. It too will be in the Geometry section. Notice that this function takes to arguments: the geometry (geom) and distance. You will use a negative number (-4000) for the distance which will create an interior buffer (Figure 3.5). This dataset is in UTM with units in meters so this will create interior buffers of -4000 meters.

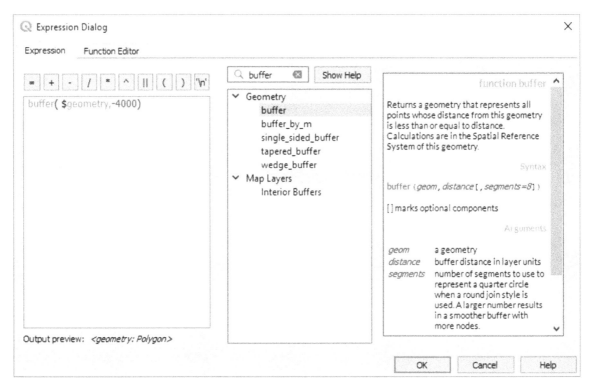

Figure 3.5: Interior Buffer Expression

7. Click OK to accept. Keep the Geometry type to Point/MultiPoint. Select the Simple Fill component and change the Fill color to (7 | 234 | 254) which is a bright blue (Figure 3.6, on the next page). This takes a little longer to render because it is a more complicated geometry to compute.

8. Save your project.

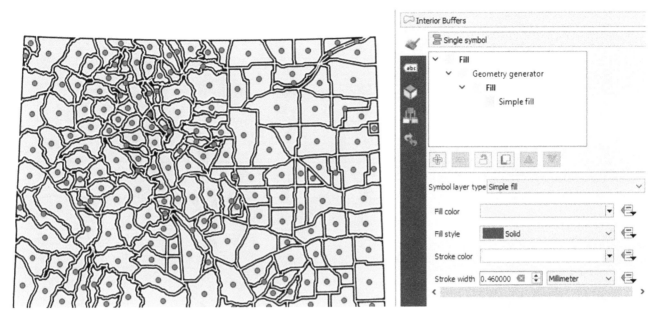

Figure 3.6: Interior Buffers

3.5 Task 3 - Creating Label Callouts

So far you have seen fairly simple examples to illustrate how Geometry Generators work. Next you will work on a more practical application using geometry generators to create label callouts.

1. Open QGIS and open `Gila.qgz`. This map document has several layers covering the Gila Bioregion in south-western New Mexico, USA. The key dataset is a grazing allotment layer produced by the Gila National Forest. It has several fields with information on the grazing permits. This is an area that has very large wilderness areas, a population of endangered Mexican wolves and a long history of cattle grazing. The last two create constant conflict (Figure 3.7, on the following page). As part of a mitigation effort you have been asked to create a map which labels some of the key grazing allotments with callouts. These callouts must have data from several attribute columns. QGIS supports labeling expressions, so composing a label with the appropriate attributes is straightforward. However, creating callouts that you can position against a busy map is more challenging. It will require use of geometry generators and a combination of the `make_line()` and `make_point()` functions.

2. The map needs to show several specific grazing allotments which are candidates for retirement. These need to be labeled with the allotment name (`UNIT_NAME`), the grazing permittee (`Permitte`), acres (`RepAcres`) and number and type of permitted livestock (`Permits`).

3. A copy of the grazing allotments layer with a filter has already been created for you Grazing allotments to label. You will set this layer up with both a labeling expression and rendered using a Geometry Generator to create the callout.

4. Zoom in to the group of Grazing allotments to label in the southeast corner near the Aldo Leopold Wilderness.

5. Duplicate the Grazing allotments to label layer and Rename it *Label Callouts*. Turn the layer on. You will work with this layer from here on out.

6. The first step will be to format the labels for the allotments. Open the Layer Styling Panel ✍ with the target layer being Label Callouts.

7. On the symbology tab switch from a Single symbol renderer to a ░ No symbols renderer. This layer will just be used for labels.

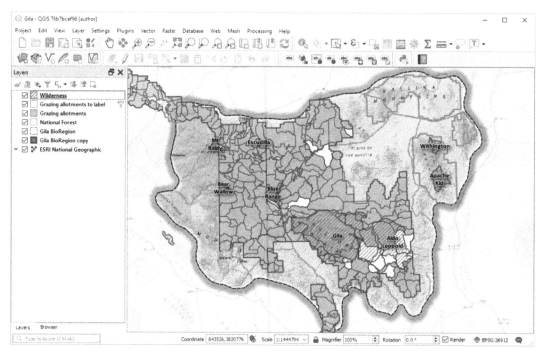

Figure 3.7: Gila QGIS Project

8. Next switch to the Labels abc tab. Choose Single labels based on the UNIT_NAME field. Choose a Font of Calibri Size 9.

9. Next you will set up a background for the labels. Switch to the Backgrounds 🛡 tab.

    a. Click the Draw background setting. Then set the Shape to Rectangle.

    b. Select a Size type of Buffer.

    c. Set both the Size X and Size Y to 1.0.

    d. Set the Stroke color to black and give it a Stroke width of 0.2. (See the result in figure 3.8).

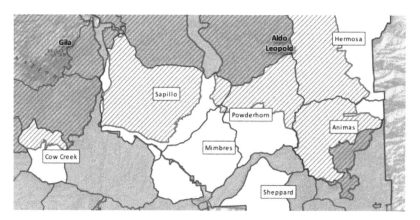

Figure 3.8: Labels with Rectangular Background

10. Next expand your labeling expression to add the Permitee column on a new line. You will open the labeling Expression window by clicking the Expression ε button. Click the String Concatenation ‖ operator followed

by the New Line `'\n'` operator. Enter one more String Concatenation operator followed by the `Permitee` column. Your expression should now look like `"UNIT_NAME" || '\n' || "Permittee"`. Click OK to accept and see the result. The new field will be added on a new line in the Rectangular background.

11. The labels will look better with a center alignment. Switch to the Formatting `tab` tab and set the Alignment to Center.

12. You will now add the `RepAcres` field to the expression and onto a new line. You will use another set of String Concatenation `||` operators around a New Line `'\n'` operator. Then you will add the `RepAcres`. Doing this alone would just result in a number being displayed. The map reader would not know what that number represented. To make it more informative you will add another String Concatenation operator after the `RepAcres` field followed by the text *acres* with a space preceding it. Your additional expression code will look like: `|| '\n'|| "RepAcres" || ' acres'` (Figure 3.9).

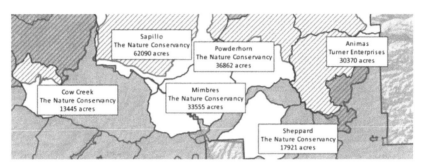

Figure 3.9: Labels with Three Fields Incorporated

13. The acres data would be much easier to read with thousands separators. You can use the `format_number()` function to accomplish this. This function takes two inputs: the number and the number of decimal places. Use the `RepAcres` field as the the number and 0 as number of decimal places. Note that this is a really useful function when you need to reduce the number of decimal places in a field. This part of the expression will now be: `|| '\n'|| format_number( "RepAcres" ,0) || ' acres' ||`.

14. Finally append the `Permits` to the end of the label, and onto another new line.

15. The labeling expression will look like figure 3.10.

Figure 3.10: Label Expression

16. Now that you have the labels set up correctly (figure 3.12, on the following page) you will work on the Geometry Generator component to create leader lines.

17. Switch to the Symbology tab then switch the renderer back to a Single Symbol. Select the Simple fill component and set the Symbol layer type to Geometry generator.

18. Set the Geometry type to LineString/MultiLineString.

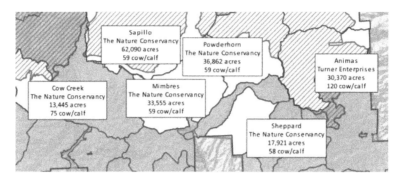

Figure 3.11: Labels with Four Fields Incorporated

19. Open the Expression dialog. You will use the make_point() function nested inside the make_line() function. Start with make_line(). This function takes two points as input. Here the first point will be the centroid($geometry) which you used in Task 1. The second point will be created by the make_point() function. This function takes two points. Here the two points will be found in fields:

- auxiliary_storage_labeling_positionx and

- auxiliary_storage_labeling_positiony

The Geometry Generator expression will look like the figure 3.12.

Figure 3.12: Geometry Generator Expression

20. Select the Simple line component of the symbol and increase the Stroke width to 0.46.

21. Highlight the Label Callouts layer. Then use the Move Label and Diagram tool on the Labeling toolbar. You will be prompted for the Auxiliary Storage Primary Key. Choose the default fid field and click OK.

22. Move one of the labels and notice the callout appear. You can now move each label to the desired position and the leader line will follow (figure 3.13, on the facing page). The leader lines go from each features centroid to the new label position. The new label position is stored in the auxiliary_storage_labeling_positionx and

auxiliary_storage_labeling_positiony fields. These fields are stored in the project QGD database nested within the Gila.qgz project zip file.

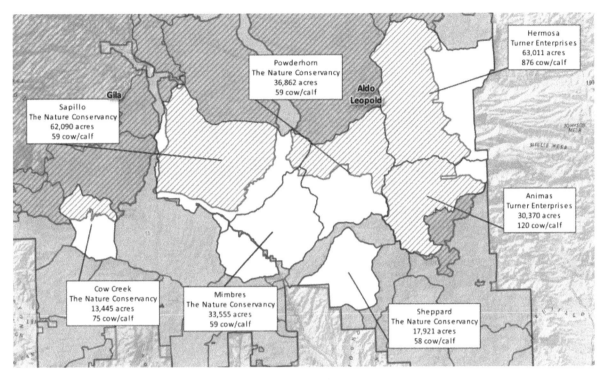

Figure 3.13: Final Label Positions

23. Remember you can open Layer Properties for the Label Callouts layer and switch to the Auxiliary Storage Auxiliary Storage tab. Here you can see the fields storing these callout positions.

24. You can also have the option to use Live Layer Effects in combination with these label callouts or make the label callout backgrounds semi-transparent.

3.6 Conclusion

This exercise have seen three examples of geometry generators, one point, one line and one polygon. You will see another example in the final task of the next exercise. Geometry generators are an extremely powerful tool and you can leverage the full power of the expression engine with this renderer.

3.7 Discussion Questions

1. How else might Geometry generators be used in labeling feaures?

2. Review the examples, here https://gitlab.com/GIS-projects/qgis-geometry-generator-examples and discuss potential use cases.

Exercise 4

Mapping Photopoints

Objective – Learn Tools for Mapping and Visualizing Photopoints

4.1 Introduction

Most smartphones and many modern cameras record the location of the photograph. This data is stored in EXIF data (https://en.wikipedia.org/wiki/Exif). This data is typically embedded in the png or jpg file. In addition to the latitude and longitude, EXIF data can include elements like camera type, camera settings (F-stop, focal length, exposure etc.), data and time, and azimuth. The exact data elements vary from camera to camera. Here you will learn a new tool that extracts the latitude and longitude from the EXIF data and uses it to create points where each photograph was taken.

This exercise includes the following tasks:

- Task 1 – Importing Geotagged Photos

- Task 2 – Using Widgets and Identify Features

- Task 3 – Creating Wedge Buffers and Using a Raster Image Marker

- Task 4 – Geometry Generator Challenge

4.2 Objective: Learn Tools for Mapping and Visualizing Photopoints

Learn to import geotagged photos as points and visualize the direction the photograph was taken in using the EXIF azimuth information to generate wedge buffers. Learn more applications of Data Defined Overrides and Shapeburst fills. Apply the new Raster Image Marker.

4.3 Task 1 - Importing Geotagged Photos

In this first task, you will learn how to use the Import Geotagged Photos tool.

1. Open QGIS 3.x. and then open `CedarCityFO.qgz`.

2. This project contains three vector layers: Potential ACEC (Areas of Critical Environmental Concern), BLM Lands with Wilderness Characteristics, the Cedar City Field Office (BLM administrative unit) and a Google Terrain basemap. This map is has information from field surveys for potential new wilderness areas. Field Offices are the management units of the Bureau of Land Management. Cedar City covers west central Utah. One of the important pieces of data are field photos. Here you will learn some tools for mapping those photos as points. You will also learn about wedge buffers.

351

What file format are these layers in?

What special effects are being used on these layers?

3. With QGIS 3 came a new tool for mapping photographs using the EXIF information. Using the Processing Toolbox, search for and open the Import Geotagged Photos tool and set it up as shown in figure 4.1. The output should be saved to the existing CedarCity.gpkg and named photopoints. To do this click on the ellipsis […] button and choose Save to GeoPackage from the context menu. Then select the CedarCity.gpkg and name the layer. Click Run.

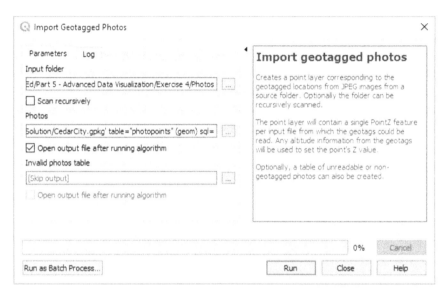

Figure 4.1: Import Geotagged Photos

4. Zoom to the new photopoints layer and give them a bright red point symbol. (Figure 4.2)

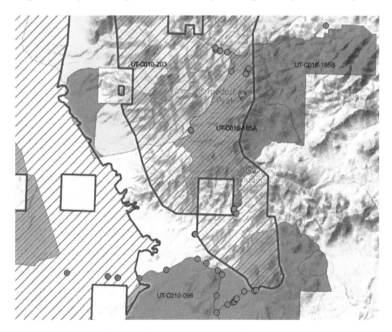

Figure 4.2: Photopoints Mapped

5. Open the attribute table and review the attributes associated with these points.

What data did this tool pull from the jpgs and add as attributes?

6. Save your project.

4.4 Task 2 - Using Widgets and Identify Features

In this next section, you will learn how to see the photo with the Identify Features tool.

1. Open Layer Properties and select the ⊞ Attributes Form tab for the photopoints layer (Figure 4.3).

    a. Select the photo column

    b. Select a Widget type of Attachment.

    c. Scroll down in the Widget type section and find the Integrated Document Viewer sub-section. Set the Type to Image.

    d. Click OK to close Layer Properties.

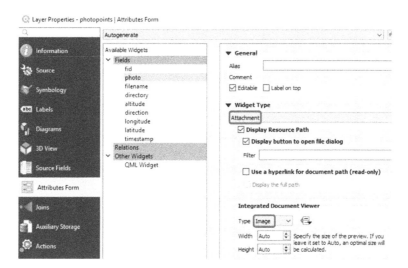

Figure 4.3: Attributes Form

> These Widgets have many uses beyond what was shown in this task. Often they are used to constrain values in a field to avoid data entry errors. This can be done via a numeric Range of acceptable values. With the Range widget you have the choice to edit numeric values in the table cell via a slider or spin box. Constraining values can also be done with the Value map widget. This one creates a drop down list to select from. Date/Time opens a calendar widget to enter a date into a date field! There are over a dozen widgets for use in field forms. Refer to the QGIS Documentation for more information (https://docs.qgis.org/testing/en/docs/user_manual/working_with_vector/vector_properties.html#edit-widgets).

2. Now click on a photopoint with the Identify features tool. In the upper left corner of the Identify Features window click the View feature form ⊡ button.

3. The photopoints - Feature Attributes window will open. Resize it so you can see the photograph. (Figure 4.4, on the following page)

4. Close the photopoints - Feature Attributes and Identify features panel when done exploring. Save your project.

Figure 4.4: Feature Attribute Window

4.5   Task 3 - Creating Wedge Buffers and Using a Raster Image Marker

In this next task, you will learn about wedge buffers (Figure 4.5) and why they are perfectly suited to visualizing photopoint data. Along the way you will also learn more ways to employ Data Defined Overrides and will use another new renderer.

Figure 4.5: Wedge Buffers

1. Using what you know, reproject the photopoints layer to UTM zone 12 NAD83 (EPSG: 26912). Save the new layer into the CedarCity geopackage and name it photopointsUTM. This step is necessary because to create the wedge buffers you need to photopoints to be in a Cartesian (projected) coordinate system with units in meters vs latitude and longitude.

2. Copy and paste the Style from the original photopoints layer to the new UTM version. (Figure 4.6, on the facing page)

3. Now find and open the Create Wedge Buffers tool in the Processing Toolbox. This tool creates wedge shaped buffers from points.

    a. Input layer = photopointsUTM.

    b. Azimuth – Click the Data Defined Overrides ⬅️ dropdown and find Field type. Choose the direction field (Figure 4.7, on the next page). This will orient the wedge buffer in the direction the photo was taken! Once you set this the Data Defined Overrides button will become highlighted ⬅️ because it is now active.

    c. Wedge width = Leave default setting. This controls how wide the pie slice is.

    d. Outer radius = 300. This controls how long the slice is in meters.

    e. Output Buffers = Create temporary layer.

    f. Click Run.

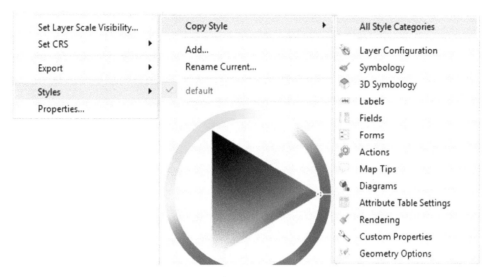

Figure 4.6: Copy/Paste Style Context Menu

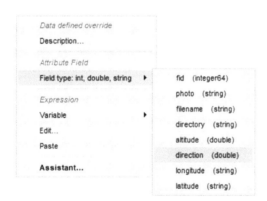

Figure 4.7: Azimuth Data Defined Override

4. The wedge buffer gives a very intuitive *field-of-view* perspective to the photopoints. Using what you know, experiment with symbolizing the wedge buffers. A shapeburst fill can be a nice way to go! Figure 4.7 shows them symbolized with a shapeburst fill from black to transparent and a Set distance of 5.

5. With raster fills you can take this visualization one step further.

   a. Make the photopointsUTM the target layer in the Styling Panel.

   b. Select the Simple Marker component of the symbol. Change the Symbol layer type to Raster Image Marker.

   c. Here you will use another Data Defined Override. In this case you will be using the override to point to the field containing the path to the photograph. Set the Data Defined Override for the image to the Photo field. Figure 4.9, on the next page

   d. Now increase the size of the image with the Width and Height parameters. Try something in the range of 20-40 each.

   e. You can take this one step further by using another Data Defined Override to point the Rotation parameter to the direction field. This will cause the Raster Image Marker to rotate in the direction the photo was taken.

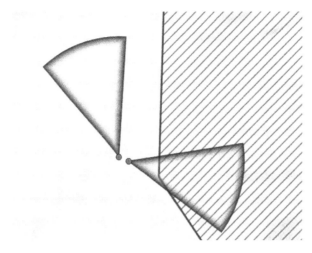

Figure 4.8: Wedge Buffers Styled with a Shapeburst Fill

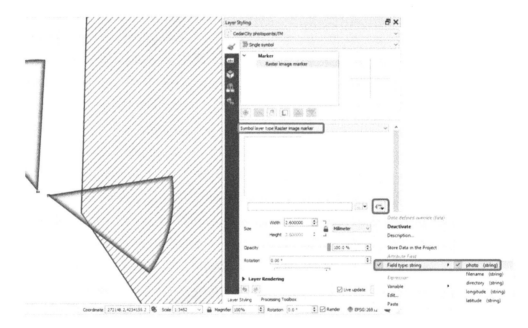

Figure 4.9: Setting the Data Defined Override for the Raster Image Marker

6. Now you have both a wedge buffer showing the direction the photo was taken, along with the actual photo instead of a point! (Figure 4.10, on the facing page).

7. Let's take this visualization yet one step further. You can also use a variable to scale the size of the image as the map scale changes!

    a. Click the Data Defined Override for the Width parameter.

    b. Choose Edit from the Data Defined Override context menu.

    c. In the Expression String Builder window, enter the following expression: `sqrt(5000000/@map_scale`
       `)`. The key to this expression is the `@map_scale` variable. This returns the current map scale. Using the `sqrt()` function with it, allows you to create a constant size at any scale. The value of 5000000 was chosen as a round number that returns the approximate width value already set. In the Expression String Builder you can see the Output Preview of the value generated.

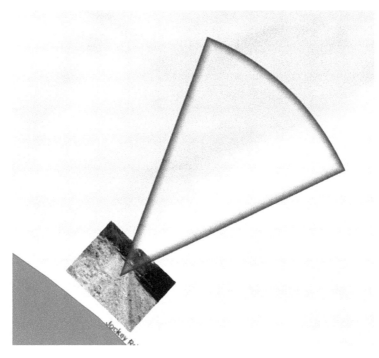

Figure 4.10: Raster Fills Combined with Wedge Buffers

    d. Click OK to close the Expression String Builder.

    e. The Data Defined Override icon will now be active and have an expression symbol.

    f. Repeat this step for the Height parameter.

8. Now as you zoom in and out the size of the Raster Image Marker will stay consistent. Data Defined Overrides can be very powerful, especially when used with expression and variables.

> Did you know that in addition to user created Variables, QGIS includes many standard Variables, and the list grows with each release? The next time you have an Expression window open explore the Variables section to increase your familiarity with them.

9. In Exercise 1 of this section you learned about Live Layer Effects. The Raster Image Marker is another good use case for them. Try adding a Drop Shadow or Outer Glow to the layer!

4.6 Task 4 - Geometry Generator Challenge

To this point you have used the following techniques to visualize photopoints:

- Run the Import Geotagged Photos algorithm.

- Used Widgets to preview the photos in the Identify Features Feature Form.

- Run the Create Wedge Buffers algorithm.

- Used Data Defined Override to orient the wedge buffer and create the *field-of-view* effect.

- Symbolized the wedge buffers with a Shapeburst fill.

Figure 4.11: Raster Marker Fill with Live Layer Effects

- Used the Raster Image Marker in combination with two Data Defined Overrides to show the actual photos on the map and orient them to the *field-of-view*.

- Used a Variable in an expression with a Data Defined Override to scale the photographs.

In the last exercise you learned about Geometry Generators. In this final challenge task, you will learn another application them. There is a `wedge_buffers()` function! This means you do not need to create a physical wedge buffer layer as you did in the previous task. Using Geometry generators you can render the photopoints as wedge buffers!

1. Duplicate the photopointsUTM layer.

2. Rename the duplicated layer *Geometry Generator* and turn on its visibility.

3. Open the Layer Styling Panel 🖌 and make the Geometry Generator layer the target layer.

4. Select the Simple fill symbology component. Change the Symbol layer type from Raster Image Marker to Geometry generator.

5. Click the Expression 𝜀 button to open the Expression Dialog window.

6. Search for the `wedge_buffers()` function and create the expression for wedge buffers as you did in Task 3.

What is the expression you used?

7. The benefit of using Geometry Generators here is that the using wedge buffers is being used as a data visualization technique. They are really effective in showing the direction the photo was taken. You likely don't need an actual wedge buffer layer. Plus using Geometry Generators you can easily tinker with the Wedge width and Outer radius parameters and immediately see the result.

4.7   Conclusion

In this exercise you have learned how to map and visualize geotagged photos. There are numerous applications for mapping photos. If you want to try another challenge, download some of the photos from a vacation off your smartphone. Try repeating using some of these techniques with them!

Exercise 5

Rendering Points

Objective - Learn techniques for rendering points.

5.1 Introduction

Points pose specific cartographic challenges. It is not uncommon for them to be clustered too closely together to distinguish. When this occurs, the cartographer must either aggregate points, or separate them slightly, so that the magnitude is evident. Here you will learn about several renderers specific to point data which can help in these situations.

This exercise includes the following tasks:

- Task 1 - Using the Point Cluster Renderer

- Task 2 – Using the Point Displacement Renderer

- Task 3 – Generating Heatmaps

5.2 Objective: Learn techniques for rendering points

QGIS has several unique renderers for points. There are the typical Single symbol, Categorized, Graduated and Rule-based renderers available for each geometry (point, line, polygon). For points there is also Point displacement, Point cluster and Heatmap. This exercise will focus on the latter.

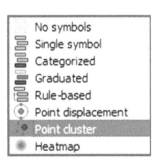

Figure 5.1: QGIS Point Renderers

5.3 Task 1 - Using the Point Cluster Renderer

In this first task, you will get familiar with the Point Cluster renderer.

1. Open QGIS and open Parks.qgz.

2. This is a project with a point layer for all the parks in the State of New Mexico. Right-click on the parks layer and choose Show feature count from the context menu.

How many points are there?

3. To accurately portray the magnitude of points, even where they are stacked on top of one another, you will use the Point Cluster renderer.

4. Make sure that the target layer in the Layer Styling Panel is parks.

5. Switch from a Single symbol renderer to a Point cluster renderer (figure 5.2).

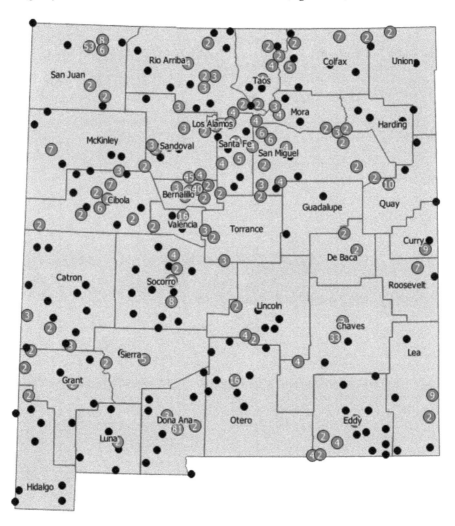

Figure 5.2: Parks Rendered with the default Point Cluster Settings

6. Click on the button for the Cluster symbol. Select the Simple marker component'. Change the Fill color to black.

7. Select the Font marker component. Change the Font family to Arial Black. Reduce the Size to 3.0. Click the Go back ◁ button to return to the main Point Cluster symbology panel

8. The cluster renderer will recompute the clustering at each map scale and extent. Zoom into the center of the state where some of the larger clusters are to see how the map changes (Figure 5.2).

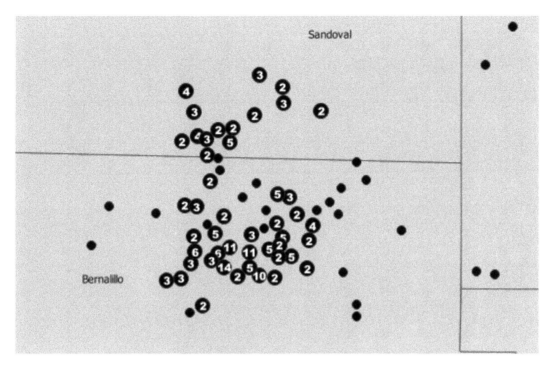

Figure 5.3: Modified Point Cluster Renderer - Zoomed In

9. Save your project.

5.4   Task 2 - Using the Point Displacement Renderer

In this task, you will get familiar with using the Point displacement renderer. This allows you to cartographically shift overlapping points.

1. Open QGIS and open `Points.qgz`.

2. This project contains populated places for Denmark. You are zoomed into the island of Zealand where the capital of Copenhagen is located.

3. Make sure that the target layer in the Layer Styling Panel is `Places`.

4. Switch from a Single symbol renderer to a Point displacement renderer (Figure 5.4, on the next page).

5. This render creates a Center symbol which is a red point by default. You can either give that the same symbol as the other points or make it transparent so it is not visible. For this exercise, you will make it transparent. The easiest way to do this is to click the Center symbol drop-down and slide the Opacity slider on the context menu to 0% opacity.

6. It also creates an displacement ring. You can make this invisible. In the Displacement lines section set the Stroke color to Transparent stroke.

7. There are three displacement methods available: Ring, Concentric Rings and Grid. Switch to Concentric Rings. You can also experiment with the Distance parameter. Increasing the Distance increases the displacement. Leave this at the default of 3 (Figure 5.5, on the following page).

8. Renderer settings allows you to change the Renderer being used while the points are displaced. By default it is Single symbol. Change this to Categorized then click the Renderer Settings button. Set the Column to `fclass` then click Classify.

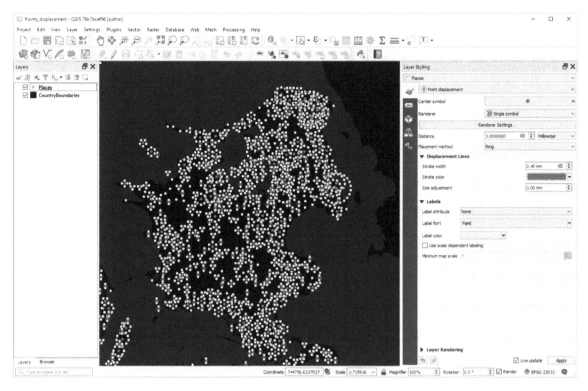

Figure 5.4: Default Point Displacement Settings

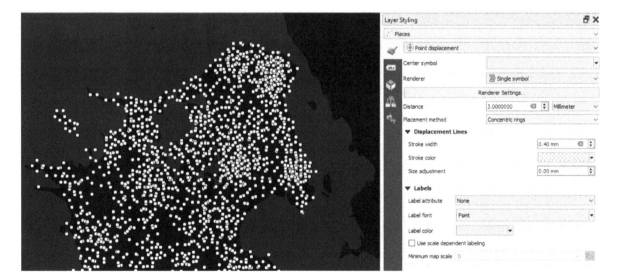

Figure 5.5: Concentric Ring Point Displacement

9. Experiment with some styling of the individual classes. This lets you combine Point displacement with a Categorized renderer (Figure 5.6, on the next page).

10. You are also encouraged to experiment with the other two displacement methods available: Ring and Grid.

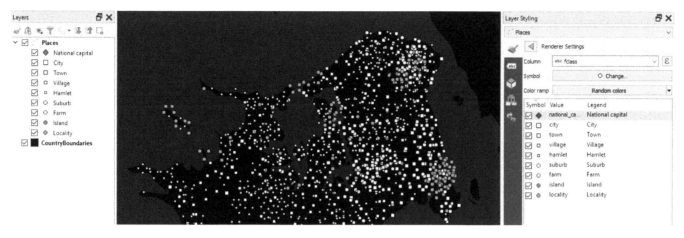

Figure 5.6: Point Displacement Combined with a Categorical Renderer

5.5 Task 3 - Generating Heatmaps

In this final task, you will learn how to render points as a heatmap. For an analysis it may be necessary to create an actual heat map raster dataset from points. However, if you just need to visualize points as a heatmap you can! Like many data visualization techniques (geometry generators), this has the advantage of creating the required visual without creating a separate file on disk.

1. Continue with the `Points.qgz` QGIS project.

2. Duplicate the Places layer and assign the copy the Heatmap render.

3. Choose the RdYlGn Color ramp.

4. Right-click on the Color ramp and choose Invert color ramp.

5. Set the Radius to 20.

6. Set the Rendering quality to Best.

7. Expand Layer Rendering and set the Blending mode to Addition (Figure 5.7).

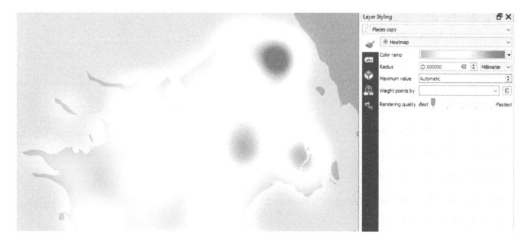

Figure 5.7: Points Rendered as a Heat Map

8. You can also weight the heatmap by an attribute field or expression. Set the Weight points by to population. Set the Radius back to 10. Then right-click on the layer in the Layers Panel and choose Zoom to Layer (Figure 5.8).

Figure 5.8: Heatmap Weighted by Population

5.6   Conclusion

In this exercise, you learned the several ways to visualize point data. All three can help show the magnitude of points when they can't be distinguished due to proximity. All three renderers are quick and easy to set up and worth remembering the next time you are dealing with cartographic challenges around point data.

Exercise 6

Animating Temporal Data with Time Manager

Objective – Learn How to Animate Temporal Data with the Time Manager Plugin

6.1 Introduction

An important component of many datasets is time. Looking at phenomena across both time and space can lead to important insights into trends in both dimensions.

This exercise includes the following tasks:

- Task 1 – Settng up the Data
- Task 2 – Animating Tropical Cyclones

6.2 Objective: Learn How to Animate Temporal Data with the Time Manager Plugin

Here you will learn how to set up a field with the data needed by the Time Manager plugin. You will then animate some spatial datasets using the data in that new field.

6.3 Task 1 - Settng up the Data

In this first task, you will install and configure the plugins. You will then animate a tropical cyclone dataset.

1. Open QGIS 3.x. and then open `Cyclones.qgz`.

2. This project contains the origin points for all tropical cyclones that occurred between 1950 and 2018.

How many tropical cyclones occurred between 1950 and 2018?

3. First you will install the plugin. From the menu bar choose `Plugins|Manage and Install Plugins`. Search for *time* and install the Time Manager plugin. Close the Plugin Manager and the plugin will appear as a horizontal panel across the bottom of QGIS (Figure 6.1, on the following page).

4. Open the attribute table for the cyclone formation points. There are fields for `Year`, `Month` and `Day`. However, you need a single field that aggregates those values formatted as *yyyy-mm-dd*. Put the table into edit mode and click the Field calculator button.

5. **Use the default Create a new field option.**

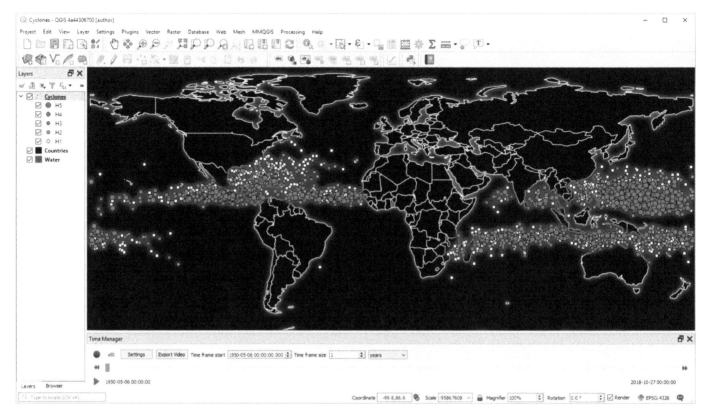

Figure 6.1: Time Manager

a. Output field name = *DateText*

b. Output field type = Text(string)

c. Output field length = 10

d. Now you will form your expression. Expand the Fields and Value section and double click on the Year field to begin your expression. Next click the String concatenation ‖ button to add that to the expression. This is required between any two pieces of text to be appended. Next enter an apostrophe and a dash followed by another apostrophe. Then another String concatenation. Add the Month field and repeat to add the Date field (Figure 6.2, on the next page).

e. Click OK.

6. Ensure that the DateText field contains values formatted as *yyyy-mm-dd*. If so, toggle out of edit mode and save your edits. If the values do not look correct, revisit the Field Calculator and try to recalculate the values this time using the Update existing field option.

> The use of the Field Calculator here allowed you to add the field and populate it all in one step. You could have also used the New Field button to first add the DateText field, then the editor widget or Field Calculator to then populate the values.

6.4 Task 2 - Animating Tropical Cyclones

In this task, you will learn how to animate the cyclone with the Time Manager plugin. You will be using the DateText field you just created.

1. Continue with the Cyclones.qgz project.

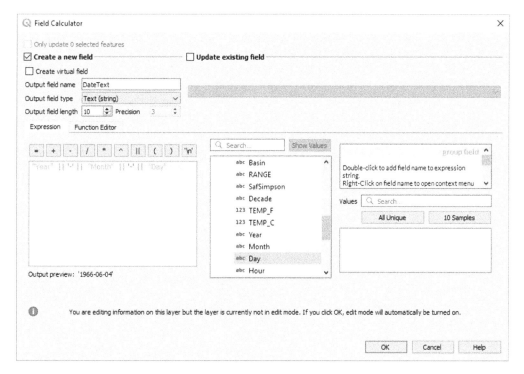

Figure 6.2: Creating and Populating the DateText Field

2. To begin click the Settings button on the Time Manager panel.

3. In the Time manager settings window click the Add layer button and the Select layer and column(s) window opens.

    a. Set the Layer to Cyclones

    b. Set the Start time to the DateText field.

    c. Set the End time to Same as start.

    d. Click OK. (Figure 6.3)

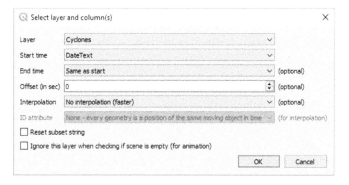

Figure 6.3: Select Layer and Columns

4. Now back at the Time manager settings window click the Time display options button to open the Options window.

5. The Options window let you control how time is displayed as the animation plays. You can choose the Font size, Text color and the units of time. Here you will only need to have years displayed.

    a. Set the DateTime setting to just %Y (for years).

    b. You can also change the font if you'd like. Although you might want to first play the animation once to see how the default settings look. In this example, it has been changed to Arial with a Font size of 30.

    c. You can also set where on the map canvas the time label appears via the Placement direction control.

    d. Click OK when done (Figure 6.4).

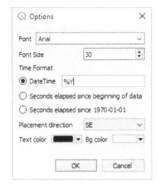

Figure 6.4: Time Manager Display Options

6. Now back at the Time manager settings window again there are a few more options. The Show frame for 500 milliseconds is the default setting. In your case this means each year will be displayed for half a second. It is a good default for this exercise, so leave it as is, but remember that can be changed.

7. There are also controls here for Play animation backwards, Looping animation and Do not export empty frames in time managed layers. You will leave these unchecked.

8. Click OK on the Time manager settings window to close it and finish the configuration.

9. The final setting you need to make is to the Time frame size. In this case, you want a Time frame size of 1 years. Set that.

10. Activate the plugin by clicking the Power ⏻ button. It will turn green ⏻ when you have done that (Figure 6.5, on the facing page). Notice that the Cyclones layer now has a filter ▽ applied to it using the DateText field. Also note there is an Archaeological Mode 🏛 button! This can be activated for use with dates in the format of 0003 BC or 0012 AD.

11. To run the animation click the Play ▶ button (Figure 6.6, on the next page).

> Notice that there is an Export Video button. This allows you to export the result in one of three ways. A) You can export Frames Only. This will save out the individual PNG files for each frame. You can then use a software like GIMP (https://www.gimp.org/) to create an animation from those. B) You can choose to create an Animated GIF if you have installed ImageMagick (https://www.imagemagick.org/). c) Or you can export a Video if you have installed the FFmpeg software (https://www.ffmpeg.org/). You will install this during the final exercise animating Mesh data. So you may want to revisit this option when you have installed FFmpeg.

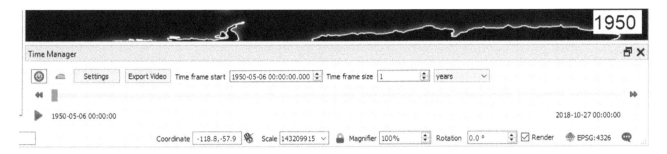

Figure 6.5: Time Manager Panel Ready to Run

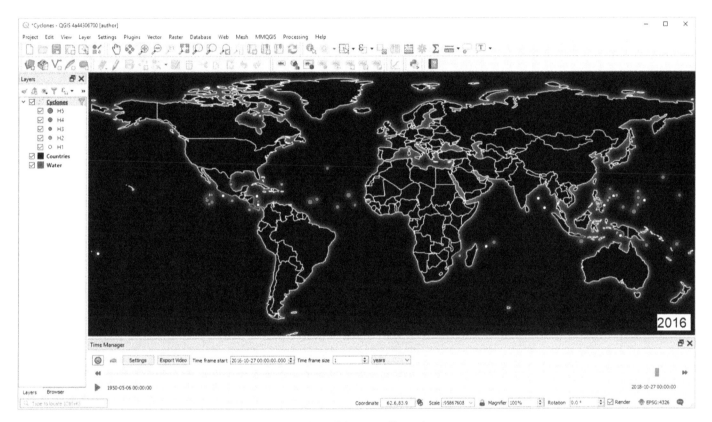

Figure 6.6: Time Manager Running

6.5 Conclusion

Temporal data is an important component of many datasets. Many consider time to be the fourth dimension. With what you have learned in this exercise, you now have the ability to animate data based on time. Time Manager is indeed one of the most widely used and important plugins.

6.6 Challenge Assignment

1. The photopoint data in the previous exercise contains a `timestamp` field. Zoom to the extent of the layer and set it up in Time Manager to play a frame per hour.

2. Also try rendering the photopoint layer rendered as wedge buffers with the Geometry generator. It still has all the same fields. Increase the Outer radius so that they are easily visible at that scale.

Exercise 7

Working with 3D Views

Objective – Learn about working with native QGIS 3D views

7.1   Introduction

The 3D environment is one of the most intuitive ways to visualize data, probably because we experience the world in 3D. For most of it's existence the 3D environment was only available in QGIS from plugins. One of the more exciting developments that came with QGIS 3 is a native 3D viewer.

This exercise includes the following tasks:

- Task 1 – Working with the 2.5D Renderer
- Task 2 – Setting Up a 3D View
- Task 3 – Adding the View to a Print Layout
- Task 4 – Creating an Animation
- Task 5 – Working with 3D Vector Data

7.2   Objective: Learn About Working with Native QGIS 3D Views

You will learn how to set up and use a native QGIS 3D view. You will also learn how to create key frames and animate a view.

7.3   Task 1 - Working with the 2.5D Renderer

Before you explore the full 3D environment you will learn about the 2.5D Renderer.

1. Open QGIS 3.x. and then open `manhattan.qgz`. This project is focused on lower Manhattan in New York City. It contains a building footprints layer and the Google Road basemap being served via the QuickMapServices plugin.

2. Open the Layer Styling Panel ✎ with the target layer being lower_manhattan_buildings.

3. Switch from a Single symbol renderer to the ▰ 2.5D renderer.

4. The 2.5D renderer has Height and Angle settings. It also has settings for Roof color and Wall color. The default settings for Height and Angle are 10 and 70 respectively (Figure 7.1, on the following page).

Figure 7.1: 2.5D Default Settings

5. Open the attribute table for this layer. Notice it includes a field that could be useful for extruding this layer into 2.5D space.

6. Click the Expression [ε] button to open the Expression Dialog window. Replace the default value of 10 with the following expression: "NUM_FLOORS" * 4. This will take the number of floors field and multiply it by a factor of 4.

7. Change the Roof color to an RGB value of: 253 | 191 | 111. (Figure 7.2).

Figure 7.2: 2.5D Settings

8. The buildings are now extruded into 3D space (Figure 7.3, on the facing page). This renderer is named 2.5D, versus 3D, because you cannot adjust the view of these buildings. They have a 3D appearance, but you cannot tilt and navigate through a true 3D scene. The benefit is that this is a very quick and easy renderer to set up, and it works for many cartographic purposes. You will learn how to work with a true 3D scene next.

7.4   Task 2 - Setting Up a 3D View

Here you will see how easy it is to create a 3D view. Specifically you will work with a DEM for Mt Rainier.

1. Open QGIS 3.x. and then open Mt_Rainier.qgz. This project contains two raster layers, DEM and a hillshade for Mount Rainier a prominent peak near Seattle, Washington, USA. At 14,411' (4,392 m) it is the highest peak in the Cascade Range and the highest peak in Washington State. It is also an active stratovolcano.

2. Apply a Blending mode of Multiply to the Mt Rainier Hillshade layer to create a color shaded relief effect (Figure 7.4, on the next page).

3. From the menu bar click on the View menu and choose New 3D Map View. The 3D view window is a panel. As such it will behave like all other panels (Layers Panel, Processing Toolbox etc.). You can either have it docked or free floating. The examples that follow will show it as an undocked free floating panel.

> Did you know that there is also an option under the View menu to open New Map Views. These are additional views of your 2D map canvas, and are also panels. You can open as many Map Views as you require. They can be linked to the main map canvas from their settings by choosing, *Synchronize View Center with Main Map*. You can also set their *Scale*, *Rotation* and *Magnification*. Plus you can assign them to a *Map Theme*!

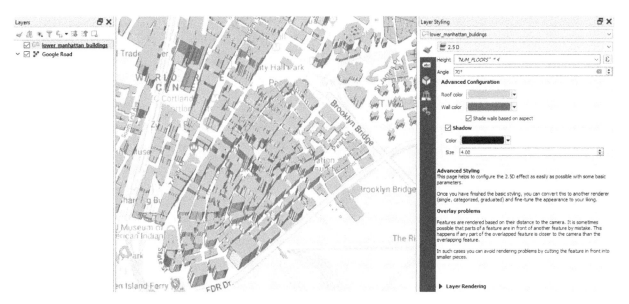

Figure 7.3: 2.5D View of Lower Manhattan

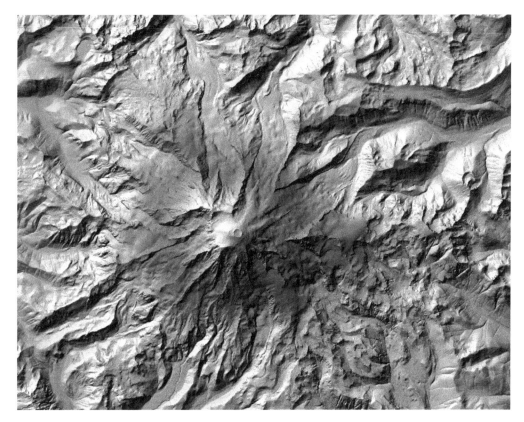

Figure 7.4: Mt. Rainier Color Hillshade Effect

4. Open the Configure 🔧 button to open the 3D Configuration window.

5. There are a lot of options. For now just set the Elevation to Mt Rainier DEM and click OK (Figure 7.5, on the following page).

Figure 7.5: 3D View Configuration

6. To start with, the 3D view shows the same extent and view as seen in the 2D canvas. Also note that there is no dedicated toolbar for navigation in the 3D canvas. You can zoom in/out and pan in the 3D canvas in the same way as in the main 2D canvas. Learning how to navigate through a 3D scene will take some practice. Below are specific instructions for maneuvering the 3D View:

Panning the Map

- by dragging the map with left mouse button pressed
- by using up/down/left/right

Zoom Map In/Out

- by using the mouse wheel
- by dragging mouse up/down with right mouse button pressed

Tilt / Rotate the Camera

- by dragging the mouse with middle mouse button pressed
- by pressing Shift and using up/down/left/right keys

Additional Camera Control

- Page up/down to move the camera up/down
- Shift and drag and the camera rotates around a point on terrain
- Ctrl and drag to rotate the camera while it stays in one position.

7. Tilt the camera to get a side view of the peak. (Figure 7.6, on the next page).

Did you know there is a really useful 3D plugin? The *QGIS2ThreeJS* plugin allows you to publish a 3D map to the web.

7.5   Task 3 - Adding a 3D View to a Print Layout

In this task, you will learn how to add your 3D View to a Print Layout.

1. Open QGIS 3.x. and then open Mt_Rainier.qgz.

2. There is a Print Layout started for this project and you will open it now. Click on the Show Layout Manager button to open the Layout Manager. Select the Mt Rainier layout and click Show to open the layout. You can close the Layout Manager once this has been done.

Figure 7.6: Mt. Rainier 3D View

3. Click the Add a new 3D map to the layout ![icon] button. Drag a box for the new map view in the space below the current 2D map view. Initially the box will be empty with the message Scene not set.

4. On the Item Properties tab you will see 3D Map properties. In the Scene Settings section click the Copy Settings from a 3D view drop down and choose 3D Map 1 (Figure 7.6).

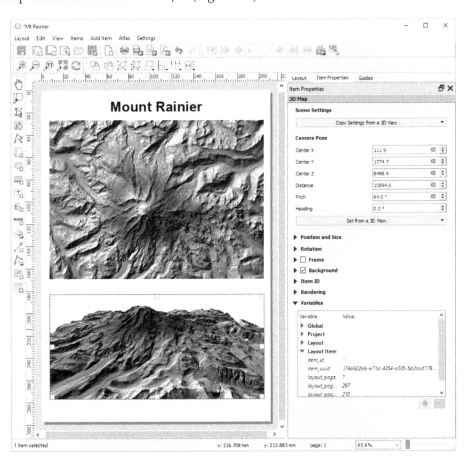

Figure 7.7: Mt. Rainier 3D View in Print Layout

7.6 Task 4 - Creating an Animation

Here you will learn how to create a fly-through of the 3D scene. This is done by setting the view to certain locations and adding those as Keyframes. The Keyframes have the camera location and time associated with them. This allows them to be used in generating an animation.

1. Open QGIS 3.x. and then open Mt_Rainier.qgz.

2. Open the 3D Map view and click the Animation ▶ button. The Keyframe panel will appear at the bottom of the view (Figure 7.8).

Figure 7.8: 3D View with Keyframe Panel Enabled

3. Navigate in the scene until you reach the point where your animation will begin. Perhaps zoom out a bit and your second Keyframe can be zoomed in. Then you can set up subsequent keyframes rotating around the peak. Once you are at what you want to be the first point click the Add Keyframe ⊞ button. The Keyframe time window will open. Set the Keyframe time [seconds]: to 1 and click OK (Figure 7.9).

Figure 7.9: Keyframe Time Window

4. Use the Add Keyframe ⊞ , the Remove Keyframe ⊟ , the Edit Keyframe ▨ , the Duplicate Keyframe ▤ tools as needed. You can step through your keyframes with the Keyframe drop-down menu (Figure 7.10, on the next page) or with the time slider at the bottom.

Figure 7.10: Keyframe Drop-down Menu

5. Continue to add Keyframes until you are done. Initially just try adding 5 or 6.

6. When you are done click the Play Animation ▶ button.

7.7 Task 5 - Working with 3D Vector Data

In this final 3D data task, you will learn how create a 3D scene of lower Manahattan buildings. These data were obtained from http://maps.nyc.gov/download/3dmodel/DA_WISE_Multipatch.zip.

1. Open QGIS 3.6 or greater. Note that if you are working with QGIS 3.4 you can still complete this task. You will just see some minor differences in the options on the Layer Properties | 3D View tab.

2. Using the Data Source Manager browse to the exercise folder and add the Buildings_3D_Multipatch layer from the DA12_3D_Buildings_Multipatch File Geodatabase. (Figure 7.11, on the following page).

3. This is a 3D buildings layer covering lower Manhattan.

4. Open Layer Properties for the buildings layer and switch to the 🔲 3D View tab.

5. Switch from No symbols to a Single symbol renderer. The remaining settings are optional. Since this is a 3D building layer, it does not require the Height or Extrusion values to be set. Explanations for the remaining settings are below.

- Height is the elevation of the base. By not setting it here, these buildings will sit on a flat plane, which is fine for this exercise.
- When working with non-3D features you can set the Extrusion value to an attribute column. For instance, if you were working with the Manhattan building footprints data from Task 1, you could set the Extrusion value to the NUM_FLOORS field. Again since these are 3D polygons, this isn't necessary.
- Depending on the quality of your 3D polygon data, enabling Add back faces may help the rendering, but will also consume more graphical memory. It is not necessary for this dataset.
- Diffuse is the color of the the buildings. You can change that to a lighter warmer color if you wish.
- Ambient is the color of of an object when it is in shadow. In this example this has been set to a dark gray versus black.
- Specular is the color of reflection on a shiny object
- The Shininess value controls the reflectivity of the objects.

Note that by QGIS 3.8 the QGIS 3D environment will likely support rendering of building edges!

6. Click OK when done with the 3D View settings (Figure 7.12, on page 379).

Figure 7.11: Lower Manhattan 3D Buildings

7. From the menu bar click on the View menu and choose New 3D Map View.

8. This is a fairly large and complex dataset and it may take several moments to finish rendering. Be patient.

> Note that you do not need normal 2D symbology for these buildings. You can switch the normal 2D symbology setting from *Single symbol* to *No symbols*. Then you will not see a flat 2D version of this layer underneath the 3D rendering.

9. When the buildings appear, return to the main QGIS window and use the Quick Map Services plugin to add a Google Road basemap. You are doing this as a second step because the basemap is a global dataset. If you were to add this before your 3D view had been established, QGIS would attempt to render a global 3D view. Therefore it is best to first establish a view with the buildings, and then add a basemap.

10. The basemap should now also appear in the 3D View panel. Next tilt and rotate the camera by:

- dragging the mouse with middle mouse button pressed
- pressing Shift and using up/down/left/right keys

11. This data includes some iconic building in midtown manhattan such as the Chrysler Building, the Empire State Building and the MetLife tower. Navigate around to find some interesting views. If you like you can return to the Layer Properties 🧊 3D View and experiment with those settings (Figure 7.13, on the facing page).

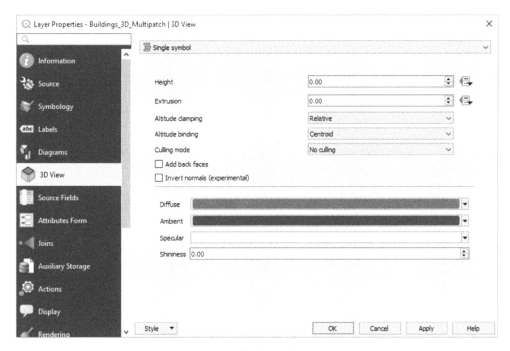

Figure 7.12: 3D Layer Properties

Figure 7.13: 3D Buildings in Midtown Manhattan

7.8   Conclusion

In this exercise, you have learned about how to work in the new native 3D environment in QGIS. This is function-ality introduced at version 3.0. As such it is still very new. The functionality in the 3D Views is likely to grow in future releases.

7.9   Challenge Assignment

Create a 3D Animation from the lower Manhattan buildings data used in Task 5.

Exercise 8

Working with Mesh Data

Objective – Symbolize and Animate Mesh Data

8.1 Introduction

Mesh data is a fairly new hybrid data model. It is a collection of vertices, edges, and faces (see figure 8.1). It is very similar to a triangulated irregular network (TIN). Unlike a TIN, mesh data are not typically used to model terrain. Rather they are used for meteorological, hydrological, and oceanographic datasets and model outputs. A mesh data file can contain multiple datasets. For example, the data you will work with contains wind, temperature and precipitation values. These values are stored at each vertex.

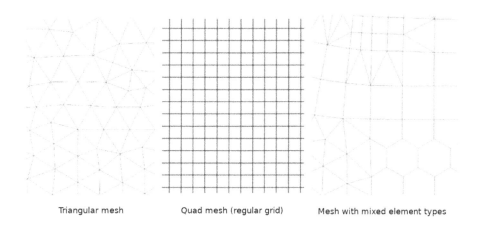

Figure 8.1: Mesh Data (Used with permission of Lutra Consulting)

There are several file formats which support this structure: GRIB, NetCDF, HDF (HEC-RAS), XMDF, XDMF, FLO-2D, Selafin files, SMS DAT and SWW (Anuga). In this lab you will be working with a NetCDF file.

This exercise includes the following tasks:

- Task 1 – Loading Mesh Data
- Task 2 – Symbolizing Mesh Data
- Task 3 – Using Crayfish to Plot Mesh Data
- Task 4 – Animating Mesh Data

8.2   Objective: Learn How to Work With Mesh Data in QGIS

Using the built in support for mesh data, you will use QGIS to explore and symbolize a mesh dataset. You will also work with the Crayfish plugin to generate plots and animations from the data.

8.3   Task 1 - Loading Mesh Data

In this first task, you will get familiar with adding mesh data to QGIS.

1. Open QGIS 3.4 or greater. Note that this chapter deals with very new functionality and there are likely to be enhancements in subsequent releases. The screenshots for this exercise are from QGIS 3.6. However, you will be able to complete all the tasks using the current long-term release.

2. Open the Data Source Manager and switch to the [icon] Mesh tab.

3. Click the Browse button to open the Open MDAL Supported Mesh Dataset(s) window. MDAL (`https://github.com/lutraconsulting/MDAL`) is a new library for reading mesh datasets. Click the drop down menu to the right of File name. Here you will see the file formats supported by MDAL. Set the filter to GDAL NetCDF. Select the `Atlantic_Sept2017.nc` and click Open. See figure 8.2.

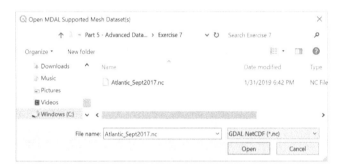

Figure 8.2: Open MDAL Supported Mesh Datasets(s) Window

4. Back at the Data Source Manager click Add. Depending on the speed of your computer this can take a few moments. Be patient. When it has finished click Close. See figure 8.3, on the next page. This dataset covers the north Atlantic Basin for the entire month of September 2017. This was a historic hurricane season in the north Atlantic with six major hurricanes including Harvey, Irma, Jose and Maria. The damage done by Harvey, Irma and Maria was catastrophic (`https://en.wikipedia.org/wiki/2017_Atlantic_hurricane_season`).

5. Notice that if you use the Browser Panel there is a special icon [icon] for mesh datasets.

6. Next add the vector layer `ne_10m_admin_0_countries.shp` to QGIS. This is a country boundary layer from Natural Earth (`https://www.naturalearthdata.com/`).

7. Reposition if necessary so that this layer is the top most layer. Give this layer a white fill and the default black stroke and apply a Layer Blending Mode of Multiply.

8. Save your project as `exercise7.qgz` in the exercise folder.

8.4   Task 2 - Symbolizing Mesh Data

In this task, we will learn how to symbolize different aspects of a mesh dataset.

1. Continue with the `exercise7.qgz` project.

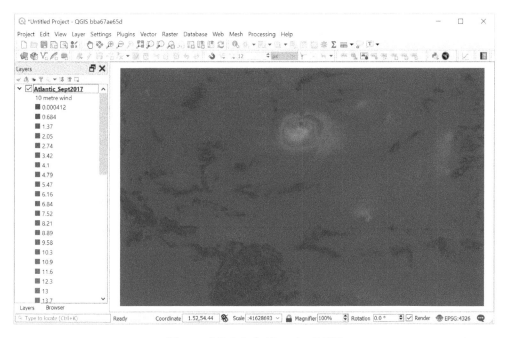

Figure 8.3: Mesh Data in QGIS

2. Open the Layer Styling Panel ☝ with the target being the mesh layer.

3. You will see a set of tabs specific to the mesh data type. The first tab on the left is the Groups ☇ tab. Here you will see the different component datasets: 10 metre wind, 2 metre temperature and Total precipitation. Initially you will see the ☝ icon next to 10 metre wind indicating that the raster on the map canvas represents wind. The ↘ icon is grayed out indicating vectors are currently disabled. Below the Group is a time slider. For datasets like this one that have a time component you can use this to view different points in time. (figure 8.4)

Figure 8.4: Layer Styling Panel for Mesh Data

4. The second styling tab ☝ is for what are called Contours which is the raster component. Switch to this tab. Change the Color ramp to RdYlBu. Right-click on the color ramp and choose Invert Color Ramp. Next change the Max setting to 25 (figure 8.5, on the next page). This lets you control the stretch of the color ramp and highlights the higher winds more.

5. The third styling tab ↘ is for the Vector component. Switch back to the Groups ☇ tab and click the ↘ icon to enable vectors for wind. Next switch to the Show Vectors tab. With default settings the vectors will overwhelm

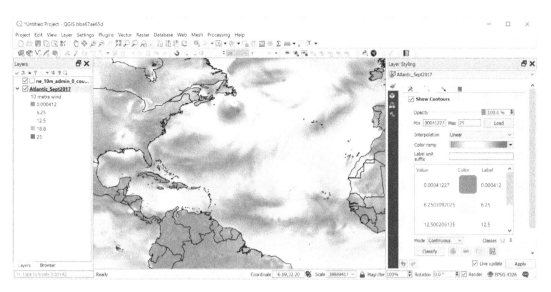

Figure 8.5: Styling the Mesh Contours

the map at this scale. Check the Display Vectors on User Grid option, then set both the X Spacing and Y Spacing to 15. This setting lets you control the density and spacing of the vectors. Next change the Arrow Length setting to Scaled to Magnitude and the Scale by a Factor setting to 1. The vectors are now sized in proportion to the wind speed.

6. Switch back to the Groups ⚒ tab. This dataset has a temporal component. As mentioned previously this dataset covers the entire month of September 2017. This data has information from four times each day of the month: midnight, 6am, noon and 6pm. You can look at any of these points in time via the time slider. It has both a drop down menu `19 d 00:00:00` ⌄ with each of the 120 points in time available, and a set of arrows

|< < > >| you can use to step through the data in sequence. Use the dropdown to set the time slider to 18 d 18:00:00. You will see Hurricane Maria as the first Category 5 storm to hit the island nation of Dominica. Over the next day it will be downgraded to a high-end Category 4 storm before hitting Puerto Rico. You will also see Hurricane Jose as a Category 1 storm raking the eastern seaboard of the U.S. Zoom in a bit to get a closer look at both storms. (figure 8.6, on the facing page)

7. The fourth styling tab ▦ is for the mesh itself. Switch to this tab and check the Native Mesh Rendering box. You will now see the actual mesh rendered. You can zoom in to get a closer look at the mesh structure. Disable the Native Mesh Rendering when you're finished.

8. Here you have selected the contours and vectors from the same wind component of the dataset. However, it is possible to choose contours from one component like Total precipitation and vectors from another like wind.

9. You can also choose to just show vectors. Select the Contour ⌇ tab and uncheck Show Contours. Next switch to the Vector ⬉ tab and change the color to white. For a background basemap use the QuickMapServices plugin to turn on Google Satellite. (figure 8.6, on the next page)

10. Save your project.

8.5   Task 3 - Using Crayfish to Plot Mesh Data

In this task, we will install the Crayfish plugin and use it to generate plots from the mesh data.

1. Install the Crayfish plugin produced by Lutra Consulting.

2. From the menubar choose Plugins | Crayfish | Plot to open the Crayfish Plot panel.

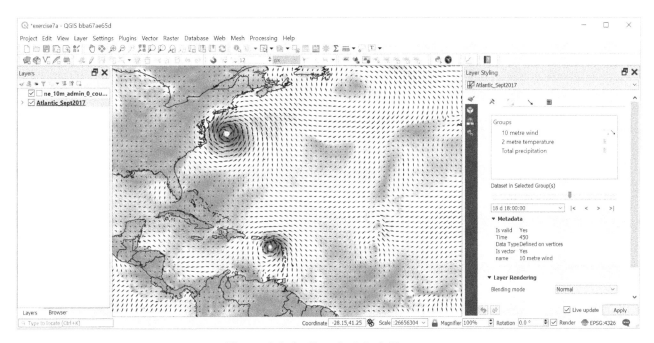

Figure 8.6: Styling the Mesh Vectors

Figure 8.7: White Vectors on a Google Satellite Basemap

3. The panel has a series of controls across the top that let you specify Layer = the mesh layer, Plot = whether the plot is a time series or cross section, Group = which group to pull data values from, From map = a plot from a point or a line or from layer = from a point layer.

4. Set the panel up like the figure 8.8, on the following page above. Click the From Map: Point setting and move your cursor around the map canvas. You will see a dynamic time series of wind data plot as you move your cursor over the map canvas. The X axis has the time values as hours from 0-n for the dataset. Here the dataset covers 30

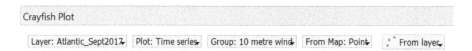

Figure 8.8: Crayfish Panel Settings

days and therefore has a time scale of 0 to 720 (30 x 24 hours). Click on a spot near Hurricane Maria. An X will be placed on the click location. The plot line will become fixed and will have the same color as the X. In the plot the right-hand peak represents the spike in wind at that location as Maria passed by. The left-hand peak shows the wind at the same location as Hurricane Irma passed by about 10 days earlier. (figure 8.9)

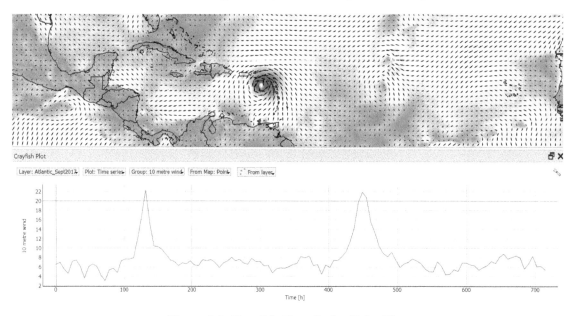

Figure 8.9: Crayfish Time Series Point Plot

5. Next you will explore a Time Series plot. Switch Plot to Time Series. A new parameter is added named Time. Keep this set to Current. Click the From map button and drag a line on the map to see a cross section plot generated. Right-click to end the line. (figure 8.9)

6. Note that there is also a Mesh menu which gives you access to a Mesh Calculator. This is similar to the Raster Calculator but is configured for Mesh data. It includes some special Operators such as: sum(aggr), max(aggr), min(aggr) and average(aggr). It treats each Group of a mesh dataset as a separate dataset and allows you to do calculations on those data. For example, these temperature data are in degrees Kelvin. To create a layer in Celsius you could create an expression as seen in figure 8.11, on the next page.

> A new feature of QGIS 3.6 is the abililty to use the Identify Features tool with mesh layers. It will display the value of the scalar and vector components of the mesh at the current time.

8.6   Task 4 - Animating Mesh Data

In the prior sections you learned how to animate data via time with the Time Manager plugin and create 3D animations. In this final task you will learn how to use the Crayfish plugin to animate Mesh data.

> Note that a new feature in QGIS 3.6 Noosa is support for Mesh data in a 3D view!

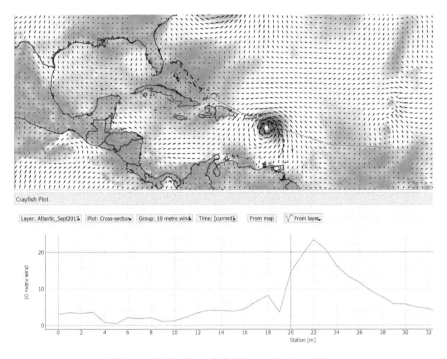

Figure 8.10: Crayfish Cross Section Plot

Figure 8.11: Mesh Calculator

1. Set up your map as in figure 8.6, on page 385 with black vectors, the wind contours enabled and the Google Satellite basemap turned off.

2. From the menubar choose Plugins | Crayfish | Export Animation to open the Export Animation window. There are three tabs: General, Layout and Video. Switch to the General tab. Set the Start Time to 48:00:00:00 and

the End Time to 642:00:00:00. Click the browse button for Output, navigate to your exercise folder and save the animation as `atlantichurricanes.avi`. For the remaining parameters on the General tab keep the defaults. (figure 8.12)

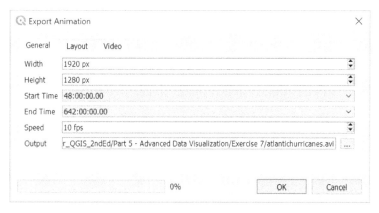

Figure 8.12: Export Animation Window

3. Switch to the Layout tab. Here you can set a Title for the video along with a Time stamp and Legend. Set the Font to Arial size 20. Enable the Background.

4. The Video tab lets you control the quality of the output. Use the default of High.

5. Click OK. This will take some time. During the first export you will likely get the message that FFmpeg is missing. There will be installation instructions for Windows, Linux and Mac users. Windows users can simple click the *download* link to install the FFmpeg software (`https://www.ffmpeg.org/`). Click OK'. Crayfish uses FFmppeg to create the AVI video from the series of png files generated. (figure :raw-latex:ref{fig.hurricanevideo.13}vpageref[unskip][unskip,]{fig.hurricanevideo.13}':raw-html:<a href='#fig.hurricanevideo.13'>fig.hurricanevideo.13</a>)

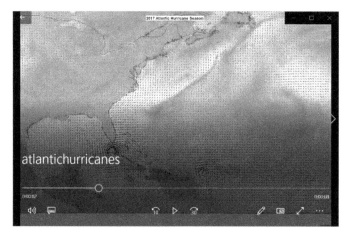

Figure 8.13: Hurricane Video

> The Crayfish Plot and Animation panels can also be accessed from the context menu exposed by right-clicking on a Mesh layer in the Layers Panel.

8.7 Conclusion

In this final exercise, you have been introduced to a new data model now supported by QGIS. The functionality around mesh data is bound to grow quickly over the next few releases. Follow the visual changelogs (`Help | About | What's New`) to find out about new features.

8.8 Challenge Assignment

This dataset was obtained from `https://cds.climate.copernicus.eu`. The site has a lot of interesting datasets. The data used in this exercise was pulled from the **ERA5 hourly data on single levels from 1979 to present**. Here you will search for data from the same dataset but for the dates that Typhoon Haiyan occurred. Typhoon Haiyan was one of the strongest cyclones ever recorded (`https://en.wikipedia.org/wiki/Typhoon_Haiyan`).

1. Create an account on `https://cds.climate.copernicus.eu`.

2. Once logged in to the site click on the Datasets tab and search for *ERA* to locate this dataset. Click on the **ERA5 hourly data on single levels from 1979 to present** link, then click on the Download data tab.

3. In the Popular Section check 10m u-component of wind, 10m v-component of wind, 2m temperature and Total precipitation. (figure 8.14)

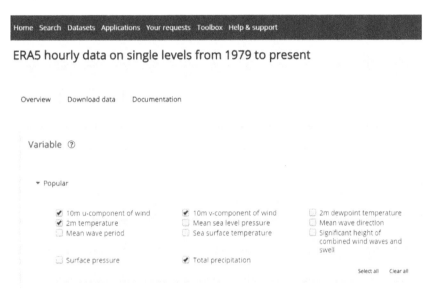

Figure 8.14: Copernicus.eu Data Download

4. Scroll down to the Year section and check the box for 2013. In the Month section check November. In the Day section check the boxes for 3 through 11. In the Year section check 00:00,*06*00,*12*00 and 18:00.

5. When done click the Submit form button. You will be redirected to the Your requests page and the Download link will appear.

6. Create an animation of Typhoon Haiyan.

> The dataset will be global. To make the data more manageable, the you worked with in this exercise, were cropped to the Atlantic basin. This was done using a command line tool named *Climate Data Operator (CDO)*. You can download this collection of command line tools here: `https://code.mpimet.mpg.de/projects/cdo`. The cropping was done in two steps. First the data were converted from GRIB to NetCDF using this copy command: cdo -f nc copy in.grib out.nc. The NetCDF version was then clipped using this sellonlatbox command: cdo -f nc sellonlatbox,-106,0,-7,50 out.nc out_clipped.nc. You can do the same to crop the dataset to the area around Typhoon Haiyan by inserting the appropriate bounding box.

Another option is to work with weather data which data can be downloaded using the **QGribDownloader** plugin. This plugin automatically downloads weather GRIB files available from `http://opengribs.org/` for the current map extent.

Conclusion

Congratulations, you have completed the Discover QGIS 3.x Workbook! I hope you enjoyed it and learned a lot along the way. Now that you have developed a well-rounded skill set, I encourage you to continue learning how QGIS and PostGIS - along with GDAL/OGR, R, GRASS GIS, and other FOSS4G tools - can be used to analyze and visualize spatial data. QGIS in particular, evolves rapidly with new features being introduced regularly. Below are some resources for staying abreast of the latest developments, and continuing your geospatial education.

As Anita Graser says QGIS is a *Do-Occracy*. You have the power to contribute to QGIS. I encourage you to get involved. As a user you are an important member of the community. Appendix C focuses on this. In short, to learn how to Report bugs, Translate QGIS, Develop a plugin, develop new features, and sponsor/donate to QGIS read more here: `https://www.qgis.org/en/site/getinvolved/index.html`

There is a new release every 4 months and a new long-term release annually. Stay current on new features by browsing the **Visual Changelogs**. `https://www.qgis.org/en/site/forusers/visualchangelogs.html`

Learn more skills via the **QGIS Training Manual**: `https://www.qgis.org/en/site/forusers/trainingmaterial/index.html`

Refer to the **QGIS User Guide** when technical questions arise: `https://docs.qgis.org/3.4/en/docs/user_manual/`

Look on **GIS.StackExchange.com** for solutions to issues you encounter: `https://gis.stackexchange.com/questions/tagged/qgis`

Subscribe to a **QGIS Mailing List**: `https://www.qgis.org/en/site/getinvolved/mailinglists.html`

Read about, *How to ask a QGIS question* before posing your first question to a mailing list (listserv): `https://www.qgis.org/en/site/getinvolved/faq/index.html#how-to-ask-a-qgis-question`

Read about how others have used QGIS in **QGIS Case Studies**: `https://www.qgis.org/en/site/about/case_studies/index.html`

Explore maps others have made using QGIS in the **Flickr Map Showcase**: `https://www.flickr.com/groups/qgis/pool/`

Read blog entries about new features and how-tos: `http://plugins.qgis.org/planet/`
- Anital Graser: https://anitagraser.com/
- North Road: https://north-road.com/blog/
- Klas Karlsson: https://www.youtube.com/channel/UCxs7cfMwzgGZhtUuwhny4-Q
- Spatial Thoughts: https://spatialthoughts.com/blog/

Explore other QGIS Applications such as QGIS Server and QGIS Web Client: `https://www.qgis.org/en/site/about/features.html`

If you require commercial support for QGIS you can go to this page to see companies providing a variety of support options: `https://www.qgis.org/en/site/forusers/commercial_support.html`

Join your local user group or start one if one doesn't exist. Visit this page to see where there are established user groups: `https://www.qgis.org/en/site/forusers/usergroups.html`

Visit the **Open Source GeoSpatial Foundation (OSGeo)** website, to stay abreast of other FOSS4G project news and conference announcements: `http://www.osgeo.org/`

Appendix

A - Keyboard Shortcuts

Project Management

New Project - `Ctrl + N`

Open Project - `Ctrl + O`

Save Project - `Ctrl + S`

Save Project As - `Ctrl + Shift + S`

Project Properties - `Ctrl + Shift + P`

New Print Layout - `Ctrl + P`

Universal Search - `Ctrl + K`

Help Contents - `F1`

QGIS Home Page - `Ctrl + H`

Exit QGIS - `Ctrl + Q`

Layer Management

Open Data Source Manager - `Ctrl + L`

New GeoPackage Layer - `Ctrl + Shift + N`

Add Vector Layer - `Ctrl + Shift + V`

Add Raster Layer - `Ctrl + Shift + R`

Add PostGIS Layer - `Ctrl + Shift + D`

Add SpatiaLite Layer - `Ctrl + Shift + L`

Add MSSQL Spatial Layer - `Ctrl + Shift + M`

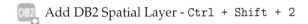 Add DB2 Spatial Layer - `Ctrl + Shift + 2`

Add Oracle Spatial Layer - `Ctrl + Shift + O`

Add WMS/WMTS Layer - `Ctrl + Shift + W`

Remove Selected Layer or Group - `Ctrl + D`

Filter - `Ctrl + F`

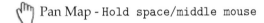 CRS Set CRS of Layer(s) - `Ctrl + Shift +C`

Show All Layers - `Ctrl + Shift + U`

Hide All Layers - `Ctrl + Shift + H`

Layers Toggle Layers Panel - `Ctrl + 1`

Browser Toggle Browser Panel - `Ctrl + 2`

Toggle Styling Panel - `F7`

Navigation & Map Management

Pan Map - `Hold space/middle mouse`

Zoom In - `Ctrl + Alt + +`

Zoom Out - `Ctrl + Alt + -`

Zoom Full - `Ctrl + Shift + F`

Zoom to Selection - `Ctrl + J`

Refresh Map - `F5`

New Map View - `Ctrl + M`

New 3D Map View - `Ctrl + Shift + M`

Show Bookmarks - `Ctrl + Shift + B`

New Bookmark - `Ctrl + B`

Data & Analysis Tools

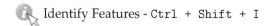 Open Attribute Table - `F6`

With Selected Features Only - `Shift + F6`

With Visible Features Only - `Ctrl + F6`

Identify Features - `Ctrl + Shift + I`

Select Features By Value - `F3`

Select All Features - `Ctrl + A`

Deselect Features from All Layers - `Ctrl + Shift + A`

$\sum$ Statistical Summary - `Ctrl + 6`

Measure Line - `Ctrl + Shift + M`

Measure Area - `Ctrl + Shift + J`

Processing Tools

Processing Toolbox - `Ctrl + Alt + T`

Graphical Modeler - `Ctrl + Alt + M`

History - `Ctrl + Alt + H`

Results Viewer - `Ctrl + Alt + R`

Python Console - `Ctrl + Alt + P`

B - Popular Plugins

There are hundreds of plugins available for QGIS. In the change from QGIS 2.x to 3.x a new PyQGIS API was developed. This meant that all plugins had to be adapted to operate in 3.x. This has taken time but as of this publication there are more than 350 plugins available—including the most widely used ones—and the list is continually growing (figure 8.15, on the next page). The main plugin site is: `https://plugins.qgis.org/`

Note that there are some important options on the Settings tab of the Plugin Manager. There you can Show also experimental plugins and add other Plugin repositories (figure 8.16, on the following page).

The following list highlights some of the more popular plugins by category. You have used many in this book.

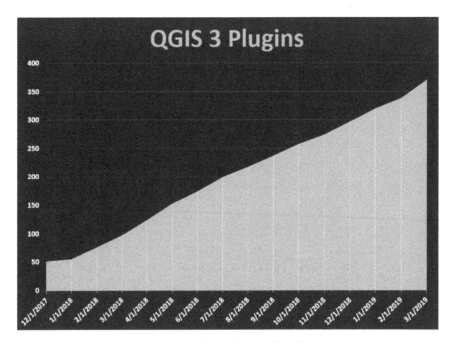

Figure 8.15: QGIS 3.x Plugin Development

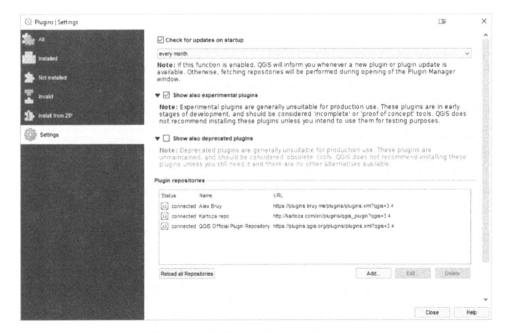

Figure 8.16: Plugin Manager Settings

Data/Data Download

- **OSM Downloader** - A plugin to download OSM data by area, using a selection by rectangle. The plugin can also automatically load the osm file into QGIS in a transparent way.
- **QGribDownloader** - Suggested for use in the **Challenge Exercise in Part 5 - Exercise 8**, this automatically downloads weather GRIB files via http://opengribs.org/.
- **QuickOSM** - Download OSM data via the Overpass API. You can also open local OSM or PBF files. A special parser is used to let you see all OSM keys available. (Experimental)

- **Sentinel Hub** - SentinelHub plugin transforms any layer created in Sentinel Hub Configuration Utility into QGIS layer. It allows exploration, customization and image download. An instance ID for Sentinel Hub services is required (`http://www.sentinel-hub.com/`).

- **Spreadsheet Layers** - This plugin adds an "Add spreadsheet layer" entry in "Layer" / "Add new Layer" menu and a corresponding button in the "Layers" toolbar. These two links open the same dialog to load a layer from a spreadsheet file (*.ods, *.xls, *.xlsx) with some options (use header at first line, ignore some rows and optionally load geometry from x and y fields). When this dialog is accepted, it creates a new GDAL VRT file in same folder as the source data file and layer name, expanded with a .vrt suffix which is loaded into QGIS using OGR VRT driver.

- **SRTM Downloader** - Included in the **Challenge Assignment in Part 3 - Exercise 5**, this downloads Shuttle Radar Topography Mission (SRTM) tiles from a NASA server based on the extent of your map canvas.

- **Vector Tiles Reader** - This reads vector tiles according to Mapbox's Vector Tiles specification as QGIS layers in a group. Styled vector tiles are typically used as high quality base maps. Sources can be an internet server, an MBTiles file, or a directory of files. If an Mapbox GL JSON style is configured, the style is (partially) converted to QGIS styles.

Data Editing

- **Digitizing Tools** - Used in **Part 1 - Exercise 3 - Task 3**, this is meant to be a compilation of tools missing in basic QGIS, especially when digitizing on existing features. It is a collaborative effort and does not contain CAD like functions meant for construction.

- **Shape Tools** - Shape Tools is a collection of geodesic shapes and tools. Create ellipse, line of bearing, pie wedge, donut, arc wedge, polygon, star, ellipse rose, hypocyloid, polyfoil, epicycloid, and heart shapes. Tools include "XY to Line" tool, densify lines and polygons along geodesic paths, geodesic line break, geodesic measuring and create a measurement layer, geodesic scale, rotate, flip and translate tools, and digitize points at an azimuth & distance tools.

- **Split Features on Steroids** - Split one or more polygon/multipolygon features showing the resulting areas on each side of the cutting line. Adjust the vertices of the cutting line before splitting.

- **Topology Checker** - Used in **Part 3 - Exercise 3** this is a plugin for finding topological errors in vector layers.

Cartography/Graphing/Data Visualization

- **Cartogram3** - Creates continuous cartograms from polygon layers.

- **Crayfish** - Used in **Part 5 - Exercise 8** to animate and plot mesh data. This plugin aspires to be a time explorer for various grid and vector datasets within QGIS supported by MDAL. This allows users to flick quickly through the various output steps in the result files and to create animations.

- **D3 Data Visualization** - Creates a D3 circular histogram heatmap from date and time fields in the data. It outputs an interactive web page.

- **Data Plotly** - Introduced in **Part 2 - Exercise 3 - Task 5.2**, this is a tool for generating D3 charts and graphs from attribute data. Based on Plotly and includes 10 different plot types.

- **Dot Map** - Allows you to create dot density maps.

- **FS3** - Use this to quickly generate, display, and compare basic statistics and graphs for numeric and text fields of vector layer.

- **go2streetview** - The plugin gives you a panel with Google Street View or Bing Bird's Eye, by clicking and dragging the cursor on map to set location, and direction of the desired view.

- **Layout Loader** - This plugin makes it simple to apply your map to a layout template from your standard templates folder.

- **MapSwipe Tool** - Allows you to peel the active layer off and on in both a vertical and horizontal direction. Very useful for comparing one raster layer to another.
- **Project Colors Dock** - A dock widget for live modification of linked project colors.
- **QGIS2ThreeJS** - allows you to build 3D views of DEM and vector data in a web browser. Simple to use and very responsive. You can try this on data from Part 5 - Exercise 7.
- **Qweetgis** - This plugin allow to download and visualise on a map twitter messages that contain coordinates in real time, without locking/freezing the main thread. The plug-in uses Twitter's Data Streaming API. The plug-in is based on the third party Python package Tweepy, thishas to be installed separately, instructions in the docs. Also, to access the Twitter API you will need the two API keys Twitter and the two OAuth tokens.
- **TimeManager** - Used in **Part 5 - Exercise 6**, this adds time controls to QGIS. Using these time controls, you can animate vector features based on a time attribute. There is also an experimental raster layer support and support for interpolation beween point geometries. You can create animations directly in the map window and export image series.

Statistics

- **GroupStats** - A tool which allows you to generate summaries on layer attributes. Similar functionality to pivot tables.
- **Statist** - Calculates and shows statistics on any (numeric or string) field of vector layer and shows frequency distribution histogram. (Experimental).

Web

- **QGIS2Web** - Generates a web map from your current QGIS project, either as OpenLayers or Leaflet. It replicates as many aspects of the project as it can, including layers, styles (including categorized and graduated), and extent. No server-side software required.
- **QuickMapServices** - One of the most widely used plugins, this was Introduced in **Part 3 - Exercise 4 - Task 1**, and used in several other exercises, this plugin provides access to over 150 basemaps.

General

- **Georeferencer GDAL** - Used in **Part 1, Exercise 3, Task 2** this allows you to georeference rasters using GDAL. It is a core plugin and only needs to be enabled.
- **Go2NextFeature3** - This plugin allows to select a layer and jump from a feature to another. It's possible to select an attribute of the the layer (usually an ID) and follow it. Press F8 to go to the next feature. It's possibile to use a PAN function or a Zoom function. The plugin was created for checking the position of every single feature of a layer without using the attribute table.
- **Lat Lon Tools** - Tools to capture and zoom to coordinates using decimal, DMS, WKT, GeoJSON, MGRS, and Plus Codes notation. Provides external map support, MGRS & Plus Codes conversion and point digitizing tools.
- **MemoryLayerSaver** - Makes layers with memory data providers persistent so that they are restored when a project is closed and reopened. The memory provider data is saved in a portable binary format (QDataStream) that is saved with extension .mldata alongside the project file.
- **MMQGIS** - Used in **Part 3 - Exercise 6 - Task 1**, MMQGIS is a set of Python plugins for manipulating vector map layers in QGIS: CSV input/output/join, geocoding, geometry conversion, buffering, hub analysis, simplification, column modification, and simple animation. MMQGIS provides an alternative to the Processing toolbox, with verbose progress reporting, an intuitive user interface, direct shapefile/CSV-file access, and some additional capabilities missing from other plugin sets.
- **Plugin Builder 3** - Creates a template for a QGIS plugin. A good place to begin on your first plugin.

- **QGIS Hats** - Adds QGIS icons with user designed hats to the QGIS logo in the system tray and on the interface. It notably adds a QGIS Christmas hat icon and splash screen each December.

- **QGIS Resource Sharing** - Developed as GSoC 2016 project, this plugin allows users to search for available symbol collections and install them. Users can also create repositories to put the collections there. There are some options where to put the repository: Github, Bitbucket, local file system, or with https(s). Please read the documentation for more information.

Processing

- **Calculate Geometry** - Introduced in **Part 2 - Exercise 8 - Task 3**, this plugin allows you to easily calculate area and length in numerous common units, without typing expressions.

- **LAStools** - Tools for processing point clouds in LAS, LAZ, and ASCII formats. The LAStools plugin exposes the capabilities of LAStools within QGIS 3.2 - 3.6 using the Processing framework. You also need to download the LAStools software from `http://rapidlasso.com/LAStools/`.

- **ORS Tools** - ORS Tools provides access to most of the functions of openrouteservice.org, based on OpenStreetMap. The tool set includes routing, isochrones and matrix calculations, either interactive in the map canvas or from point files within the processing framework. Extensive attributes are set for output files, incl. duration, length and start/end locations.

- **PDAL Tools** - This plugin installs the necessary tools to integrate PDAL into the Processing Toolbox. A prerequisite to use this provider is to have PDAL installed.

- **Point Sampling Tool** - Samples polygon attributes and raster values from multiple layers at specified sampling points.

- **Processing R Provider** - A processing provider for connecting to the R statistics framework.

- **refFunctions** - This plugin adds custom user functions to the Qgis Field calculator.

- **Script Runner3** - Use this to load and run Python processing scripts. NOTE: For Windows you need the pywin32 module. ScriptRunner attempts to install it for you if it isn't represent on your system (Windows only).

- **Semi-Automatic Classification** - Perhaps the largest plugin in the QGIS ecosystem. This allows for the supervised classification of remote sensing images, providing tools for the download, the preprocessing and postprocessing of images. Search and download is available for ASTER, Landsat, MODIS, Sentinel-2, and Sentinel-3 images. Several algorithms are available for the land cover classification. This plugin requires the installation of GDAL, OGR, Numpy, SciPy, and Matplotlib. For more information please visit `https://fromgistors.blogspot.com`.

- **TauDEM for Processing** - Add the suite of TauDEM tools to the Processing Toolbox. TauDEM (Terrain analysis using Digital Elevation Models) is a suite of DEM tools for the extraction and analysis of hydrologic information from topography as represented by a DEM.

- **Visibility Analysis** - Viewshed analysis calculates visible surface from a given observer point over a digital elevation model. Additionally, this plugin can be used for modelling intervisibilty networks between groups of points. It is particularly performant for multiple viewshed calculations form a set of fixed points. (Experimental)

- **WhiteBox Tools for Processing** - Adds the suite of Whitebox processing tools to the Processing Toolbox. This plugin is available from this site (`https://plugins.bruy.me/processing-whitebox.html`) which includes installation instructions.

C. Getting Involved

There are many people who make QGIS what it is. QGIS in addition to being a piece of software is an open source project and a vibrant community. Much of what needs to be done to keep QGIS developing is done on a volunteer basis. It is not entirely altruistic however. Most of the core developers earn their living by doing so. In fact most people involved, even on a volunteer basis, are making a living by providing services with QGIS.

There are numerous roles to be filled. You can read about the QGIS organization here: `https://www.qgis.org/en/site/getinvolved/governance/index.html`.

QGIS is what it is, because of the community. If you find value in using QGIS with your work, consider giving back in some way. The most obvious way is to donate money to the project. You can do so here: `https://www.qgis.org/en/site/getinvolved/donations.html#qgis-donations` You can even visit the QGIS store. Part of the purchase of a shirt or mug is a donation back to QGIS. `https://qgis.org/en/site/about/shop_goodies.html` Simply put, if people stopped donating to the project it would die. It is truly important even if it is a small personal donation.

There is a list of current sponsors you can find here: `https://qgis.org/en/site/about/sponsorship.html#list-of-sponsors`

You may also encounter a bug. It will not be fixed unless it is reported. You can read how to participate in this very important way here: `https://qgis.org/en/site/getinvolved/development/bugreporting.html`

After working with the software you may think of a feature you wish it had. The good news is that you can develop it yourself. If that isn't within your skill set, you can pay one of the developers to do this for you. All you need to do is scope out the feature, get an estimate from one of the developers and pay for it. I've done this and seen the new feature appear within weeks! It is a truly empowering experience. Imagine, you can have direct control over getting a new feature developed, and everyone benefits. That is how this works. This article by Nyall Dawson of North Road is an important read if you are not familiar with how this works: `http://nyalldawson.net/2016/08/how-to-effectively-get-things-changed-in-qgis/`

There are other ways to get more directly involved. As mentioned previously QGIS evolves rapidly. One area that the community struggles to keep up with is documentation. Anyone can contribute to the documentation. You can read about that here: `https://www.qgis.org/en/site/getinvolved/document.html`

Similarly you can work on translating QGIS into other languages other than English: `https://www.qgis.org/en/site/getinvolved/translate.html`

Join your local user group or start one if one doesn't exist. `https://www.qgis.org/en/site/forusers/usergroups.html`

Index

Books from Locate Press

Be sure to visit http://locatepress.com for information on new and upcoming titles.

Leaflet Cookbook

COOK UP DYNAMIC WEB MAPS USING THE RECIPES IN THE LEAFLET COOKBOOK.
Leaflet Cookbook will guide you in getting started with Leaflet, the leading open-source JavaScript library for creating interactive maps. You'll move swiftly along from the basics to creating interesting and dynamic web maps.

Even if you aren't an HTML/CSS wizard, this book will get you up to speed in creating dynamic and sophisticated web maps. With sample code and complete examples, you'll find it easy to create your own maps in no time.

A download package containing all the code and data used in the book is available so you can follow along as well as use the code as a starting point for your own web maps.

QGIS Map Design - 2nd Edition

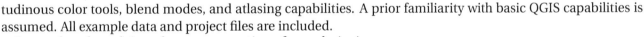

LEARN HOW TO USE QGIS 3 TO TAKE YOUR CARTOGRAPHIC PRODUCTS TO THE HIGHEST LEVEL.
QGIS 3.4 opens up exciting new possibilities for creating beautiful and compelling maps!

Building on the first edition, the authors take you step-by-step through the process of using the latest map design tools and techniques in QGIS 3. With numerous new map designs and completely overhauled workflows, this second edition brings you up to speed with current cartographic technology and trends.

See how QGIS continues to surpass the cartographic capabilities of other geoware available today with its data-driven overrides, flexible expression functions, multitudinous color tools, blend modes, and atlasing capabilities. A prior familiarity with basic QGIS capabilities is assumed. All example data and project files are included.

Get ready to launch into the next generation of map design!

The PyQGIS Programmer's Guide

WELCOME TO THE WORLD OF PYQGIS, THE BLENDING OF QUANTUM GIS AND PYTHON TO EXTEND AND ENHANCE YOUR OPEN SOURCE GIS TOOLBOX.

With PyQGIS you can write scripts and plugins to implement new features and perform automated tasks.

This book is updated to work with the next generation of QGIS—version 3.x. After a brief introduction to Python 3, you'll learn how to understand the QGIS Application Programmer Interface (API), write scripts, and build a plugin.

The book is designed to allow you to work through the examples as you go along. At the end of each chapter you will find a set of exercises you can do to enhance your learning experience.

The PyQGIS Programmer's Guide is compatible with the version 3.0 API released with QGIS 3.x and will work for the entire 3.x series of releases.

---

pgRouting: A Practical Guide

WHAT IS PGROUTING?

It's a PostgreSQL extension for developing network routing applications and doing graph analysis.

Interested in pgRouting? If so, chances are you already use PostGIS, the spatial extender for the PostgreSQL database management system.

So when you've got PostGIS, why do you need pgRouting? PostGIS is a great tool for molding geometries and doing proximity analysis, however it falls short when your proximity analysis involves constrained paths such as driving along a road or biking along defined paths.

This book will both get you started with pgRouting and guide you into routing, data fixing and costs, as well as using with QGIS and web applications.

Geospatial Power Tools

EVERYONE LOVES POWER TOOLS!

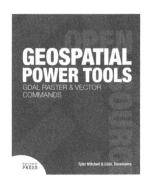

The GDAL and OGR apps are the power tools of the GIS world—best of all, they're free.

The utilities include tools for examining, converting, transforming, building, and analysing data. This book is a collection of the GDAL and OGR documentation, but also includes new content designed to help guide you in using the utilities to solve your current data problems.

Inside you'll find a quick reference for looking up the right syntax and example usage quickly. The book is divided into three parts: *Workflows and examples*, *GDAL raster utilities*, and *OGR vector utilities*.

Once you get a taste of the power the GDAL/OGR suite provides, you'll wonder how you ever got along without them.

See these books and more at http://locatepress.com

For a 50% discount on the ebook, use coupon code 751508003a3 at locatepress.com

CPSIA information can be obtained
at www.ICGtesting.com
Printed in the USA
BVHW021140070819
555308BV00017B/1213/P

9 780998 547763